BLACK McCOOL

Written 2016-2018
Edited 2017-2018
Printed and published by CreateSpace 2018
ISBN - 978-1981837915

Written by James C. McCusker

Front cover illustrated by Chris Pennestri
Back and inside cover illustrated by Adrienne Wells
Edited by Adrienne Wells and Eileen McCusker

A special thanks to Michael McCusker for his major
contribution, for his legal expertise and first-hand
experience into the War in Afghanistan, Chris Rose
for his firearm and bullets for the inside and back
cover photos, Jon Kappock for his firearm
knowledge and all of my family and friends for their
advice, critique and support.

This book is dedicated to the greatest Irish I know to ever come out of Philadelphia – everyone in the McCusker and Gartland Families, both alive and not. I thank you for all your love, care and guidance over the many years.

Other works by McCusker:

Atlantic City Nights ©2013

Left in the Sand ©2016

A Girl Named Emerald ©2016

All available on:

www.booksbymccusker.com
www.amazon.com

"I don't ever wait for luck in this lifetime. Nothing is won by chance. I take the pound of gold as it shines in front of me! It may not be there tomorrow!"

- *"Black" Jack McCool*

Prologue

Twenty-Five Years Later

The kid was about to have a life-changing night...but he did not know it yet.

"What the fuck is an Irish bar doing in South Philly anyway?" he asked while he scratched his brown-haired beard. Fitzy replied, "C'mon, boy...get it together. We are all leaving in ten minutes. Everything is a green light with meeting Chris Veccuto down the street from here."

"Why does it have to be us that goes, Fitzy?" questioned the kid more, looking in his mentor's direction. He kept his hand on his jaw as he intently listened to every word.

"We report to Red Alan Connor...he is the one orchestrating this new business venture along with Veccuto and Pretty Paul Muchetta. We went over this earlier today. He gave the order for us to broker the meeting."

Who was "Pretty" Paul Muchetta? A reputed wiseguy that should have died the scandalous night he was shot at in Atlantic City in November of 1989.

After the most grueling war seen in the Philly Mob's history had ended, the worst was still ahead. It all came down to gunfire and cold indictments once the murderous don of the decade, "Little" Vinny Veccuto received a life sentence in Federal prison on multiple RICO predicates.

A few others followed Vinny to the slammer that same year. Yet, the ones who remained on the streets held the throne successfully…for about three weeks.

Coming in to grab the big seat was Vinny's older turncoat brother, Dante "DV" Veccuto along with underboss "Fat" Phil Lupistanza and Pretty Paul as *consigliere.*

It was their last night in America's Playground after the violent unrest that undoubtedly shadowed most of the year. The three were having dinner at Anthony's Pizza Grille on Iowa Avenue before hitting the road to venture back home to the City of Brotherly Love.

Once they got into the heat of discussing plans for the family's future, all three were killed by Vinny's youngest son, Chris Veccuto, avenging the trio's setup on his dad and brother. Right? Well…*not completely.*

To his advantage, Paul only took bullets to his chest and abdomen. Many thought he was dead like his two buddies on the floor who both had holes in their heads. He almost was! The entire restaurant cleared out after Chris…even the staff. Nobody wanted to have anything to do with viewing a gangland hit. In the event, Paul was all alone.

Helpless, he crawled over to the payphone in the back corner of the restaurant to dial 9-1-1, leaving a trail of smeared blood in his path.

As the first responders arrived at the pizzeria, they did not know who to help first, given Paul looked as inert as the others.

Figuring it out was only half the battle. Once they discovered he was hanging on for dear life, he was immediately rushed to the emergency room at Atlantic City Hospital.

Paul remained in a coma for weeks after the three bullets were taken out of him. Even more questions were asked about his fate during significant surgery. Miraculously, he made it. By the skin of his teeth and with probably the last favor God was looking to give him.

When the time came to return back to Philly, he nearly *wished* he had died once asked by the Commission of the Five Families in New York to take the reins of what was left of his Veccuto territory. Given New York's full partition to the imprisoned Vinny, Paul would have full control of the family as boss. This was a responsibility he never thought he would have nor want.

Hesitantly, he accepted the role right before the legendary Jimmy "Squints" Tasseno of Brooklyn died in prison. His last words to him during their final visit were simple, "Bring justice to streets, Pretty Paulie…however you need to do it!"

His first order of business was a contract he put out on Young Chris Veccuto who was on the run and hiding on Vinny's last dime. Paul made it clear that $500,000 would be the grand prize for the kid's head…a million for beaten and bruised, still breathing.

The next action item for Paul was growing the family's net worth again. He needed to bring the streets back to their eminence.

He made the most money where he always saw the most enormous opportunity: narcotics. Except going into the 1990's, he did not want to deal in heroin anymore.

Something more lucrative and extensive was coming about to the country: ecstasy. Triple the revenue!

Everyone was trying it. More importantly, everyone started demanding it. A widespread operation was set up across the city, stretching into Delaware and over to South Jersey. Paul oversaw manufacturing at a warehouse in North Philly.

Aligning with "Red Alan" Connor, an old friend from prison, Paul relied on him for mass distribution. He grew close to Alan, his brothers, and the Kensington & Erie Crew. In short, they went by *K&E*. They were the Irish gang in the Northeast part of Philly. The next twenty years brought a surplus for both allied family forces.

Although the return on investment was not comparable to the prime of Vinny and the AC casino empire in the 80's, it was still a profitable era. Things were going well.

Hitherto, the adage 'things only *stay* good for so long' held true. The War on Drugs and The War on Terror combined caused the perfect storm in the years that followed 9/11. The problem more than ever was the *heat*.

From 2009-2014, the FBI spent an enormous amount of money attempting to weaken the ecstasy empire and the crimes surrounding it domestically and internationally.

Just as predicted, guys started to fall again in every kind of way. As a result, money began to go down the toilet.

With it being exactly twenty-five years after the official end to Little Vinny's "halcyon days," the streets grew uncertain, even in the better of times. Pretty Paul, now in his mid-70's, was starting to *deteriorate*. A change was necessary.

Part One

Black and Red

CHAPTER ONE

On a cold November night when the city needed all the hope it could get, the full moon barely lit up 17th Street and its surrounding grim alleyways. However, the darkest moments were yet to come.

With the wee hours of the morning arriving, the sky still had a long wait until it would burst with the gold of the dawn. Too much time for one to linger, yet plenty of time for trouble.

McCluskey's Tavern sat in the middle of the old block. It was a South Philadelphia icon. Rustic and modest in its appearance, the bar held centerpiece to decades of local history; both good and bad.

It was most recognized for its large and gaudy green shamrock, shining in the middle of the rotted wooden door. Many of lads and lasses over the years entered through. For the old Irish still around in the neighborhood, this place was their saving grace, their salvation.

Whether it was the suits and ties or the drunks and derelicts, all were welcome…including the renowned K&E Crew.

Although for as far as a hike it was from their usual northeast section of town where they ruled, they felt just as far out of the place where they were sitting.

The four hoodlums rested on stools at different points of the circular bar, watching the beats on the clock tick, bit by bit and in rhythm.

After sipping their Guinness and humming two bars of 'Danny Boy,' the jukebox filled the air with folk sounds of The Dubliners for all to enjoy and sing along to.

Mush-a ring dumb-a do dumb-a da!! Wack fall the daddy-o! Wack fall the daddy-o! There's whiskey in the jar!!

The same two bartenders who had been there the past forty years were still serving drinks. The only things they would keep fresh were lemons in a bowl on top of the bar. They barely washed the mugs anymore. They would just reach for an old tankard, tap the brew into it and exclaim, "Here!" slamming it in front of you. After a shot or two of Jameson whiskey, it didn't matter…nobody knew what they were pouring anyway.

Echoing chimes of glass on glass carried on as the only real dame in the place mixed her cocktail slowly. The noise was muffled by timpani notes that jumped and danced from the music, amplifying the old cavern.

Her black dress hung from her shoulders, hugging her curvy form as she stared at the same clock on the wall that the fellas of the K&E Crew were gazing at the past hour.

It was 1:45 in the morning.

Last call…

The girl switched her twinkling emerald eyes to the middle-aged man on the stool next to hers and asked him politely for a napkin from the silver caddy.

Like a gent, he pulled one out and handed it to her, smiling ear to ear. "Here ya go, doll." Immediately, she looked away after taking the napkin. Not a *thank you*. Not even a grin back.

With a quick and soft chuckle, the man stood up, took a deep breath as he looked ahead and made his way over to a member of his crew on the opposite side of the bar.

As he was walking his six-foot-three frame across the room, he began to ponder slowly, scratching his salt-and-pepper-like hair. He then put his hands in the pockets of his gray slacks.

"How did that girl not know who I was?" he asked himself. "I guess I really am out of the Northeast...this south side just ain't the fuckin' same."

The man was not a bigheaded chauvinist, looking for recognition. In truth, he was well-known, near and far. However, to the pretty green-eyed lady in the black dress, perhaps it *was* too far.

The name was Michael "Fitzy" Fitzgerald – the oldest member of the K&E Crew after its three founders. He had been around for it all. The good, the gruesome and the *glorious*.

From its humble beginnings on Kensington and Erie Street to its lucrative business networks in cities surrounding, Fitzy worked under the legendary

Connor Brothers of County Wexford for years as a jewel thief. They built what became the most dangerous gang on the streets of Philadelphia into the 1990's and 2000's together with, of course, the well-known Veccuto Crime Family.

He quickly glanced over the bar to Sean O'Hara, his number one. Notorious for stealing top-of-the-line automobiles throughout the city, O'Hara was ready to take any kind of ride.

He was worth his weight in American steel, literally. He was a massive fella...as wide as an interstate highway. They even called him "Highway O'Hara" because of his size, as well as his repertoire of stolen vehicles. Everywhere he went, there was an open road.

Next to O'Hara at the bar was his third cousin-by-marriage from Dublin, Brian Duffy. Quiet and stern most of the time, Duffy was far from shy...when it came to *killing*. There wasn't a soul still soaring who would ever doubt this short and stocky terror...him or his signature wool flat cap.

He had almost as many notches on his gun as Fitzy. He also had enough support from the Irish Republican Army back home in the motherland to help him slay even more if he wanted to. This allegiance came in handy. Duffy was the best hitman in K&E.

As a matter of fact, it was Duffy's clan who brought the most active muscle during the Easter Rising when Ireland had its most significant years of rebellion. Legend has it, the nation's leader Michael

Collins would not have won the Civil War without the firm alliance of the Duffy family support.

Nevertheless, Highway O'Hara and Duffy were not of the uppermost importance on Fitzy's mind this night. He trusted them with every decision he made. Yet the third and youngest member of his crew was his greatest concern and held his deepest care.

He directly and affectionately called him "kiddo" or "the kid." Fitzy loved him more than anything. In fact, he helped raise him since he was five-years-old after his parents were killed in a car accident. Over the years, he groomed him to be one of his own in K&E.

Fitzy gradually sauntered over and sat down next to the kid at the bar, gazing at the clock with him. They wasted no time before they started talking.

The kid was about to have a life-changing night...but he did not know it yet.

"What the fuck is an Irish bar doing in South Philly anyway?" he asked while he scratched his brown-haired beard. Fitzy replied, "C'mon, boy...get it together. We are all leaving in ten minutes. Everything is a green light with meeting Chris Veccuto down the street from here."

"Why does it have to be us that goes, Fitzy?" questioned the kid more, looking in his mentor's direction. He kept his hand on his jaw as he intently listened to every word.

"We report to Red Alan Connor...he is the one orchestrating this new business venture along with Veccuto and Pretty Paul Muchetta. We went over this earlier today. He gave the order for us to broker the meeting."

McCluskey's Bar was starting to clear out, even more as the two carried on with their conversation. The last of the drunkards were being hauled, drug, or thrown out, one by one like they were bad pieces of food in the fridge.

"The whole thing is as foreign to you as it is to me," continued Fitzy to the kid. "But, it could end up working in our favor." He readjusted the gold Claddagh ring on his right hand, clenching his fist at the same time. The ring was two hands that met in the middle with a heart and crown on top. Luminous in its appearance, it burned when it shined. It was a priceless piece to many, considering it was hand-made in Ireland centuries ago.

"Pretty Paulie is a motherfucker to deal with, just like Alan is." The kid nodded his head up and down while Fitzy went on.

"With Chrissy V being on the lam all this time, he is reluctant to see Paulie face to face now that he is back home. But with us going…it will make him feel better, more comfortable. This new operation is going to explode and make a lot of money for everyone involved. We definitely want to be on the front lines of it all," detailed Fitzy.

He seemed overly-excited about this meeting. Young Veccuto had come upon a new undertaking and was presenting it as his peace offering while hoping for a way back home.

"What is really in it for us though, Fitz? Raw figures?" asked the kid. Smiling, Fitzy took his last shot of Jameson for the night, wiping his mouth before he responded.

"A mountain of opportunity. As a matter of fact, I spoke with Red Alan...I want you spearheading the thing for us, kiddo. Your connections from when you were in Atlantic City will be crucial for bringing this all together. It's time for you to show the higher-ups what you're worth."

The kid could not believe it. As much as he was skeptical about what the night had in store, this sounded like the break he needed. What it exactly entailed, he wasn't sure of yet. However, between his old days of counting cards and new ones running the executive poker game, this could have been the chance to make more than both rackets combined.

"That's dynamite, Fitz!" he told him.

It was now a few minutes before 2 AM.

Throughout time, Chris Veccuto had been known as a stand-up guy. Born into a household of high-profile criminals, he was the only real hope left in making the family name a legitimate one.

The last thing he wanted to do was follow in the footsteps of his brother, uncle, and father. He tried to make his mark by rising to the occasion. Initially, there were plans for college and a dream of a more fulfilling life. It was always his goal to do well.

Yet now, he was somewhat of a street legend since the night of the pizzeria. It was the single-most fearless ambush with gunfire at high-ranking Mob guys in one sitting the family had ever seen. As much as he tried to escape the Veccuto curse, it was in his blood. It followed him all the way to the end.

Additionally, his lam was a remarkable one. It was the longest anybody in the family had gone off the grid without any mishap during.

Given such depth of history in the entire situation, there were plenty of theories about what was in store for the young blood.

This would be the first time the city would hear from him since the infamous night on the shore. Not even Vinny, his own father, spoke to him during his time away. No risks were taken on either end.

However, at this point, things were different. With the recent passing of Chris' mother, Lorraine, he knew he had to come home. It was time to set the record straight.

Whether it was the safest decision or not, Chris did not care. He had to make things right by coming head-on with the shadows of his past that were haunting him for so long.

It was not going to be easy. Chris was aware of this. Jumping into a new business opportunity, it appeared to be phenomenal timing. He would potentially avoid the wrath of Muchetta, who was still holding on dearly to the twenty-five-year-old grudge. This was the price he knew he had to pay to come to his mother's funeral and to show his face to everybody.

The venture was not about the money. It was about the freedom to say goodbye to another loved one. Being able to walk with his head held high again was top of the agenda for the now forty-four-year-old Veccuto.

As he always claimed, "it is up to us to be the change." He was looking to start over and bring some good to his life and to others.

The clock struck 2:00 on the dot.

"Let's get out of here," stated Fitzy to the kid, signaling over to Duffy and O'Hara to do likewise. The boys stood up simultaneously in perfect unison, ready to leave.

The kid stopped Fitz once they began walking. "Thank you...really," he said. The old man smiled, putting his hand on the kid's shoulder. "I love you, boy. You have proven yourself time and time again as a good earner with your AOH card game. Just keep doin' good and good things will keep comin' your way!"

"I appreciate that, Fitz."

"You will work well with Young Veccuto, kiddo. He is forty-four, you are thirty. You guys are the future of this city! Soon enough, you'll be the ones taking the reins."

Smiling, the kid patted Fitzy's back, reminding him that he would give him nothing but his full allegiance in those days to come. As the four collectively joined together, they headed towards the shamrock door to exit. It was time for the meeting.

On his way out, the kid gave an enamoring stare to the young girl in the black dress as her bright emerald eyes flashed back. He winked at her, nodding his head in her direction. She nonchalantly smiled in return as she tucked her jet-black hair behind her ear. She then went to finish her last drink.

It was brisk outside. Everyone tensed up as soon as the cold air hit their faces. "That cocksucker Red Alan better be appreciative. He should be out here freezin' his fuckin' ass off with the rest of us!" exclaimed O'Hara, rubbing his hands vigorously together.

"Believe me, I can't stand him any more than you guys. But, I am in immense debt to him. I got to stay on his good side," responded Fitzy, putting his two cents in.

The walk was short yet bitter. The K&E Crew arrived at an old, abandoned and boarded up deli. It also served as a corner store, decades ago. It was just about a block away from McCluskey's on Shunk Avenue, intersecting 17th Street.

At the entrance, two brawn and burly men dressed in all black, guarded the door. The only way you could see them was from the gleam of the spotlight above. The rest of the road was dim. The entire city rested quietly for whatever was next.

"Everything out of your pockets!" one of the guards demanded. Duffy gave some pushback. "Who the fuck is asking, lad?" inquired the native Irishman with the thick brogue he was known for.

The guard came an inch away from his face. One could smell his lousy cologne as he quietly retorted, "Pretty Paul Muchetta, you fuck head." The other guard brought his gun out and aimed it in the direction of the boys, assuring the seriousness of the situation.

"Whoa! Whoa!" said Fitzy. "No need for all that. Duffy, it is ok. Everything out of our pockets...especially our guns." He said it with a smile.

Duffy huffed and puffed with his bull-like temper, pulling all his belongings out. He even took off his signature flat cap. O'Hara and the kid acted accordingly as well.

"Is Chris Veccuto inside?" asked Fitz. One of the guards rapidly countered, "It is after two in the morning. Neither Paulie nor Red Alan has time to waste. Young Veccuto is in there. Let's get this over with, could we?" Fitzy nodded his head and calmly chuckled, ready to get it over with as well.

Patted down and checked carefully throughout their bodies, the four Micks were clean. It was their time to go in. There was an eerie feeling with the way the guards were acting. Yet, the boys reminded themselves as to why they were there. This had to be done, once and for all.

Anxious to see Veccuto, they hurried into the deli. The stable wooden door swung shut with the swish of a sonic boom. It was so loud and quick, they jumped out of their skin.

What was witnessed next would be horrific. Nobody said a thing. It was like they were all staring at a ghost. Their eyes were wide open, glued to the center of the room. The scene was so chilling, it felt cold to the bones.

It was both sad and scary to see Chris Veccuto, hanging from the ceiling in a noose, gutted like a fish. His insides were all over the floor beneath him.

As the blood continued to pour like a waterfall from his open stomach, it was a clear indicator this was a fresh kill.

They were dumbfounded. Fitzy, O'Hara, Duffy, the kid. Each one of them stood there in awe, jaws dropped. Nobody would have put money on this outcome.

Fitzy turned to the front door to try and open it. It was no use. It was bolted shut, locked from the other end. Nobody could escape.

Puzzled, Fitzy and the guys looked for another way. The only windows were boarded up from the outside. There were no other exits. The place was enclosed like a military fort. It became more evident as the seconds went by that this was a setup. How could they have not seen it? Their fate was determined way before they arrived.

On the spur of the moment, they heard ticking. It was the same type of tick the boys listened to on the clock at McCluskey's.

However, this time, the clock was jammed inside the blown open stomach of the ravaged Chris Veccuto. It was strapped to an old-fashioned nail bomb.

The kid ran behind an old glass counter in the corner, looking for a miracle while the others continued trying to break open the front door. It was then the kid found a meat cleaver all the way behind the dust and cobwebs of the shoddy work table.

"This should break the door!" he yelled, holding the great chopper up high.

It was too late. Before Fitzy could utter his last words to the crew he adored, the device went off. The room went up in smoke.

Anyone within a mile radius would have heard the explosion. It was loud enough to shatter windows and powerful enough to keep ears buzzing.

As a matter of fact, that was all the kid heard before he ducked behind the counter...a loud, echoing whistle. He took cover just in time as the bomb went off to save himself. Although the glass in front of him shattered, he remained together.

Yet, it was still so brutal. He could barely breathe. It was even harder to see. The cloudy haze was overbearing all senses.

He stared at his leg, bloody to its pulp, and held it tightly. It was his only major wound. How the flying metal and debris made its way to his lower limb, he did not know. Yet, he was confident that now was not the time to try and figure it out. He was lucky to be alive...that, he certainly knew.

With the last bit of energy he had left, he crawled across the floor with the cleaver, around the counter, and towards the front access. The nails did enough damage to the wooden door that it was now in a fragile enough state to break down.

He stood up once he was close enough to his getaway, trembling on his one good leg with minimum balance. He swung the cleaver at the door multiple times, breaking down the wood like a lumberjack.

He then threw his body with full force at the door, crashing through the remains to make it outside. Once he escaped, he never looked back…not once!

Lying face down on the street, the fresh chilly winds were now relieving after the blaze of heat inside the deli.

He had very little after the frisk; no phone, no wallet, no gun. The only things in his possession next to his driver's license were a matchbook from the bar and a business card for a carpet cleaner from Duffy he received earlier in the night tucked in his back pocket. The guards must have missed those items.

He knew he had to get moving.

The kid got back up on his only decent leg and hopped in the direction of McCluskey's. His lungs were filled with smoke. His ears were still ringing as if an alarm clock kept going off inside his head. Blood was all over his body. Nails were still stuck in his left leg. The stare in his eye was cold as stone. The fact he made it out alive was stunning. How he made it this far, he was unsure.

The owner of McCluskey's was now in his view, locking up the bar for the night. The kid did his best to yell. "WAIT!!!!!" he panted from across the street, waving his hands in the air. "Hang on! Help me, please! Help me!!!!" The owner was shocked and bewildered to see this young man stumbling and limping in the street. As the kid got closer, the owner realized he was just pouring his drinks nearly a half an hour ago.

"Call 9-1-1. Call…fucking…9-1-1 NOW!!!" shrieked the kid, exasperating. The owner panicked, fumbling for his cell to call an ambulance and asked, "What is your name, kid?"

The kid's arms stretched, and knees buckled as he fell down face first to the concrete. He rested his battered body at the feet of the owner, uttering, "Jack McCool…*Black* Jack McCool."

CHAPTER TWO

Once I woke up in the hospital bed, it felt like I was coming out of a six-month coma. Yet, it was barely twenty-four hours later. The horrid white walls in this off-putting room were closing in on me. All I could do was look around for another escape.

Get me the fuck out of here!!

I felt like shit. I could barely think either. It was like being in Hell on earth. This was far from comforting. Nothing like the hospital in my neighborhood I grew up going to.

Sitting upright in the bed, it was moments after the nurse came in to tell me the perturbing news. The fact that none of my crew made it out alive with me from the deli explosion. They were obliterated. Blown away beyond recognition!

Now, all I wanted to do was find the fuckin' piece of shit who killed Fitzy, Duffy, and O'Hara...as well as the legendary Chris Veccuto. The same one who *almost* killed yours truly. Instead...I am sitting here...doing nothing.

So – *why me?* I asked. How the fuck did I make it out, breathing? Sure, a gimpy leg was my rite of passage. Yet, how was it not worse? How does a no-good bastard of a kid like me be the lone survivor? I guess it is just the McCool Family blasphemy...we don't die quick enough. God likes to kill us softly...slowly.

Luckily, the sexy nurse I couldn't stop eyeballing reentered the room just as my headache came back. She was far from the green-eyed beauty I saw the night prior at McCluskey's, but she was still stunning. She was the only thing worth living for in those very moments. "You here to give me my sponge bath?" I asked her, still half-awake.

She laughed innocently as her pearly white teeth shined bright in her mile-long smile. You could see her radiance from any angle you watched her.

Her mocha skin complimented her hazel eyes. She had a grace to her that followed her around. "No. You have a visitor, Mr. McCool," she said, with a gentle tone. "Who could it be?" I asked.

"He said his name is Alan and that you know him." I tensed up. The anxious feeling that I was having in my chest spread throughout me immediately like a lightning bolt. I could even feel it in my bad leg.

Breathe in, breathe out, McCool...he is only your boss. He is coming to pay tribute...right?

I cleared my throat, preparing for whatever was next. "Dynamite! Send him in, darling." The best part of the nurse's walk was the way she moved her hips. It's like she knew her ass was the "second coming" to anyone who had the pleasure to feast their eyes. It bounced up and down, one cheek after the other. Breathtaking!

Once she left my white-walled cell, Red Alan Connor arrived. In he trotted with that big ginger beard of his, taking over the bottom part of his face. You couldn't even see his lips. His shirt was untucked, and his pants sagged past his rear-end. I don't even think he wore a belt the way his belly would burst out. He looked like he slept in a hamper.

For a man who was so influential in our world, he sure appeared weak in his unkempt presence. Embarrassing!

I hard dark features, like an Italian. So, it was hard to imagine Red and I both had family that hailed from the same set of four green fields. His skin was as pale as a piece of Wonder bread. Yet, I was from the South and his family was from the North...two different countries practically. They called my kind "Black Irish."

"How are ya, Jackie?" he asked as he came over to my hospital bed, reaching out to holding my hand. He felt colder than I did.

Immediately, I looked back at him. With a scowl, I replied, "I have been better, Alan!" I then shifted my attention towards the television that was on. Wheel of Fortune was booming with excitement compared to this guy. "You are not happy, Jackie...I know. This, I understand."

"Not happy? My fucking crew is dead. Your crew as well, Alan!!! Not happy? I am miserable! What is being done about this?" I inquired. My fury was starting to boil over like water on a hot stove. I wanted justice. I wanted it immediately.

Dismissing me, he quietly replied, "I'm handling it." This was a guy who would typically have a mouth like a motor. Yet at this moment, it was hard to get any clear dialogue from him on current events. It made me wonder where he really stood in the situation.

Out of nowhere, he changed the subject. "I want you to have this," he told me while he shoved his hand in his pocket. I was leery of seeing what he was reaching for. Was it a wad of cash? A loaded gun? Who knew?

With Alan's other hand, he rolled his fist over, and gradually opened his grasp to reveal one of the most sacred gems we had ever known about. It was Fitzy's rare gold Claddagh ring, the one I always adored. I couldn't believe it.

My eyes then grew as wide open as a two-way tunnel. I was shocked. "I do not know what to say. How did you get this?" I replied as Alan handed it over, telling me he received it at the autopsy.

"Now he will always be with you…bringin' you luck." After that, Alan winked at me, trying to hold back from shedding a tear. He smiled, coming in and squeezing my hand once again. Yet, I wasn't sure how to feel. I wasn't entirely buying it.

Nonetheless, I played along. "I loved him, Red…he was the father I never had. Always looked out for me."

"He loved you too, Jackie. That is for sure."

Alan's defenses were down. I felt this was an opportune time to get down to business. It was now or never. "Say, Alan…the night at the bar…ya know, Fitzy was telling me about a venture that Young Veccuto was bringin' to the table for Paulie Muchetta to consider."

Before I was able to finish, Alan stopped me right in the middle of the beat of my words...quick enough to make my head spin. "I got to go see my brothers, Edward and Patrick. Call me in a few days when you get out, kid. We will all sit down."

I didn't even get to say goodbye. He was already heading towards the exit with his final statement rolling off his tongue on the way out.

That's when I knew. Red Alan did not give a fuck about me. He didn't give a fuck about Fitzy, the other two...nobody! Just himself. He felt I was as useless as the hospital I laid in, trying to fix me! *Cocksucker!*

I'd like to say his attitude made me upset. Yet, it didn't. It just made me want to find a way to escape more. From there, I'd see my revenge on who planned the hit. Afterward, I'd get back to my routine: the gym, church and running my poker game.

Nothing was around me for a moment besides the end of Wheel of Fortune on television and those revolting white walls. I always imagined *white* being the actual absence of color one sees when they die. It seemed more poetic than looking at a black *nothing*.

My eyes were closing quicker than a trap door. I was fuckin' tired. I would have loved to say Red Alan was the only disruption of the night. But, he wasn't. Hardly ten minutes went by until what seemed like an army came barreling into my forsaken hospital room.

I wasn't sure if I was getting arrested or killed. Perhaps both…the night was young. The three guys that came in could have gotten away with either one.

"Mr. John McCool…I am Federal Agent Jay Martinez!" the first one spoke, holding his polished badge out for all to see.

Talk about a crime stopper. His voice echoed throughout the hospital and its hallways like a train arriving at its station. You would have thought he was coming in to take down Whitey Bulger the way he charged through the door.

The man had fit the bill too…a real debonair kind of G-man. He could not have been much older than me. Tall as a giraffe, crew-cut hair as black as coal, and a suit so prim and pressed, James Bond would look like a hobo next to this stud.

I sat upright again in my hospital bed to get a glimpse at the agent, checking on my bandaged, mummy-like leg on the way up. "My last words when I got out of prison were that I was never going back," sternly, I told him. "You better put me down before you put me in, Mr. Federali."

Not even a grin cracked on his striking face. The two flunkies behind him weren't fazed either. It was like being at a memorial during the moment of silence.

"Those options are up to you, Mr. McCool," said Martinez. Every little bit of his badge shined as he put it away. "We may have similar interests here."

"Hah!" I chuckled. "The only things we have in common are our initials, Agent. Even that I question. Is your name really Jay Martinez? Let me see your real papers! Where were you born, Mexico?"

I had a way of making women laugh, but I was no comedian in the eyes of the law. The other Hispanic-appearing agent with the mustache behind Martinez looked like he wanted to strangle me with his bare hands after the jab I gave. He was shifting his weight around so much, he was ready to pounce. This was no joke to any of them.

"Okay, I am kidding," I assured. "Take it easy. I really just don't like you guys. Or the Staties, for that matter. They gave me five years in the can and robbed me of my early twenties."

"You robbed yourself, Mr. McCool...along with a lot of money that did not belong to you. I did my research."

I was starting to dislike this guy more with every word he uttered. He had no empathy. He was as cunning as they trained him to be in the academy. He went on as I remained silent.

"I am going to cut right to the chase, Mr. McCool. You are in severe danger!"

"Tell me something I don't know, Agent Martinez. You think I want to be in this fucking place right now?"

"We are just trying to figure out who is behind all this, Mr. McCool. For our sake and for your own good...before things get worse."

I wanted to laugh again. Not to insult the FBI, but I already had the answer. There was no denying who was behind this ordeal. It was no mystery. Yet, it sure wasn't a riddle I was revealing to them.

"Sir, things like this tend to figure themselves out. We all meet our maker eventually," I said in the coyest way I could have.

Martinez was trying to tell me otherwise. "There is a force bigger than both Paul Muchetta and your bosses, the Connor Brothers. There's a greater power holding the strings. There is no doubt they were behind the hit on you, Chris Veccuto, Michael Fitzgerald and your whole crew. However, there is more to it than just revenge on the now-slain," he told me.

"Oh yeah? Like what, smart guy?" I asked, entertaining the notion. I wanted to jump out of my bed in wrath. I wanted to wrap their clean black blazers around their heads and shoot them all. They made me sick…just as much as Red Alan did earlier.

"At this time, we do not know. The department is trying to figure it out. All we can determine is that there is something hateful in the city of Brotherly Love…and we would be appreciative if you would cooperate to help us bring it down. You're in *the mess* now…you can make it right by cleaning it up! Help us out!"

Martinez and his quick word use were far from charming to me. I ran my hands through my long brown hair and trimmed-up beard, thinking of the kindest way of how to tell these gentlemen to "fuck off."

"I am all set, Agent. Being in a mess, haha…I was never clean in the first place! Don't try to change me now."

"We know you ain't clean, McCool. Aside from the fact you're Black Irish, your mysterious discharge from the Army during the War in Afghanistan was a great start to the shit storm you brought home before you went to state prison. When are you gonna make things right already?"

He hit a nerve. That was it! I had enough! Now I wasn't thinking of how to tell them to leave, I was as frank as I could have been.

"GET THE FUCK OUT OF HERE, YOU SPICK COCKSUCKER!!" I exclaimed. "AND TAKE THE OTHER TWO CABALLEROS WITH YOU!"

I felt terrible making it racial. I didn't mean to say that part. My temper caught up with me. Yet, I hadn't thought about my military days until he brought it to my attention. There were many of nights I chased the bottle of whiskey, trying to forget it once I came home.

I wasn't going to go back to remember it now. Not even with a little provocation from a few fancy agents.

After those sour grapes left their business cards on my nightstand, they exited the room. Then, the apple of my eye came back in. The sweeter-than-wine nurse with the smile that could steal a heart.

Only this time, she wasn't smiling. "You have a phone call, Mr. McCool," she hesitantly murmured. "He sounds like a smoker, ya know…with the weird voice."

I wasn't even aware there was a phone in the room. It was one of those old rotary dials with a cord. The antique sat on the table next to my bed, yellow-colored and faded. I picked it up as soon as I was instructed.

"Someone is coming to kill you. The same one who gave you the gold ring," the voice on the other end stated. Whoever it was had an electrolarynx, one of those speech boxes. "Leave now! Go to 17th and Passyunk and call the number written on top of the payphone!" The other line then hung up.

My heart-rate accelerated. I could feel it pounding out of my chest. I looked over to the nurse, instructing her to come over. "What's wrong?" she asked, standing near the edge of my bed.

"Get my shirt, my jeans, and my cane. Then get me the fuck out of this hospital…NOW!!!!"

CHAPTER THREE

The hours were silently slipping away. Many in the city were already asleep. McCool, now restless for two days in a row, was on the run in the streets. He was looking for answers. Yet, he wasn't the only one burning the midnight oil, second-guessing every little thing. There was a dazzling men's suit store on South Street spotlighting another set of questions.

Red Alan and his two brothers were just entering the store. Also known in the Northeast as the "Irish Twins," Patrick and Edward Connor were less than a year apart. Affectionately, Alan called them Patsy and Eddie. Unlike him, big and red, they were both small and light brown-haired.

After being granted access by a few quiet wiseguys guarding the front door, the three stood and waited. Another man with a barrel chest came out from the back to greet them. "I will bring you to the office," he said.

From there, the brothers were escorted through the classy boutique. Smells of leather, shoe polish and starch sailed to their nostrils and span around like a whirlwind while their footsteps pounded along the rickety wooden floor.

Creek after creek, each section of the store held a different kind of clothing in sight of their walk. Vintage style slacks, classy three-pieces, and a myriad of dress shirt cuts.

The next area held the most excellent hand-made belts, cufflinks, and accessories. Across the room, there were custom-made shoes and Argyle socks.

Everything from penny-loafers to wing-tips. Right above it, a rare assortment of cashmere fedoras and embellished hats.

As Alan marched along this path of such high-class clothing selection, several thoughts became clear. He scratched that big old red beard of his, thinking, "Man, I really need to start dressing better." Behind the cash register's platform and into the stockroom, the barrel-chested guard led the Connor Brothers to a black wooden door.

Just on the other side sat the boss of the family in his leather-bound chair at his mahogany desk. Sangria-colored carpets, finished velvet walls, and a mini-chandelier lighting up every corner. He even had his initials embroidered in gold on the seats. This room had more elegance than the Oval Office. As if the suit store wasn't beautiful enough.

The entire store and all its possessions belonged to no other than "Pretty" Paul Muchetta. Along with the guards out front of the store, he had a few in the office with him. It was like he had his own Secret Service there for his protection. He wasn't taking any chances these days after his experience at the pizza place in Atlantic City.

"The Irish hoodlums!" he exclaimed as the brothers walked in. "There they are!" Paul stood up and came over to greet each one of them with a hug.

He did not move as quickly as he used to. Yet, Paul rarely moved for anyone.

"Ally! Patsy! Eddie! What do you say? What do you know, ya three stooges yas?" he asked, smiling and laughing from cheek to cheek.

"Happy 75th birthday, Paulie," said Alan. The pretty one laughed as he countered, "You are late, Red…my birthday was on Sunday. But I won't fault ya, I know you've been busy!"

"Well, Paulie…measures were taken the past few days. Things had to be dealt with in ways that work in both our favors!"

"You ain't kidding, boy. I've never felt prettier than I do at this very moment!"

Paul still dressed as extravagantly as he did back in the day. He donned the same powder blue double-breasted suit and peach collared shirt without a tie in full pride. Although, these days, it had a noticeable shine…one acquired in a way only twenty-five years could give you.

Besides his attire, the one thing Paul remained self-righteous of was his long hair he kept in a ponytail. Although a bit more gray over black these days, he still let it hang with honor.

Patrick and Edward sat down in chairs on either side facing the desk with Alan in the middle. Paulie maintained his smile as if it were painted on his face as he walked back over to his leather seat. He plopped down and looked towards the guard by his stylish mini-bar.

"Pour us all some Johnnie Walker there, Umberto…it is a celebration! And not just my birthday!" he exclaimed. He was satisfied with more than himself.

Alan then went on in detail. "It sure is. That cocksucker Fitzy was in up to his eyeballs in debt with me. He knew what was coming to him. His crew stood behind him instead of me...so they all had to be dealt with!"

Paul then reached for a cigar in the wooden box at the edge of his desk, offering one to each of his guests. They declined. High and low, he searched his drawers for a cutter and matches before asking a question...one of vital importance.

"What about the kid? The one in the hospital that survived the deli?" he inquired in a concerning tone, finally finding the cutter to prep his cigar. Simultaneously, Edward and Patrick both looked at Paulie then immediately to Alan.

Red replied, "We are dealing with it. After I checked on him to see what room he was in, Eddie made the call to send somebody. They will then bring back the ring I gave to the kid as proof the job is done!" Patsy and Eddie shared a glance as they nodded their head, concurring with the statement. The guard finally brought over a glass of Scotch Whiskey to each of the four.

Paulie smiled once more as he finally lit his cigar. "That is good," he commented, both to the stogie and to the update on McCool.

"We can't have him live to avenge us. He's a hot-headed pistol, that one." This was more than obvious. With his jaded past, McCool had a chip on his shoulder; it was known...an appetite for destruction. The pretty one continued, "Meanwhile, find new guys for your crew, Connors. There is still business to be done. You know what I'm saying?"

Alan and his brothers were a big part of the ecstasy distribution for Paul's manufacturing. Fitzy and the boys always helped with the legwork, peddling it to dealers on the street.

However, they needed more manpower than ever for the brand-new business endeavor that was to come. The greatest cash cows were ahead.

"And for that naive cocksucker Chris Veccuto thinkin' he could just come back home to peace? He was crazy...I wasn't going to let him buy himself off. That piece of shit needed to be made an example of that not all debts can just be bought...some you have to pay with your life. I'm glad he was gutted like the fish-out-of-water he was! He and his fuckin' brother, Primo can rot in Hell together!!" Paul, more passionate than ever, enlightened the boys.

His intense glare felt painful and piercing. It was tearing apart anyone who dared to look directly into his eyes.

"If only I had the chance to kill their father as well. That cocksuckin' snake in the grass, Little Vinny had it out for me more than anyone. Fuck, I wish he wasn't in jail just so I could slice open his throat in broad daylight, Alan!"

"I know, I know. I remember well, Paulie...I was the one who took you into hiding when you were on the run from him. Back when he wanted to kill you and his brother, Dante!" Alan said calmingly.

"I am forever indebted to you for that, Red. You were good to me then and are still good to me now. I'm extremely grateful."

Alan retorted with the most exceptional deal of sincerity. "Hah! Well...I knew once we met in the joint, we'd stay close. We've done a lot of good cohesively."

He thought very genuinely about Pretty Paul. They went way back. However, the one thing he cared about as much as their friendship was their business relationship.

"So, Paul...tell me more of how we have now taken upon this new overseas venture for ourselves! Give me the details!"

Paulie then stood up, pacing back and forth behind his desk. He puffed his cigar in-between statements. "Still ironing out the details, but we have finally made arrangements to sit down with Young Veccuto's guy in Costa Rica. He goes strictly by the *Caribbean Connection.* Someone from the family will be chatting more with him next week."

"Who from the family?" asked Alan.

"You-know-who...," quickly replied Paulie.

It was then Alan and Paul came to their famous gridlock in conversation. Red never met this *mystery man*, remaining behind the curtains of the regime for years. However, he knew it was this particular guy who helped Paul rise to power. He brought the family to glory at a time where it was at its critical low, after Vinny went to the can.

"When am I going to be able to meet this enigma-of-a-wiseguy, Paulie?"

"Alan, believe me…he does not make many public appearances."

"Well, tell me more about him then...more than just his first name!"

All that was known to many was that he wore a long black overcoat and a fedora at all times. Just as Paul was about to elaborate on more than simply that fact, a ringing sound went off.

Out of the blue, Eddie's cell phone chimed loud enough to wake the dead. It sounded like a smoke alarm in a blaze of fire. "Go ahead, pick it up!" instructed Patsy, holding his ears. Eddie looked at the screen of the phone, checking to see who was ringing. It was a number he recognized. "This is my guy," Eddie told them. Alan and Paul asked him to answer it as well.

Eddie stood up from his seat to take the call in hopes of receiving some good news. "Hello?" he asked. Then, he was quiet. Silence hung in the air while the others waited with baited breath.

All of a sudden, he hung up the phone. With all eyes on Eddie, he began to deliver the message to all. "The kid…McCool." Paul stopped pacing.

"He left the hospital. My guy, when he got there…all he saw was the nurse," continued Eddie. He thought to himself, "The kid must have known."

Paul froze in his furious state. His knuckles were pure white from clenching his fists too hard. He gritted his teeth from an effort to remain silent. The smile he wore the entire time had suddenly disappeared. A thick, dark scowl was now all the guys could see.

Alan snapped his neck and looked directly at Eddie. His face was red as his name suggested from suppressed rage. When he swung around and lurched, he yelled, "ED!! What the fuck do you mean he left? His leg is barely hanging on!"

"Where the fuck would he have gone?" asked Paulie.

"I don't know. My guy went in there and his nurse said he checked out," responded Eddie.

Nearly three blocks down from South Philadelphia Hospital, one of the last payphones left in the area lit up the bleak street corner.

Staggering towards it, Black Jack McCool felt the agony in every step he made. Three blocks to him seemed like three miles, walking with a bad leg and a cane. The journey was long. However, the goal was clear.

He searched for the few quarters he pleaded strangers for during his walk. McCool pulled out from his jeans pocket, the only other possessions he had left. The matchbook from McCluskey's Tavern, a business card with the name of a carpet cleaner, and Fitzy's gold Claddagh ring.

It was then when he let out a chuckle. He looked at the carpet cleaner's business card carefully and began to reminisce about his final conversation with Duffy the night of the explosion:

All four ruffians exited the cab. Walking towards the illustrious McCluskey's Tavern, it was 11:36 PM once they were dropped off at the parking lot.

After a long night out at Trinity Pub in the Northeast, the K&E Crew was looking to let the good times continue. Yet, they knew this was the last place they wanted to celebrate.

Trinity was their usual hangout. It was where they spent nearly every occasion. Nowhere else seemed appealing, especially anywhere down in South Philly.

Highway O'Hara joked with the boys about how they were heading into the *"Paison* territory" and were looking for trouble.

"Eh, Fitzy, you better tell Ol' McCluskey when we get in that he ought to greet us with some cannoli," said O'Hara, holding his belly while he chuckled. Everyone laughed…except for Fitz.

"Enough out of you. It is going to be a long enough night. I don't need your wisecracks. The last thing you need is a cannoli anyway, O'Hara…ya fat fuck," replied Fitzy. As much as he was serious, it was still funny once he said it. The fellas cackled even more. So much, their breath could be seen in the cold air.

Before walking through the shamrock-covered door, McCool tapped Duffy on the shoulder. "What is it, kiddo?" asked Duffy, thick with the Irish brogue.

Smiling, McCool hesitated at first. "Duffy, is it true you are close with the IRA in Dublin?" he then built up the courage to inquire.

Without hesitation, Duffy shoved him. He was much shorter than McCool, so he did not move him too far. The kid towered over the middle-aged, short and stocky bruiser. Not even his jeff cap helped his height.

"You shut the fuck up about them in public, kid...you hear me?" yelled Duffy. Jack put his hands up in surrender. "I only speak of them when it's necessary...know what I'm tellin' ya, McCool?" Duffy tiptoed to get closer to the kid's face.

"Alright, alright, Duffy...I am just saying that we are all family here. If I was ever in danger, I want to know if I could reach out to you and yours for help," admitted the kid. Duffy could sense he was being genuine. He held his cards close to his chest long enough...literally.

Reaching into his coat pocket, Duffy pulled out his money clip. "You don't come to me for that kind of help, Black...it doesn't work that way," he said as he scuffled through his dollar bills.

McCool was puzzled. "I don't understand," he told him. "No understanding is necessary...just be quiet," Duffy responded, finally seeming to capture something in his clip, pulling it out quickly like the big prize in a game.

He handed McCool a business card. The text looked like that done on a typewriter. It had the name of a local carpet cleaner on it. No pictures or graphics. It looked old. The card was beige, folded and faded. There was what seemed like a water stain of some sort on the end. If one had to guess, Duffy had this card for a long time.

"Two of these cards exist. The one I keep and the one I'm giving you now," Duffy told him. "If ever another presence is necessary for a certain situation, you call this number. Let it ring and go to voicemail. Don't leave a message, just hang up once it beeps. Your coordinates will be found and the help you need…will be there. They'll know."

As much as the kid was puzzled, he was gracious. "Thanks, Duffy…I really appreciate it," he said. He lent his hand out for Duffy to shake. Instead, the old man brought him in for a hug.

"We love you, Jackie…me, Fitzy, O'Hara. We have high hopes for you. Far and above what the Connor Brothers offer. Never forget that. Harness your youth." He then walked away, winked at him and headed into the bar.

While Jack stood and stared at the card, he remained thankful. Although, he was still confused whether Duffy was serious or not.

He slowly put it into his back pocket while an arm, out of nowhere, came around him. It was Fitzy! "Hey, Jackie…you asking Duffy for money again?" He then snickered and brought McCool in for a hug, telling him what a good boy he was.

Man, he sure loved him.

Even at the payphone on such a grim night, McCool smiled, thinking back to what he had which was now gone…those he loved dearly.

Right before he was about to shed a tear in memory of his deceased friends, he bucked up and put the card back into his pocket with the matchbook. He slid Fitzy's ring on his right finger before looking on top of the payphone as instructed. He proceeded to dial the written-out phone number.

Although he had no idea what he was getting into, he went for it. Picking up the phone and putting it to his ear, he dialed away. The buttons felt icy cold under his fingertips.

Whether this was a way out of a setup or into another, Black McCool was a betting man. He gave the odds of this outcome fifty-fifty, but he was all in. There was no looking back.

The phone, only ringing once, was the same electronic voice he heard on the line at the hospital. "It's me," said an annoyed Jack. The voice on the other end asked, "So, you do value your life?"

"I'm here, man. 17th Street and Passyunk, right outside of the gas station like instructed!"

"I will come get you now."

"I'll need a little more information. Where would we be going? And who is this?" It was then there was a dark silence. "Hello? Are you there?" McCool could hear breathing on the other end.

The voice then replied, "It can't be discussed on the phone. Look for a phantom gray Cadillac in a few minutes. First thing in the morning...*he* is expecting you. We do not have time to waste."

"Who? What the fuck, man?" Jack asked, demandingly. The other end of the line clicked into a hum.

CHAPTER FOUR

While Pretty Paul, Red Alan and Black Jack were plotting to get ahead, The Federal Government was in the midst of doing the same. The young, suave Agent Jay Martinez and his diligent Philadelphia division were fighting tooth and nail in the heart of the concrete jungle in an attempt to reveal some of the city's darkest secrets.

At FBI Headquarters on Arch Street, the rising star and his team gathered in the main conference room that very next morning to discuss their "war on crime." Although it was an ongoing fight, they were sure there were some key battles they could triumph upon to indeed push towards the path of victory.

While the nine other agents gathered around the long discussion table with small talk and gossip for a few minutes, Martinez swung the door open at the very last second he could. The young go-getter made his entrance a thunderous one. He marched with a great stride to the giant whiteboard in the center of the room as if he were General Patton. His blaring words resounded to his agents as if he was commanding his soldiers in the trenches.

"Good morning to all!" he alerted. "Good morning, Special Agent Martinez!" the room he led rejoined together in one sound, standing up briefly out of respect to their leader.

Martinez reached for a big black marker on the edge of the whiteboard. "Agent Davey…could you come up here please?" He signaled for his partner sitting at the head of the table, pointing the marker in his direction as if he were handing him a grenade to throw at the enemy.

Davey Leodore was the Fed who was known for his big mustache. He was one of the suits who accompanied Martinez to McCool's hospital room the night prior. He was also the one taunted at for being Hispanic like his partner.

Truth is, he was as Irish as McCool. He was hailing from the Boston division to give Martinez a hand with the never-ending case against *The Mob.*

He had a dark enough complexion to be mistaken for several different types of ethnicities. This worked to his benefit many times when he was working undercover.

"Bean Town's finest. Hey, there are enough Micks and Guineas down here to chase to make ya feel at home, Davey boy," joked Martinez. Everyone thought it was funny. "Not enough Latinos though…they are all still at the border with your cousins!" countered Davey, laughing as the room grew louder.

"Okay! Okay! Now down to business!" exclaimed the head agent, putting his arms in the air, palms out to all. Looking to genuinely make a name in the department, he knew he had to detail the mission at hand very clearly.

"Paul Muchetta." He pulled out a photo of the elder Mafioso, pressing it onto the center of the whiteboard for all to see. It was an aerial photo recently taken by a traffic light camera on a street corner in South Philly.

"This is our guy. We need to bring him down as soon as possible."

One of the agents raised their hands at the table. "Go ahead, Agent Rock," accepted Martinez, signaling for the man to speak at once.

"Agent JM…what about the Class of 2014? They have all been released recently. These past few weeks or so. Aren't these guys loyal to the old Veccuto crew? Ya know, the ones who hung around his eldest son in the 80's?"

Federal Agent Rock was not referring to the graduating class at Temple University that year. These guys were coming out of the school of hard knocks.

The dubbed "Class of 2014" referred to a set of wiseguys who were arrested in 1993, a few years after the end of Vinny Veccuto's reign. They were the last of a dying breed…the only allegiance the little one had left coming back to the streets.

They were also known as "The River Boys" during their youth, growing up in the South Philly section by the Schuylkill River. They were primarily remembered for their affiliation with Primo, Vinny's older son. They had a mixed reputation around the city, stemming from the infamous gangbang at a Brooklyn café in 1989.

At the end of Vinny's tenure, these young guns became tighter after Primo was killed. They rose to the occasion. They did their best to counter against Muchetta's takeover before they went away.

There was Carmine Copetelli, the oldest of the pack. Then, "Tony Boy" Tomasello, known as 'the man behind the plan.'

Finally, Virgil "Skinny Caz" Cassimo. He was the smartest of the bunch. Known for being the "master of cracking safes," he paid his dues many nights with high-price heists. The Feds had no doubt he was coming out of the prison cage, flying like a free bird towards the ultimate prize of claiming the family throne.

What was of utmost importance was the common denominator that the River Boys represented with the Feds: their hatred for Muchetta and the way things were being run in the city. Now with Chris dead, the assumption was that they were ready to do whatever it would take to bring down the ruthless regime that ruled. Twenty years of bitter rage in the making.

"What are you implying?" asked Martinez, taking a deep breath and striding closer to Rock. "Let's get one of them to flip," he spoke.

Shaking his head sideways with a smile, Martinez took another deep breath...this time exhaling loud enough to let the room know he didn't hear what he wanted. "Not going to happen, Rock. They did their time...there is no leverage," he finalized.

"More importantly than just the release of The River Boys is figuring out their next move. Will they try and whack out Pretty Paul before we get to him? Will they form an alliance and move up the pecking order? That's our focus. Either way, it brings us closer to the Holy Grail, Muchetta. With him off the throne, it brightens upon others hiding in the darkness!"

As Agent Martinez was explaining this, everyone was on the edge of their seat. Where he was going next with this story was as cryptic as his tactics: sporadic and without much warning prior.

Next, he directed attention above Paul's picture on the whiteboard. It was then he plastered a blank printer-paper page with a massive black question mark drawn on the majority of the sheet.

"Someone is telling Paul what to do...and it sure ain't the sloppy Red Alan Connor, his brothers, or the shit bag K&E Crew! The glue that has been holding the family together the past twenty-five years is an enduring conundrum."

"Your mystery guy," chimed in Davey, drawing an arrow from the big question mark down to Paul on the whiteboard.

Everyone was listening. Yet, nobody knew what to say next. The looks exchanged around the room were as blank and unanswered as to who this puzzling figure was. Many questions, zero clues.

All while this was happening, Martinez went over to his briefcase. Slowly, he pulled out a picture taken by Federal surveillance a few nights prior at McCluskey's Tavern.

There were various photos in the beige folder. These were taken by hidden cameras around the city as well. He passed them around the table while each agent took a glance for a second. One photo in particular though was top of mind.

"Another mystery yet to be solved. Black Jack McCool…young kid, last of his kind in K&E. The only one who survived the deli explosion the other night." Agent Davey pulled out a piece of scotch tape and snatched the photo from Martinez's hand. He then mortared the pic onto the whiteboard. "A real wild card," said Davey.

"I need to know what the little shit's part is in all this," commented Jay.

"Is he that important?" asked Rock.

Martinez made it clear. "Fitzgerald held him in high regards from what I gather."

"This little fuck head! You really think he has any clout whatsoever, Jay?" inquired Davey. He then spat on the picture of McCool, enough for it to run down the entire length of the whiteboard slowly like molasses falling from a spoon.

"I don't know yet. That's a part of why we're here, Davey. One arrest, putting him in state prison from 2003-2008 for armed robbery…that's all we have on him so far."

Suddenly, another robust man barged into the room during the meeting. It was the Bureau director of the division. He made the entrance of Martinez look like the opening act. The real show was beginning. He looked like a lineman, ready to make a tackle on the football field.

"Get your Teflon on and pack your pieces, everybody. We are going to North Philly!" he boomed, standing as if he was ready to go wrestle anyone he came in sight with.

"Director, what the fuck is going on?" asked Martinez, upset that his grand meeting was interrupted.

"We have someone ready to talk about the ecstasy manufacturing. This is our chance to bring down Muchetta and finally bring your mystery guy to light!" exclaimed the director. Martinez then rallied the troops.

The night prior was just as unnerving. Most of the car ride was silent between McCool and the man who scooped him up at the payphone in the phantom gray Cadillac XTS. He let him take shelter for the eve on an old cot in the back of the gentlemen's club he owned. It was just a few blocks away from the pickup.

The man was one of few words. He gave very little instruction. Why this was all happening still remained unclear to Jack. He felt as lost as a redwing flying north for the winter.

The eerie sounds of the night were not soothing either. The wind's velocity was ferocious. It warped at such a high decibel, it sounded like piping hot tea was incessantly being made outside on a stove. There were constant creeks in the olden wooden floor from every corner of the room.

Crick! Crock!

Jack knew he wasn't alone. Needless to say, he did not rest easy…or much at all for that matter. Nevertheless, once the sun pierced its light into the windows the next morning, the Cadillac man came into the back room to waken the young Irishman. He brought McCool a few items. There was soap, a towel, a change of clothes, and a black leather wallet with a money clip on the back of it with a small sum of cash tucked in it. This was to get him through a few days, living at sustainable levels.

After freshening up in a hot shower, McCool changed into the polo shirt, black hooded sweatshirt, baseball cap, jeans and sneakers he was given. Immediately after, he tucked the carpet cleaner business card and the matchbook into his brand-new leather wallet. He grinned looking at it, still laughing in his head at Duffy's story.

Suddenly, the strange man came back again to check on the kid once more. "You ready, McCool?" he asked, strolling in. Jack took a deep breath as he stretched his arms out, looking around the room. He was still unsure of what to be prepared for. He didn't even know who he was dealing with yet. "What is your name anyway?" asked McCool.

Hesitant at first, the man took a few seconds to reply. He knew if he gave it away, he'd be revealing more than just a simple name. "Virgil Cassimo. They call me Caz, Skinny Caz…or just plain Skinny. Your choice," he told him.

There he stood, the River Boys' own fearless leader sans Primo Veccuto. He was tall and lean as his nickname suggested.

He had long, slicked-back brown hair that was combed to perfection. With a clean-shaved face, his skin shined in the only dimly lit light in the back of the club. What resonated more than his smooth voice was his reputation over the years. Everyone knew about Caz and the River Boys...especially McCool. All the stories, from the streets to the cell block.

"Wow, it's you. You cracked a lot of safes in your day! Word on the street is that you just got out of the joint. I didn't even recognize you. I have heard plenty about you though, I must say," replied McCool, giving his full tribute. Caz scuffed with a smug 'hah' while he walked over to get his keys from the table.

"And I don't know enough about you, McCool. Yet, I am sure I am bound to find out very soon," he responded.

Black didn't like the way Caz was acting. It was as if he was upset he had to shelter him for the night. He never asked to be there in the first place. "Who are you working for? Pretty Paul? Red Alan?" asked Jack.

The skinny one then approached Black, inches from his face. "Kid, I would rather chop my dick off and have it fed to me! Don't bring up those names to me or I'll put a bullet in your fuckin' head! Just be happy I saved your life!" he exclaimed.

"Then what the fuck am I doing here, Mr. Caz and what do you want? And how did you know about the gold ring?" questioned McCool.

Before he even decided whether he was going to answer the kid's questions or not, Caz turned his head away. A crashing boom echoed from the front entrance. What sounded like a pile glass shattering on the floor rang all the way to the back. Caz walked out to see what was going on while McCool hopped behind him.

"Who goes there?" he asked, yelling loud enough for whoever it was to be alarmed. It could have been anyone at the door, breaking any type of thing. There was no room for error. Caz reached to his side, holding tight onto his Glock nine that rested on his belt.

It was nothing serious though. Caz sped his skinny frame up and trotted his way over to a guy resting on his knees at the front door. He was cleaning up the glass in front of him. Cardboard boxes scattered on each side, open and crumpled. "I ask again, who are you?"

"I'm the mug delivery guy. You ordered two boxes of glass earlier in the week for your bar. I just dropped them coming in. I am sorry. I will have a new shipment sent today."

"Make it fuckin' happen then. Expedite that shit!" an angry Caz demanded. He then took his hand off his gun to reach into his pocket for a few twenty-dollar bills to the floor. He threw whatever he had in front of the delivery guy.

"For your troubles."

McCool and his cane made it towards Caz's direction, passing the bar and stripper poles to his right. The smell of the entire club was peculiar. It was a combination of cigarettes, Mr. Clean, perfume, cocaine, and cash. He knew, just like anyone else;

after the glitz and glitter of the night came the reckoning of the new day.

Before he got too close to him, Caz stopped McCool in his hopping. "Just get outside and get in the fuckin' car. I will answer all questions on the way." He grabbed his overcoat and a comb for his perfectly fixed coiffure.

Moving towards the door, Black could not help himself. He was growing more and more agitated. "I want answers now!"

"Pipe down, kid. I'm not in the fuckin' mood."

"Just tell me where we are going, Caz."

The skinny one paused once again. He was not about to start taking orders from a kid he barely knew. Yet, he responded just to keep him quiet. "Federal Correctional Institute in Fairton, Southern New Jersey."

CHAPTER FIVE

There was something grand about the majesty of a winter's morn. I noticed it more than ever looking across the meadows of the Garden State. It was unlike any other scene. I could still see the snow on top of the thick and sandy-brown colored grass that fell nearly a week ago.

Blankets of white powder piled on tussocks in the wide-open fields. It laid calmly underneath the gray skies, curtaining the sunlight from above.

The trees shivered in the bitter wind. Gatherings of twigs, gnarled and twisted, extended out like the very hands of old man winter, ready to catch the next batch of soft falling snowflakes...whenever that would be.

It was a relaxing ride, sitting in the passenger seat of Caz's Cadillac. The open roads were a delight for me to see. Peaceful. With the uncertainty of what was in store at our upcoming destination, it had the possibility of being the last view I'd have pleasure in witnessing.

Except for continually tapping his thumb on the steering wheel, Caz was quiet again for most of the drive. But, that was okay...I wasn't necessarily looking for conversation myself. It had been one hell of a forty-eight-hour sleepless binge, and I did not imagine myself coming to rest anytime soon.

"We are almost there," he blurted, putting on his right turn signal. I looked around again, sighing once more at the deserted countryside before us. I had no idea what was coming next.

It was then I replied, "Where? Old MacDonald's Farm?" turning my Phillies baseball cap around backward to get a better glance of the no-mans land. In the distance, the first building in many miles became visible.

Caz quickly shifted his face in my direction, raising his voice, so I heard it well. "No, cocksucker!" His temperament changed from being impatient to on edge once we came into plain sight of the prison. *Gee that didn't take much.*

"Somewhere I spent many years," he finished.

At this point, we were in front of the compound. The vast white-bricked building had barbed wire fences around it, enclosing a countless amount of criminals with various types of stories as to why they were in there. One of those tales, I was about to learn.

As Caz parked the car in the visitors' lot, I took a deep breath before I attempted to get out. I tried to think of a time Fitzy gave me great advice. Of course, one of the many. It resonated so well in my mind, it was as if I was hearing it for the first time as I reflected.

We never know the cards the dealer is going to give us. But, how we play the hand...that's all we can control.

I smiled, pondering on this because of how accurate it was. Most importantly, with my current situation. Thinking about the man, I looked down at my Claddagh ring with pride. I was glad that not only his wisdom but a piece of him was still with me. I then stretched my fingers out before I put them on the door handle. As I reached, all I heard next was, "wait!" from Caz, grabbing my other arm.

I could tell he had something to say yet he was hesitant. We sat in silence for a few more seconds. Looking in his direction, I kept a blinding stare on my face. I was raising the obvious question of what exactly I was sitting still, waiting *for*.

Finally, the one they called "Skinny" answered. "Listen, Black. I don't mean to be a hard ass with ya this whole time," he admitted. There it was…the first nice thing he said to me. I couldn't believe it.

"There's something you should know. It's just that I loved Chris Veccuto…the same way I loved his older brother, Primo. This is all still as hard for me as it is for you. I know you miss your crew, Jackie…I heard nothing but the best about Fitzy and them."

Maybe I did have an ally. Then again, this could have been his ploy. Whatever we were walking into at the Federal prison was just as much a mystery to me as the night at McCluskey's Tavern still was.

"We are fightin' the same fight…believe me," pleaded Caz, lending out his hand to shake. He even took off his black leather glove…a sign that he was serious. Whether he was being genuine or not, I still could not decipher. Yet, I had nobody else to depend on. I took my chances. I shook it back.

"Means the world, Caz!" I replied. "Not sure what we are doing here at a Federal penitentiary or if this answers anything for me."

Caz winked one eye, opening his door and responding, "You are bound to learn, kiddo." He then got out of the car, adding into his conclusion with telling me, "Take the fuckin' hat off. A little respect, eh?"

Rolling my eyes, I acted accordingly, grabbing my cane and opening my door. There he was, back to being an asshole.

I wobbled out of the Cadi and took a deep breath, standing tall. It was the first clean, deep inhalation I enjoyed in days. Something about the woodlands around me seemed ominous. The quiet gave me a feeling of serenity.

Slowly and silently, we walked into the correctional complex. The air was different once we got inside. For a moment, I wasn't able to put my finger on it.

Suddenly, it occurred to me. The smell of the fresh pine was gone. There were no sounds of happy trees and sights of winter skies. There was nothing left but the eerie chill in the air. We could feel the icy grip of death lurking in the concrete walls around us, waiting to capture the many who were banished to an eternal stay here.

Among the condemned was the man we were about to see. Once we got to the visitation room, the glass wall separating society from solitude revealed all the answers. There he was! I was speechless!

Little Vinny Veccuto, an absolute living legend. He certainly did not look the way I remembered him or how he appeared in his pictures from the 80's. Then again, he had been away in prison since I was five-years-old.

The old man's grey-white hair encircled his balding, motley scalp. He had a weathered face and big thick reading glasses. His back slightly hunched from the weight of his past. You could see by the way he sat in his orange jumpsuit, he was a man with much to regret.

With each movement, there was the creak of old bones. He had the resigned look of one who knows that at his age, life has stopped giving and only takes away.

The prison guard who escorted him in stood directly behind him. He seemed to be very accommodating to Vinny. I noticed it mostly with the way he pulled his chair out for him.

Leisurely, Vinny picked up the phone that was resting by his booth. It was a short movement to bring it to his ear. Caz and I sat down on the other side. There were two receivers we each had to use as well. We picked ours up, one each. There was an awkward stare-down for nearly ten seconds until the old man broke the ice.

"Jesus Christ...twenty-five fuckin' years, kid. I remember seeing you as a little runt when Fitzy brought you in as his own...he was a good guy!" said Vinny, looking deep into my eyes as if he already knew everything about me.

It was amazing. I was talking to somebody I heard about all my life. Somebody who ran the city and its outskirts for so long. Somebody I forgot was still around.

I responded to him, "That he was, Mr. Veccuto. I can't tell you how much of an honor this is right now. Your name still rings bells in Philadelphia and South Jersey."

"Hah! Spare me the homage. The real heroes of the street have fallen."

Vinny readjusted his glasses as he looked over to Caz with a smile. "Except for this man sitting next to you, Jackie…eh? Skinny Caz…ya look good, boy."

Caz leaned in, pressing his hand on the glass to Vinny as if he were saying a prayer in his honor. "Thanks, Vin. It's good to be out," he told him, nodding his head up and down.

"How long now?"

"About three and a half weeks."

"What about the others?"

"Tony Boy and Carmine have been out two weeks."

"Good for you all. And thanks for bringin' the kid in."

"You got it, boss."

The more I sat quietly, the more I realized I needed to speak up. This was the kind of opportunity for one to seize. What I wanted to let out and vocalize to all was of vital importance. It was on the tip of my tongue.

Before I even made a peep, Vinny took the words right out of my mouth. "You're probably wondering why you are here now...aren't you, Jackie?" he asked me. It was like he read my mind.

I choked, uttering a simple, "Mmm-hmm." There was little reason to say 'yes' back. The old man already knew the question and the answer. With a smile, he folded his hands, beginning to unravel the details I had been waiting to hear before I even requested them.

"Caz and I have an old friend who runs the morgue back home," he said, cracking his neck to the left and right, readjusting the way he held the phone to his ear. "The night of the deli, 'the brothers' were there...and our friend overheard the plan about them coming to you to finish some business at the hospital. He let us know about it the following day."

I was all ears. Although I had my suspicions, it was nice to finally hear it confirmed. That son of a bitch, Red Alan and his two brothers!

"He gave you Fitzy's gold ring only to get it back. Whoever was coming for you was to retrieve it to him as a sign the deed would be done," he continued.

What a miserable prick. I knew it! Now my blood was running hotter and quicker than the veins of a volcano. My hands were shaking so quickly, Caz could see me flexing my fists, sitting next to me.

"He had been in cahoots with Muchetta from the beginning. It was both of them involved in the plan for the explosion. Thought you should know," finished the old man.

I told Vinny I was appreciative of him telling me all this. When I reflected on the past few days, I realized he saved my life. Yet, I wasn't satisfied yet. I wanted to do something about it. I wanted to end this madness, once and for all. "So, now what? We goin' after Red Alan and Pretty Paul to put them both in the ground like the piles of dirt they are or what?" I questioned.

Right away, Vinny looked to Caz through the glass and laughed for the first time during his entire prison sentence. For a brief moment, it felt like I was there for entertainment.

"You must have inhaled too much smoke after that nail bomb went off. Don't even think of retaliating…it is not worth it, kid. That isn't why I brought ya in," said Vinny looking back at me, shaking his head sideways. He then turned around to the guard behind him, nodding his head. Shortly after that, the guard left his side of the visitation room.

Disagreeing with his notion immediately, I countered, "What the fuck do you mean it's not worth it? They took out my crew…he took out your son, your second one is now gone!"

Maybe I went too far. The old man stopped laughing and slammed the phone on the glass. I'm sure he really wanted to smash my head with it if he were on our side. "You little cocksucker! I want to rip Muchetta and that miserable red-headed fuck to pieces…but it's not going to happen," he stated.

This was a passionate subject, one for considerable debate. I did not fully understand his reluctance. To let those animals merely get away with what they did would be a sin. I wanted justice…street salvation. "I'm sorry. I don't mean to insult you," I pleaded.

The little one's voice then grew calmer and softer. It was as if he wanted nobody else to hear him even though we were already confined and secure to a glass wall and phones. Plus, Vinny had it very good with those on the inside so that his calls weren't listened to or recorded. Nonetheless, he was extra cautious.

"My sons are dead, my brother is dead, and my ex-wife is dead. When I die…so does the Veccuto family name. I'm all that is left. I have more a motive to wipe out anyone involved in that night than you can imagine. There was a time in my life I would have simply done just that!"

"All due respect, Vinny…what's holdin' ya back then?" I wondered.

There was more he wanted to say…this I knew. Two and a half decades of balled-up emotions. He made it clear that he had a troubled mind, one that he held locked away much like the chains that held him imprisoned.

"I'm an old man. I may be losing my marbles in here but I ain't completely fuckin' stupid."

"What do you mean?" I asked.

"Red Alan ain't runnin' the show nor is that faggot Paul Muchetta. Trust me, kids."

The puzzle was getting bigger and the pieces were getting harder to find to fit together. "Then who is?" I asked.

Vinny leaned back in his chair. He looked up to the ceiling before he spoke, perhaps just to be extra careful no cameras were capturing the chat.

"The night of the explosion…Muchetta wanted revenge on my son and Connor wanted it on Fitzy. But the bigger motive…the cash cow, the Caribbean Connection that Chrissy had ties to."

I was on the edge of my seat like a kid in class who was actually paying attention to the teacher. *For the record, that was never me when I was in school.* Nonetheless, I wanted to hear more.

"So why would they take out the whole K&E Crew? Why not just Fitzy and your son and call it a day?" I asked.

"Lessens the interest and potential hands in the pot. More money coming in and a chance to cut out any middlemen tryin' to take a piece of it, including yourself. But see…neither Alan nor Paul are smart enough to plan that out…they aren't that ruthless. I know who has been running the city since I have been away, calling every single shot on the street."

As I looked to Caz, I noticed he was hanging on Vinny's every word as well…every predicate for that matter. However, he already knew the answers.

"Paulie's first cousin from the 'other side.' He goes by *Lou Gorgeous*," stated Caz, sternly looking in my direction.

"Who the fuck is Lou Gorgeous?" I questioned, looking at them both, back and forth, waiting for a response.

"I honestly do not know much," replied Caz, turning his head back to the old man.

Vinny then quickly took over the conversation. "Nobody does. He came in from Caccamo, Sicily in the 80's when he was in his early twenties. He worked for one of the New York Families, not Carlo Felonacci's outfit. Yet once I was gone and the family went to Paulie, it was Jimmy Tasseno who told the Commission to send him down to Philly. Paul didn't like it, but he learned to live with it…especially given the fact he is his cousin."

In all my time, I never heard once about this 'Lou Gorgeous' character. Then again, I didn't care. All I wanted was to see Paul and Alan choke on their blood and die a slow death. They tried to kill me, for Christ's sake. I now knew for sure!

"What the fuck is it with this Muchetta family? One calls themselves 'Pretty,' and the other goes by 'Gorgeous.' Are they that vain? Vinny, I don't give a shit about this cocksucker…who does he think he is?" I inquired, laughing at the terrible nicknames.

"He's incognito is what he is. He was set up at an auto garage on Reed Street and stayed quiet all these years. He told Paulie what to do and how to delegate. He doesn't make public appearances, he keeps it low key. That's why the Feds don't know him. I shouldn't even be telling you this, but you asked," said Vinny.

"So what the fuck then, Vinny? Are you saying Caz and I are supposed to be afraid of this Lou cocksucka and run away?"

"For your own good," he demanded. I wasn't having it. Yet, Vinny went on. "I requested you here today to thank you and tell you I am going to have Caz get you up to Maine tonight, far and away from this bullshit. Out of respect for you standing behind my son. He'll get ya more cash before he drops ya off…enough til' you get on your feet."

Vinny put me in a weird place, mentally. My conscience began yelling at me. I could hear it screaming from the depths of the deepest and darkest parts of my body.

Was this a way out? I began asking myself different types of questions. *Could this be a chance to embark upon a new beginning? A fresh start?*

The offer seemed enticing for a brief moment. I never traveled to The Pine Tree State, but I heard it was serene. Big blue lakes and vast green forests. It would be the same type of peace I experienced on the car ride here to the prison. Nothing spoke to me quite like the different views of nature.

This would be mean no more hustles. No more hoodwinks or bamboozles. The days of counting cards and running the executive game would be over. There would be no madness.

Yet...at the same time…

There would be no real message sent to those who fuckin' deserved it!

Up I stood. "No...no fuckin' way!" The skinny one tried to sit me back down immediately, tugging at my hooded sweatshirt. Feeling insulted, I asked him, "Is this why you brought me here, Caz?"

Vinny squinted his eyes and looked right at me, keeping the same mellow pitch despite my short tone.

"Jackie, you think this is ideal? You think anyone wants this? It's the fuckin' way it is. Life ain't fair."

I couldn't make sense of it. This was a man who feared nobody. Twenty-five years ago, whoever stood in his way was destroyed...even those closest to him. Yet, now...he was backing down from this revenge like a coward. Worst of all, he was asking me to do the same. I was feeling very let down.

"I ain't fuckin' runnin' nowhere, Vinny. Not from any of these scumbags!"

"Sometimes we have to make sacrifices for the greater good, kid."

"But I ain't sacrificing myself, Vin."

I could tell Caz wanted to chime in. I noticed he looked down at the floor once I stood up. His posture told me all I needed to know. He was not happy with this advice either.

"You'll be fine up in Maine. Believe me, you've done your part with staying alive. You made it this far, kiddo!" said Vinny.

I looked away and shook my head sideways, letting my thoughts get the best of me. *What did he mean I did my part, staying alive? There had to be a better way to solve this.*

The old man went on. He wasn't giving in. "Lou stands behind an army, pal. You don't want to feel his wrath, believe me! You go after those two, you're starting a war you cannot win."

"Okay, Vinny…listen. I gotta say something," interrupted Caz. Finally! *Speak up, Skinny!* I was waiting for support this whole time.

Vinny didn't want to hear him out either. "We agreed to this prior, Caz. Not even *you* would want to get into this mess, believe me. You told me you were out of the game, content with running your strip joint and staying low-key."

"I know I did. But the truth is…I don't give a fuck about Lou either. Where has he been the past twenty years? Nobody has even seen him!"

Betrayal was the only way Vinny was feeling. He and Caz spoke about ceasing fire. Yet now, Caz was making a different play in a whole new book.

"We can't let Alan and Paul get away with this just like Jackie is saying here. Chris was like a brother to me the way Primo once was. What has happened keeps me up at night. We must counter," continued the skinny one.

Silence spread. It stretched thinner and thinner, like a balloon blown big, until the temptation to rupture it was too grand for Caz to resist. "I gotta agree with Black. What's right is right. We can't wait around to make a move here."

Still nothing. I sat and hoped Vinny would see it our way. It didn't feel like we were getting through to him. Every other word from either one of us seemed to infuriate him more.

"Twenty years in the can. Let me do this last hit now that I'm a free man, that's all I ask. I'm lookin' to be done too, Vin. Just need this to finish this final job," finalized Caz.

All of a sudden, a smile cracked from the old man. It was hidden in there, along with a chuckle. "Hah! You're a lot like him, Jackie...you know that?" asked Vinny.

"Who?" I questioned.

"Fitzy. Hardheaded, Black Irish. Always had something to prove and made sure everyone around him joined in on his madness."

Caz then barreled in on the defense. "Vin, I was on the fence even before I talked to Black. But now, I see...he makes a good point."

My stare was now longer than the term Vinny was serving. "This is more than trying to prove something, Vinny. This is about what is comin' to all those pieces of shit! I just want to look them in the face when it's done...particularly Red Alan," I detailed.

A moment of hope. No response for merely a minute. Vinny was clearly contemplating what we were trying to sell him. You could hear a pin drop in the prison until the old man spoke up. "Clearly you two won't listen. Caz, you really think you can get the other two River Boys on this?"

"I will get a meeting together."

"You do what ya need do then. I can't stop you inside here anyway." Vinny slumped in his chair, crossing his arms as he held the phone between his ear and shoulder.

I made it clear this was the only route my mind was traveling on, no U-turns. "I just can't run away like this, Vinny…not after what I've been through the past few days."

"Then you have to do what makes ya feel right, kid." He smiled, looking back down to the ground. He pulled off his glasses, cleaned them and put them back on his face.

"Dynamite!" I exclaimed.

I could tell he did not want to go along with our plan. Yet, he saw where Caz and I were coming from.

"I'll make sure there are no errors, boss," said Caz, taking responsibility. We both stood up, ready to put the phones back on the hooks. That was until Vinny gave his last peace.

"What you need to make sure of is the aftermath. Just know you're all in now. You're pissing on a bee's nest. I can't prepare you for Lou Gorgeous…you guys are on your own there."

"He doesn't scare me, Vinny," I exclaimed. Caz had my back. "Me either. If he is even *really* out there, we'll fuckin' kill him too," he boldly stated.

"You two got more balls than me, I'll tell ya that." Vinny hung the phone up and gave us his best before we left.

CHAPTER SIX

Once they finished their detailed discussion with Little Vinny at the Federal prison, McCool and Caz immediately called upon the other two River Boys: Tony Boy and Carmine. They asked them to meet at the gentlemen's club Caz owned later on that night. It was called "Skinny's Lounge," a local favorite for those who appreciated the kind of thing it had to offer.

It was getting to be about that time to make sure things were ready for the show. Caz prepped for the night while McCool took a quick trot down the street to get sushi for their meeting.

Outside, the bright neon sign hung above the entrance, lighting up the club's name with a brilliant blinking martini glass on top as the logo.

Inside, young girls of all different races danced on stage over what looked like the Northern Lights. Through smoke swirled assortments of blues, acid greens, hot pinks, and gold.

While the music played, the girls danced as if they were exchanging energy. Their bodies were in sync with the rhythm.

Swiveling lounge chairs surrounded the circular stage in the center of the room for a more intimate view. Tall pub tables were scattered across the rest of the open space while the bar stood in the back with stools in front of it.

This was indeed different than the way McCool saw it the night before when he slept over. Much more alive, much more to look at!

However, he nor Caz were there to partake in the events. There was no time to throw dollar bills at pretty gals for hours. There was a more important business to tend to.

Hidden in the back of the club was the VIP Lounge. A half-circled leather booth enclosed around a glass table that rested in the middle. Center of the seating was the one Skinny Caz, sitting alone…waiting for both the boys and the food.

"Over here, McCool!" he yelled, standing up, signaling to him as if he were redirecting traffic to get his attention. He put his hands around his mouth to strengthen the sound when he shouted his name.

Black finally heard him after the smell of the perfume on stage stopped making him dizzy, stumbling by it.

Although he was enamored by the glamour of the room, McCool kept thinking about the same green-eyed girl from McCluskey's, hoping he'd see her again someday.

Once he, his cane and the bags of dinner he picked up shuffled their ways over to sit down, McCool was greeted by Caz. "See anything you like?" he asked, pointing towards all different directions of the stage.

"Every piece of pussy in here…perhaps they will get my other leg working again, ya know what I mean," Jack replied, seating himself down in the booth slowly and carefully. Caz chuckled as he took another sip of his Sambuca. He then took a look to see what assortment of sushi McCool picked up for them to eat.

"Where are the others in your crew?" spoke an anxious McCool, looking around the club. He was tapping his better foot on the floor, eager to discuss the plan they had ready to sell to the rest of the famous River Boys.

Caz then pointed directly to a heavy-set bald man using the ATM next to the bar. He was in a black button-up shirt with grey slacks. His signature silver suspenders shined in the light with each movement he made.

"That's Big Carmine Copetelli, one of my top guys and a regular around here. I think we restock the ATM every morning with more cash because of him," he said.

They both watched while the large guy smiled and stacked the twenties coming out from the machine and into his massive hands. He would then take the dollar bills and smell them. Very weird…yet methodical.

Old Carmine was loyal, always true to Caz and the River Boys. Historically, the skinny one knew he could depend on him, no matter what the task at hand was. They were very close. They had been through a lot together.

"What is it, he's never seen a naked broad before?" responded a restless Jack.

"The guy has been out of the can for two weeks. He's making up for lost time," replied Caz, winking at him and finishing up his Sambuca. Jack laughed, signaling the waitress for a Jameson and a refill for Caz. The skinny one continued on.

"I'm tellin' ya, kid...back in the day, I cracked safes and Carmine cracked heads. That's how it would go."

"You think your boy over there is ready to put this plan into play with us or what, Caz?"

By the looks of Carmine dilly-dallying with the girls in the club, Black was reluctant to think he had what it took. He could hardly imagine him cracking his own knuckles...let alone, heads.

Caz responded just after the waitress came over to take their drink order. "Bring the drinks to my office, dear," he then told her, slipping a few dollars in her G-string.

"Carmine's made more collections in less than two weeks than any of the other shy locks around. He's hungry to get back in the game when the rest of us initially didn't want to at all. Plus, he has whacked out some big names in his day. I think he is more than ready for this."

Still not convinced, Jack asked, "What about the other one? Where is he at?"

Caz scooted out from the booth and signaled for McCool to follow him with the food in hand. "Let's continue this in my office, kid," he said. They both got up and made their walk to a hallway behind the VIP lounge. From a distance, Carmine could see the two getting up...a signal that it was time to go to the back to talk.

There were three doors down the hallway. One at the end, one to the right, and then a revolving one to the left. Innocuously, there was a dark turn at the end of the hallway as you came closer to the door in the center. Down that path led to another door...Caz's office. He and McCool went inside.

The office contained very little. It was as if somebody took the Staples catalog and ordered whatever was on sale that issue. There were a few filing cabinets by the entrance, a metal desk in the back corner and a circular table with four metal chairs sitting in the center. The entire room looked rarely used.

"So, Caz...where is the other guy?" asked McCool as he sat in one of the chairs, putting the food down in the center of the table.

All of a sudden, another gentleman popped open the back entrance door to the office. He practically came out of nowhere like a magic trick.

Yet, that's how he moved...quickly. One minute you would see him, the next he would just vanish. The man had thinning brown hair, a trimmed up mustache and a dirty white apron hanging from his neck. The grease stains on it were so deeply embedded in the cloth, they looked like they were there initially.

"Sorry I am late, Caz. I had to finish up working at the diner down the street," said the guy, brushing off his clothing of the day's cooking debris.

He smelled like he was behind a deep fryer all night. You could see how disgusted McCool was when he came over to sit next to him by the way his face curled up. At the same time, he slid a few more inches away, hoping for relief.

Not just because of his appearance…but at his choice of profession being a cook. He was alleged to be a dangerous man. Now, his only danger was whether he remembered to turn off the oven or not.

"That's how you dress to a gentlemen's club?" inquired Jack, smiling with an off-color remark. "Nice to meet you too, *shit-face*. Caz, who the fuck is this?" asked the guy, pointing over to McCool. The guy didn't take his humor too lightly.

"Fuck you!" replied the young Irishman, raising his voice a decibel.

Caz took a deep breath and exhaled slowly, trying to cool off the hostility that was brewing right before him. "Jack, Tony Tomasello…Tony Boy, Black Jack McCool," he introduced. The two could barely look at each other, let alone share a handshake.

For Caz, this night was turning into an absolute mess. Both at his table and inside the club. From a distance, he could hear the commotion of screaming and yelling outside his office door. They were voices of the dancers and bartenders he was all too familiar with.

"Let's get through this, boys…I got a lot of shit to do here tonight." He shook his head sideways, ready to move on.

Big Carmine finally made his way into to the office just as the waitress opened the door with the tray of drinks. She even got what Tony and Carmine liked without them asking; a Malfy Con Limone Gin and Tonic and an Old Fashioned.

Carmine looked like he just got out of a bath with the way he was sweating. "Eh, Carmine…what do you say?" asked Tony Boy, standing up for his old friend.

"Antonio, ooooh! *Que sa di?* What can I say, these babes give me a workout, ya know? They've been dipping me in holy water all night, can't ya tell?" replied Carmine, exchanging a kiss on the cheek with Tony Boy as he dropped sweat everywhere like he was ringing out a wet rag.

He did the same with Caz before introducing himself to McCool. With a firm handshake, it was much more cordial than the meet and greet he had with Tony Boy. "Ain't you a doozy, *Big Shot!*" said Black, smiling away at the heavy hitter.

"Oooo! Caz, before we get started…who the fuck let this bog-trotter from K&E into your bar, heh?" asked Tony Boy, referring to the only non-Italian in the room. McCool hopped up out of his seat with a hot Irish temper. He was holding the table for balance, ready to do what he had to do to send a message to Tony Boy.

"What did you just call me, you Dago motherfucker?" he yelled. Tony Boy remained on his feet, prepared for the young one's wrath.

"Caz! Get this fuckin' kid out of here, please…c'mon!" demanded Tony. The skinny one arose and came over to separate the two at once to avoid any bloodshed. "Both of you, sit down and shut up!" demanded Caz. They remained standing.

"Only thing I am trottin' is ya motha's twat, you greasy fuck!" bawled McCool to Tony. "Hey, Jack...that is enough! Shut the fuck up already!" yelled Caz. Finally, all were attentive. The table was silent at last.

He then took a moment, folding his hands in front of him, getting right to the point. He whispered to the three, "We are going to take out Pretty Paul Muchetta...plain and simple."

Black nodded his head while the other two sat in shock. It was as if Caz told them they were both diagnosed with cancer the way they reacted.

"Along with Red Alan and the Connor Brothers in the Northeast. We *decapitate*...and we do business with whatever is left," Jack added.

Tony then chose to be the first to respond. He looked at Caz intently, telling him, "I don't think it's a good idea, Caz. I know what you're trying to prove, but I can't stand behind it." McCool then countered, "Why not?"

"I'm not fuckin' talkin' to you, kid!" replied Tony, shifting towards McCool with his hand in the air.

"TONY!" yelled Caz. McCool sat in fury while the greasy one turned back to his old friend.

Caz spoke, "What are your concerns?"

"What do you mean? We just spoke about this a couple weeks ago. This exact topic...in your office here! We agreed to leave this alone!"

"Things have changed now, Tony Boy...people have been killed by these guys. People we knew very well. People we loved," explained Caz.

"Caz, I hear you. But, this will not go over well. We all said we are trying to go legit. I'm working on a second chance here. You, me, Carmine. I ain't goin' back to prison for nothin' stupid. There won't be a third chance, ya know?" countered Tony.

"Yeah. And how has that been going? Staying legit?" asked Caz, pointing to his attire.

Looking down at his apron, Tony Boy remained speechless. He knew what Caz was saying. He just did not know how to get on board. It was a risky move, no matter how he looked at it.

Big Carmine then spoke his peace. "I hear ya, Tony. What they did to Chrissy was wrong…we must have justice here. There is no other way. I gotta agree with Caz and Jackie Irish," he admitted.

Tony had an undying love for the Veccuto Family, especially Chris' older brother Primo from back in the day. However, he was trying to look at the reality of their inevitable consequences. "Do we really want to deal with the repercussions of all this?" he asked.

McCool then leaned in towards the man with the dirty apron sitting next to him. "You talkin' about this man, a myth…a one *Lou Gorgeous*?"

Tony looked towards the back door, preparing for his exit. "What the fuck do you think you know about him, kid?" he asked McCool.

"I know enough."

"Really? Do you?"

"I know that he isn't nearly the great power to stop me from doing what is right, Tony."

Sitting and laughing, Tony put his hand on his face. He began shaking his head sideways. He then stood up and pulled a few dollar bills out, putting them on the table.

"Here is for the drink I didn't have. Caz, I'll talk to when ya start thinkin' clearly and when you get this cocksucker out of here," he said, pointing to Jack. He began walking away.

"Tone, c'mon…for Primo, if anything!" yelled Carmine, standing up, pleading for him not to go entirely just yet.

Tony stopped, closed his eyes tightly, beginning to ponder. He was not going to let anyone change his mind. Turning around, he replied, "I just can't do it, Carmine. My love to both Primo and his little brother. I respect their old man like no other."

Out of the blue, Black hopped back up, "Vinny is behind us!" Tony shook his head again and continued his walk away from the fellas.

"Hold up!" yelled Jack, springing over to Tony on his one good foot. He had to think quickly and sweeten the pot to make this plan rich.

"Look, you don't gotta like me, and I don't gotta like you. But we are in this together, Tony. There is something we both want here."

"What do you mean?"

"If we don't do this, yeah…you can stay legit. But for how long? How long until Muchetta decides he wants to settle the score himself by wiping out anyone else he sees as a potential threat after what has happened?"

Tony stayed silent. He was not buying it. "I'm sorry, kid…can't do it." He turned back around again and headed for the exit. His mind was made up. Nothing would alter it.

Black then spoke up. It was now or never to give him all he got. He had to create the urgency for Tony to join in.

"I run an executive poker game! Once every two weeks! High rollers and big dollars that come into the Northeast, fellas! I will give you all a rake of the buy-in and pot!"

Tony looked at his apron once more then turned around. "Okay. I'm listening," he said before they both made their ways back to sit at the table. Carmine then asked, "What are you kiddin' me? Jackie Irish, I heard you used to count cards in AC after you got out of prison. Now you're running the executive game?"

"Times have changed, Carmine. This is a high stakes table. Ten G minimum on the table. Multiple players throughout the night til' sunrise!"

Black Jack McCool was a man with many ways of making money. A real hustler. He always found a way to come out on top…which is why when he offered to share his marquee racket, they knew he wasn't kidding around.

"Okay I'm in," surrendered Tony, reluctantly sitting back down to the table. Black motioned to pat him on the back. Tony reacted, flinching and said, "Don't touch me!"

"Alright, alright…take it easy," said McCool, smiling with his hands in the air.

Tony looked at Caz. "If we're going to do it, it's gotta be quick." The days were of the essence. Tony knew, much like the others, this had to be completed in a timely and orderly fashion.

"One thing!" yelled Carmine. "I want to be the one who takes down Pretty Paul myself. Let me handle it!"

Caz chuckled, knowing deep down he wanted the honor of doing the same. He wanted to see the man fall before him, begging and pleading for his life just before he took it away.

Although, at the same time, he also knew they were all equally as close to the Veccuto Family. Caz realized whoever took down the pretty one would do it coldly and ruthlessly. There would be no mercy shown.

"Okay, Carmine," he said. "But make sure he suffers. I want him to feel it all the way down his trip to Hell! Ya got me?" As they exchanged a look, Carmine nodded. One eyebrow raised with ideas.

Tony then leaned over to McCool. "What else you got up your sleeve, kid? What other secrets you holdin' out on?" he asked him.

Little did he know, there were so many things. The hardest part would be how much to actually tell him.

The depths of McCool went more in-depth than many could imagine. You could see it in his expression, there was an abundant amount that he held in. His blank stare filled his face with mixed emotions. It was all a mystery. However, it was all about to be revealed in time.

The young Irishman just smiled back, nodding his head to Tony. The four then began planning for the following day.

Jack leaned over to Caz just as he was about to speak, asking, "Skinny…what else you know of this *Caribbean Connection*? Vinny talked about it earlier. I must learn more!"

The skinny one smiled and replied, "All I know is that it has to do with offshore gambling. A 'price-per-head' kind of operation conducted online. Not your usual stuff. Big money involved."

"Who is really making the decisions on it, Caz?"

"Beats me, Jackie!" he replied, finally digging in and eating the sushi on the table. Sarcastically, he looked to Caz and replied, "*Dynamite*!" while rolling his eyes.

In the hours after McCool and The River Boys mastered their grand plan, nothing good was happening in the north part of the city. It was nicknamed "The Badlands" for a reason.

Even at dawn, the neighborhood was barely lit. Shadows lurked in odd places while strange figures lingered in the only bright ones. Not even the police made their way to these streets on a regular basis…but this day was different.

Grim secrets hid in the darkness of every corner. Garbage piles spilled into every gutter and alleyway. Cat-sized rats squeaked viscously through the blocks, scurrying swiftly to the next hole in the wall. Flocks of pigeons swarmed above in perfect accord. They traveled from the crumbling, graffiti-covered concrete walls to telephone wires draping down in-between old wooden poles.

Stenches of old musky beer and rotted food powered the air. Littering the streets were dead rodents, nickel bags, cheap sex and every type of syringe in plain sight.

However, it was on this late morning that North Philly saw its most gruesome moment above all. Everyone who walked out after it happened could not believe their eyes at the mayhem in front of them.

There at the intersection of 3rd Street and Indiana Avenue, thirty-two bodies were shot to the ground from a vicious ambush. It was led by two black, unmarked SUV's whipping by with IMI Uzi submachine guns at laser speed. The entire attack occurred in less than five minutes.

Twenty-seven were confirmed dead while the other five who were caught in the crossfire hung on for their dear lives. They crawled through the streets aimlessly, leaving a bloody trail behind them.

Walking out from his quarters at seven o'clock sharp that morning, neighborhood legend Desmond Carter stood in awe at the wasteland that he called home. He held his son's lunch, preparing to walk down and meet him at the bus stop that was picking him up to go to school. His son, Nathan, never came home the night before. Desmond figured he stayed out with his friends too late once again.

At first, he was mad that young Nathan didn't come home on a school night along with forgetting his lunch. Then, his mood instantly changed once he looked around.

Not once in his twenty-four-year career as drug kingpin had he seen such a ground-zero like this. This was inhumane.

Recognized as 'the almighty' or 'the block warden' for so long, Desmond was referred to as "King Carter" in his prime. The native African-American residents would bow down to him when he walked around, ready to kiss his feet. It wasn't that they just wanted to be on his good side. They respected him as if he were the "holy of holies" to his people.

From the late 1980's into the early 2000's, King Carter ruled the Badlands and anywhere outside where he dealt drugs. He worked closely with Pretty Paul for manufacturing. These two were very familiar with one another.

Desmond was a great success in making a lot of money, not going to prison or being killed. Luck always seemed to follow him…until this very day.

He called it quits when his son was born in 2002, his only child…Nathan. Especially after his wife, Nathan's mother died shortly after their son's birth of a heroin overdose, Desmond knew he had to make things right. He had to get out of a life of crime. He didn't want his son growing up without both his parents.

As he made his way down the street, he noticed the police cars and ambulances' blazing blue and red light shining into the formidable community. In plain sight was the old ecstasy lab on the corner that had just been torn to shreds the previous afternoon by FBI and DEA agents. Desmond figured this gangbang was somehow tied to the recent raid. He just could not connect the dots yet.

Shaking his head sideways, the retired thug was still in shock as he continued his walk, aghast at the lifeless and their pools of blood that bordered around him.

There was a time where Desmond would have two or three flunkies next to him, guarding his every move wherever he went in the city. He would not go a full block without having four or five conversations. He'd have a custom-made suit, a fancy-colored fedora and big black sunglasses on.

These days, nobody recognized him. Nobody even acknowledged him. His attire consisting of a white wife beater and old blue sweatpants with holes complimented the man who "once was" somebody.

This did not bother him though. Very little did. As he continued his path to the end of the block, there was only one thing on his mind...who was among the wounded. He gripped the lunchbox firmly and sped up his walk towards the bus stop on the corner...where all the action was.

The five who were still breathing were being taken care of by the police and EMT's. Stretchers came rushing out of the vans. Body bags followed right behind them.

More residents came sprinting over to the crime scene. "Back up!" yelled police as their radios were going off. Their attempt to keep citizens away from the horror was great…but to no avail. This was just too personal.

Among the dead and wounded were those who had it coming…and those who didn't. Guilty and innocent. The powerful and the weak. Men, women, children. There was no discretion. Whoever conducted this hit was colder than the late November freeze in the air…a heart of ice.

As Desmond came closer to the police, he shut his eyes. He prayed for the best outcome. However, he knew there was a possibility of something even more terrible than he imagined.

He didn't want to believe it…not for a second. Yet, as he came in arm's length of the first responders' commotion, there was the truth. The unbelievable. The five bullets in his 12-year-old son, Nathan's chest and abdomen.

From the middle of the street came the most hysterical crying. It was the screaming sobs only interrupted by one's need to draw breath. It was a primal sound. You couldn't ignore it. Anybody around turned their heads, caught between an impulse to help or stay out of bother.

Desmond ran to the other end of the stretcher where the paramedic was attaching IV's and cleaning up the bloody mess around him. He clenched to his son's hand. His violent shaking almost caused him to fall on top of him. From his eyes came a thicker flow of tears than he had ever cried in his entire life.

"That's my son! That's my son! Help him, please! Is he going to be okay? Please tell me, please!!" he begged the emergency responder.

"He still has a chance, sir. He is hanging on here!"

Nathan was pale as a ghost. One of the medics put a breathing mask on him as they hauled him into to an ambulance.

The police came up to talk to Desmond. However, it was no use. In those moments, the entire world had gone astray for him. There was only pain…enough to break him…enough to change him beyond recognition.

Although he had many thoughts swirling in his mind, one seemed to encompass them all. "We expect to bury our parents one day…but never our children."

In the blink of an eye, this day had changed from being a normal one to utterly unforgettable. This was a day he hoped would never occur since the very moment his son was born. All his greatest fears had come true.

CHAPTER SEVEN

While havoc was spreading in the Badlands, McCool woke up serenely in his native Northeast that very morning. Still, on the run, he took refuge at his lifelong parish, Our Lady Mother of Mercy Roman Catholic Church on Frankford Avenue.

Something about the sanctity of the place seemed safer to stay at for him than his own home. The bells of the basilica that rang in perfect accord, the smell of frankincense giving off an aroma that delivered peace. This was a haven for many including Jack. A good friend of his, Monsignor O'Brien, the high holy, set him up with shelter in the back of the rectory.

O'Brien ran the clergy for many years, starting when he emigrated from Limerick, Ireland in the mid-1950's. At this point, he could have stepped down a few times over. However, many would be lost if he did. O'Brien was the last of his kind...a devoted man, faithful to the vocation and committed to the people of the parish.

He and McCool were close. As an orphan, Jack would spend a lot his time either at his church or nearby hospital early on in his life. This overnight stay was very nostalgic for him.

Breakfast was ready early. Jack was awake for it, but he wasn't hungry. Instead, he watched the sunrise from his window.

As he stared at the orange glow, he thought about everything he needed to get done in the daylight. Confession, for starters.

He met with Monsignor O'Brien at the altar of the church for some morning prayers to start fresh. Once they finished up, they walked side by side down the aisle towards the confessional. As they slowly passed by the pews, O'Brien did his best to give the kid some proper advice.

"I worry about ya, John," said O'Brien with a deep brogue. McCool replied right away. "No need to worry, Monsignor. There are far more out there in worse situations than I am in."

Turning towards Jack, O'Brien noticed his limp. He was trying to walk without his cane. Yet, it was more than evident his leg was not fully healed.

"You should have that looked at, my son. You are not at peace, I can tell," said the wise priest. Hopping and flinching to the confessional, McCool replied, "I feel fine, Monsignor. Better than I did days ago." Clearly, he did not.

"Pride comes before the fall, my son."

His leg was still bandaged up from the initial hospital visit. Days had now surpassed without it being cleaned or checked out. Who knows what kind of bacteria could have spread?

In a joking tone, McCool told him, "Maybe I will go to Saint Isaac's Hospital, they always took care of me."

Saint Isaac's Children's Hospital, better known as SICH, was the privately ran hospital operated by the Archdiocese and was open to all adolescents in the North and Northeast sections of Philadelphia. In operation for nearly seventy years, the hospital began after World War II when the baby boom era was at its dawn.

O'Brien then shook his head sideways and told him the bad news right away before McCool even had the chance to ask. "SICH is not looking good. They are having economic problems, John."

"What do you mean?" asked McCool.

"There have been talks recently of its struggles."

"That is a sin, Monsignor. I was there all the time as a kid. They took care of me like nowhere else would have."

"A sign of the times, my son."

McCool did not like what he was hearing. Although he had a lot going on, he vowed to O'Brien that he would get over there to check out what was happening immediately.

"When I get the time, I'm going to stop over there to see if I can help," said Jack.

Not much in life was sentimental to him anymore, but this place was near and dear to his heart.

The humble priest responded, "One who is gracious to a poor man lends to the Lord. And He will repay him for his good deed."

"Proverbs 19:17," replied Jack, dipping his fingers in the holy water font on the wall.

A smile lit up on O'Brien's face. It was as if all the years spent trying to teach McCool the scripture and at least one meaningful life lesson tied to it paid off. "Very well, my son." O'Brien gave the sign of the cross before they went in to start the confession.

After spending the morning at church, McCool ventured his way over to the depths of the neighborhood…Connors' territory.

It was a bold move, but it was his only one. He wasn't going to hide anymore. Even as a courtesy, he let Red Alan know he would be there with a text message.

The place was merely called "Alan's Café," and it sat right in the heart of Kensington. For years, this was the hub for the Connor Brothers. Many big decisions were made here.

McCool arrived alone. There were only two people there; the bartender, drinking a glass of water with lemon and one of Connor's henchmen, drooling in the back, holding a gun and a beer. They both frisked Black before he sat down to have his first glass of Jameson. However, he came clean…not only in his holster but in his mind.

Once he got comfortable enough, he went over to the jukebox, putting in all the quarters that he had. There was one song he wanted to play continuously into the night. It was "Ailein Duinn." The tune spoke to him in the name alone. *Ailein Duinn* was Gaelic for "Dark Haired Alan."

He knew that whatever was about to happen next, there was no coming back. Yet, he also knew…he wouldn't be alone.

CHAPTER EIGHT

Big Carmine was getting ready for an important task, preparing at his house on Wolf Street, late that afternoon. He ventured upstairs to his bedroom, ascending the staircase to find what he needed to get things started. This would be the beginning of a very defining night.

When he went inside, he made his way to a tall wooden dresser. The thing was an antique. He looked at it for a few minutes only to pull the top drawer out slowly as if he were unveiling Pandora's secrets.

Inside, it was empty…except for a single cigar box resting dead in the center. The box was old yet opened easily. Inside was his signature silencer and the materials to clean it. They rested solemnly while he spent the past twenty years he was in prison.

Carefully, he took the old silencer and began to polish it, so it shined with the brilliance it always had in his heart. He wanted it to sparkle so bright, whoever would see it last would remember its luster like the last light you see when you die.

This was the first night it would be used on a gun in two decades. He was so thrilled, he didn't look at his phone when Tony Boy was trying to call. He even tried to text him multiple times. Carmine did not want any distractions. He then put his phone in the cigar box in place of where the silencer was.

Back on the streets of the Northeast, Patsy Connor was freshening up at the barber nearby. He was just wrapping up with a shave. Once the hot towel came out, he knew it was almost time to head out and take care of certain matters.

As he saw the sun begin to set through the window of the shop, he reached down into his pocket and glanced at his phone while they were cleaning him up.

It was then he noticed a few text messages from his brother Alan, ones of significant value. The texts prompted him to call his brother Eddie as soon as he could.

As he exited the barber shop, that is just what he did. He got on the phone and rang for Ed immediately. He came out the front entrance door and sped walked towards his car, parked nearly fifteen yards away.

"Eddie...it is Patsy. Listen, Alan needs us at the bar right away! This minute!"

Before he had the chance to hang up, he felt something fasten around his neck as he passed by an alleyway. As this happened, he dropped his phone on the concrete, shattering the screen to pieces.

Just as he was able to get his hands on this rope-like object, it wrapped around him tight like an Anaconda in the Amazon.

"Fuckin' piece of shit cocksucker!" he then heard being softly whispered into his ear. Before he knew it, he was being dragged towards the alleyway behind him by the cord.

The force responsible for the compression was Tony Boy Tomasello, holding and squeezing a garrote so strong around Patsy, his hands began to bruise and bleed.

The young Connor brother did his best to try and wrestle out of the deathly grip, but it was to no avail. The lock was snugger than a vice closing in without halt.

Coughing and gasping for any kind of relief, Patsy grew weaker as he fell square to his knees…directly onto the hard concrete. Before he knew it, the garrote was taking the life out of him, choking on his own spit.

It was then he heard the sound of his windpipe collapse as if Tony Boy was choking a plastic water bottle. In that instance, he was no longer in control of his body. He was paralyzed. The next moment, he was dead.

Tony left the shell of a man sitting up right next to a dumpster with its eyes wide open. He then detoured, scurrying out of the alleyway quietly.

Eddie was just on the phone with his brother…and then there was nothing. He tried to call Patsy back multiple times…yet no response. It didn't make sense. Now, he was a panicking, confused about what happened. When he had no success getting though, he ran out of his house on Morrell Avenue at high speed. He was going so fast down his front stairs, he jumped over the last three steps and darted to his Jaguar XF, parked in front of the house.

As he got to the driver's side door, he was fumbling for his keys in his coat pocket to unlock it. Right when he found them, his windshield cracked quicker than Patsy's phone screen did on the concrete.

"Those damn squirrels with their nuts," he said to himself, looking at the massive oak tree in front of him. That was his first thought. Of course...until the second crack. Then the third!

He ducked down behind his car, realizing it was the gunfire that was discharging closer to him...not nuts. Looking down the street, he noticed the only two cars on the far side of the block. First, there was Mrs. Peabody's Oldsmobile. "Man, she must still be mad about me parking in her spot the other day."

No way...she wasn't the one packing heat. It was coming out of the phantom gray Cadillac right across from her. Stepping out of the car was a man holding a Glock nine. He was speeding his walk down the street towards Eddie and continuing to shoot.

It was none other than Caz, squeezing his pistol off, round after round like he was at the practice range. The next two bullets hit Eddie's driver side door.

Not sure what his best move was, Eddie decided to get into the car instead of running away. He hurried in and started the engine, panicking to escape. He threw the shift into reverse.

However, he backed up so quickly, he smashed into the neighbor's Hyundai Accent. "Shit!" he screamed.

With no time to assess the damage behind him, he had to focus on escaping the chaos approaching his way. Just as Eddie reached for the gear, putting the car into drive, he caught a shot to the right arm. Caz was getting closer. His aim was getting even tighter.

"Ahhhh!" Eddie screamed, holding his arm. He was starting to think a quick getaway wasn't an option. With his left arm, he turned and reached for the gun he kept handy in his glove compartment.

Yet, Eddie still wasn't quick enough. Caz caught him with a hit to the left shoulder blade. He was now five yards away from the Jag. Eddie lost control, lifted his foot from the brake and never got to the weapon. The car started rolling forward slowly.

Caz wanted to savor the moment and get a good look at what he was doing. He moved in at point-blank range. He released four more bullets. Two to the chest and two to his eyes…Eddie was smoked!

He fell face first into the steering wheel, bleeding out a pool from his head down to the mat below him.

The Jag remained in drive as Caz ran back to his Cadi and fled the scene. Mrs. Peabody and multiple neighbors came running out immediately, screaming while they witnessed the madness in front of them.

Eddie's car then came to a stop once it hit the tree ahead. Acorns came falling down on top of it like a hailstorm.

Back at Alan's Cafe, McCool sat quietly, sipping his Jameson neat just a tiny bit every few minutes, waiting patiently. He was making small talk with the bartender about the weather. He continued being refilled when it was necessary.

"You ought to just leave the bottle there, guy," said McCool, putting down a few more dollars on the bar top. The bartender chuckled, sipping his glass of water. He then thanked Jack for his generous tips.

Just as the talk started to get a bit more personal, Jack felt the chill of icy metal on the back of his neck. It wasn't just the crisp winter air coming in and flowing down his body. It was something more tangible. The sound of a Kane K9 pistol cocked behind him.

"You son of a bitch," uttered the eerie voice behind McCool. "I'm clean, man. I did not come here for violence!" replied Jack, looking over his shoulder as he sat still, remaining calm.

"I don't believe you," said the guy holding the gun, pushing the barrel deeper into the back of McCool's head.

"Let me finish my drink, at least," pleaded Jack. He slowly moved his right hand towards the glass of Jameson that was freshly poured.

All of a sudden, he heard the cocking back of another weapon. This time…it was a sawed-off shotgun.

The bartender, holding the barrel at eye's length for Jack to stare down, told him, "I don't think so." He looked down the two dark tunnels, holding what could have been his ultimate fate.

Just as McCool was checking his watch, plotting his next move, the bell on the front door rang as it swung open. In walked a tall Irishman wearing a flat cap. Behind him was the man he was shielding the way for…the one Red Alan Connor.

Red was clapping his hands for McCool, smiling as he waited in front of the big window next to the entrance. "You're making this easy for me, kiddo," said Alan. "What did you plan on doing here?"

Jack remained silent. He put his hands in the air as he looked at the red-haired beast with disgust. Everything he hated, this man possessed. Even in what appeared to be his final moments, McCool wished he wasn't in his company.

"It's over, kid…time to finish the job," continued Alan as he pulled a silver revolver from the side of his belt, checking to make sure each bullet was packed tight.

"You actually gonna try and do it yourself this time, Alan? You chicken shit cocksucker!" yelled McCool. The guy behind Jack put his arm around his neck, squeezing him like a lime while continuing to push the gun at his skull.

Swish, boom! Everyone was caught off guard as the back door behind the bar flung open, out of nowhere. It hit the wall as if a pack of bulls were coming out to charge through the gates. Yet, there was nothing. All guns pointed to the back door in response to the noise.

Frozen, all eyes were stuck to the door in that instance. Time was of the essence. Alan knew he couldn't let this kid live much longer before any other tricks he had up his sleeve came out...that included whatever flung the door open. Alan made his move. He cocked back his revolver and aimed it at McCool. "Say goodbye, Jackie," he told him.

All of a sudden, the window behind Alan shattered. Glass was everywhere. Three bullets came through. The first two missed Alan but went directly into the back of his guard's head. The third one hit his hand he held his gun in. He dropped it like it was biting him.

In shock and pain, he fell to the floor, trying to hold the bloody mess from pouring out all over the place. It now looked like a piece of raw meat.

The guy holding McCool's neck twirled him around, continuing to hold him tightly. He started firing at the window. From behind the bar, the bartender blasted a few rounds out as well before he ducked down. They both inched towards the entrance. However, much like the door behind them seconds prior, nobody appeared to be there. They didn't know what they were up against. All theories were on the table. Whatever it was, they were ready to fight it.

McCool kept thinking about elbowing the stomach of the guy holding him as his deathly grip clenched tighter. Yet, the bartender he just poured his heart out to hours prior was locked and loaded with the shotgun, ready to fire away.

Crash!! Just as the man holding McCool and the bartender made their way towards the front, the back door flung open once again behind them. Except for this time…Caz was there, standing tall and skinny with his Glock nine.

Bang, bang! Two bullets flew out and went right to his mark…into the guy holding McCool. One lodged in his shoulder and the other in his rib as the man turned.

Pop! Another bullet soared and went into the bartender's mouth, opening up his head and splattering his brains on the bar like soup exploding in the microwave. Hot chunks were everywhere.

McCool slid out of the weakening grasp of the guy choking him and darted over behind the bar as the body fell to the ground. He ran, yelling, "You're late!" to Caz, who was now pointing his gun at the wounded Red Alan on the floor.

Picking up the sawed-off shotgun from behind the bar, McCool cocked it back once. He then took the extra bullets the bartender had in his shirt pocket. He reloaded and kept the rest at his side.

As Jack came around and walked towards Alan, the man on the floor who was holding him just seconds prior rose up slowly. He took an unexpected shot at McCool before his last breath, reaching his left arm.

"MOTHERFUCKER!" Jack yelled, holding his arm in agony. "SHIT!!!" He was caught off guard. The guy on the floor kept his gun pointed at McCool, ready to shoot again.

It took less than a second for Caz to rush over and fire back at the guy laying on the floor. This time, he was putting him to rest for good, releasing one between his eyes.

Caz turned to McCool, "Don't give me shit about being late again or I won't save your ass once more!"

McCool grinned…that's all he could do, even though he was now in dire pain. He gave Caz a fist bump with the numbed hand of his bad arm, holding his shotgun up high with the good one.

Red Alan, fading from lost blood, moving towards his gun that rested on the ground with his healthy hand. Catching him swiftly, Jack shot his reach down. The red one, now with two bloody gloves for hands, gasped and beseeched as he was screaming for his life.

Breaking down the front entrance door, Tony Boy appeared with his gun out in front of him. "You couldn't come through the window you just shot down?" asked Caz. "I like to enter in style," replied Tony, winking at him and McCool.

McCool blasted Alan's hand again. "That's for Young Veccuto!" he yelled. "Please, Jackie!! C'mon, please!" begged Alan. Another bullet went in the shotgun and exploded right out…this time to Alan's right kneecap. "That's for Highway O'Hara!"

Pull, click…boom! To the left kneecap. "That's for Duffy!" Alan laid down on the floor, crying, screaming for Jack to give him mercy. Yet, all he gave him was another bullet after he reloaded. This time to the gut. "That is for Fitzy!" shouted McCool.

Blood now poured out of Alan's mouth, running down his face and onto his shirt. It was then McCool aimed the barrels at Alan's head. "I will give you one opportunity to live," he told him.

Caz turned in McCool's direction, wondering what on God's green earth he was doing. "Tell me about the Caribbean Connection!" he demanded, keeping the sawed-off steady. Tony and Caz remained frozen, watching McCool tear the man apart, little by little.

Choking, spitting up blood, Alan kept saying one word over and over. The murmurs were so low, however, the three could barely hear him. "Ooo…ooo…ooo."

"What are you saying, motherfucker?" yelled Jack, continuing to keep the gun directly at his head. "Loo…loo!" The red one wasn't even making sense anymore.

He was delusional, losing all that blood. All of a sudden, the loudest he could scream it, Alan leaned up and yelled, "FUCK YOU!!!"

That was the last thing anyone heard him speak. Alan's head cracked open like a cantaloupe with the final round McCool let fire. He left a lake of blood under and around his draining cadaver. "That one was for me!" he told him.

The trio looked at each other and once more around the bar, making sure nobody else was breathing. They then walked out the back door, one by one…inconspicuously.

As the floors of Alan's Café in the Northeast continued to run red, more blood was about to be poured into South Philly's streets. Carmine quietly parked his Buick Lucerne blocks away from Paulie's. Far enough to be hidden yet close enough to see the light on at the suit shop.

It was this hour he knew that the pretty one typically prepared for his departure. The guards were officially off duty. The vulnerability was at its most opportune moment.

This was the ultimate time to strike. Final preparations were about to begin. He attached the suppressor to his P228 pistol, wiping it down one more time with a cloth for good luck. After that, he kissed the top of the metal, reminding it to keep its silence with its secrets. Lastly, he stuffed his lucky rag in his side pocket.

Now that he was working with the Irish, it seemed he believed more in his own superstitions than ever before. Carmine rolled his massive presence out of his car, shutting the door softly once he was on both feet.

It took him awhile to get down the road. Carmine walked as if he was dragging his past along with his weight. Yet no matter how heavy the burden, he was always willing to add more.

He noticed the light outside the suit shop was flickering as he got closer, battling to stay on. All of a sudden, it surrendered and remained off. He smiled as he thought, "This ain't the only light that's goin' out tonight."

The front door was cracked open about an inch, perhaps a notion that guests were welcome, even at the late hour. Taken back by such an embracing invitation, Carmine opened the door meticulously to make his way through the entrance.

Just before he stepped inside, he looked around every direction just to make sure there were no surprises. Now, the lights inside the store were off. The familiar scents of suits and leather were circling through the air. He could hear some type of clatter coming from the back. Unsure of whether it was music, talking, or things moving, Carmine hasted his haul and tried to be soundless while doing it.

Progressively, he passed through the store and over to the register. His full stomps allowed for some loud creeks as he paced on the old wood. He couldn't help it though. He kept at it. What was coming from the back was even more audible.

Behind the register was the door to Paul's office. He noticed two things through the bottom of the door. There was the sound of soft music and a bright light piercing through the crack. This was a radiant and vocal message for him to get in there and to finish the assignment quickly.

While holding the pistol in front of him with both hands, Carmine used his massive foot to kick and break down the door. With all his weight behind him, he charged through like a ram.

He then barged in towards Paulie's mahogany desk once it was in plain sight. Although, there was nobody in the seat. Nobody in the room...except him.

The lights were beaming bright and throwing heat like the sun. The warming waft in the room led Carmine to believe he truly wasn't alone. Additionally, a Classic Crosley 78 player was spinning and amplifying the record of "The Flower Duet" from the French opera Lakme by Leo Delibes. As comforting as the libretto was to hear, there was nothing to trust about the situation.

Carmine noticed two closets in the room. "Has to be something," he said, tiptoeing towards the first. Still, he proceeded with caution. What was behind door number one with the big old brass handle? Nothing. Just a mop, a bucket, and some cleaning supplies.

"What the fuck?" he thought. "Maybe door number two had all the answers." Still hesitant, Carmine shook the stainless steel knob a little just to see if it was going to turn. What was in the closet once he opened it? Again...zip! A few suits...but no bodies wearing them. They sat cold, hanging on the rack.

Taking a deep breath and looking around, he was wondering what he was missing. The big guy walked over to the entrance of the office, glancing out to see if he could find somebody or something he didn't notice before. Yet, he didn't. He looked back in the office and looked outside it again. Then once more!

SLICE! The last thing Carmine saw was a switchblade flying into the room like a dragonfly and cutting through his neck. Gushes of blood came bursting out of his mouth and throat as he dropped his pistol to the floor.

The man holding the blade was wearing a black overcoat and fedora, standing at the entrance while Carmine backed away into the office, making nothing but choking sounds. The man then smiled, humming to the tune of The Flower Duet as it continued playing its soothing melody.

The big guy teetered in circles, getting dizzy, not knowing where to go next as if we were just waking up from a nap. He knew in these very final moments, he wanted the pain to end as quickly as possible.

He rested his hands on Paulie's desk, trying to maintain his balance. He swayed back and forth as he felt his eyes roll back to his head like two balls spinning effortlessly.

Just as he thought he was dead and done, Carmine felt the wrath again. The man in the black overcoat came over and turned him around to face him eye to eye. He wanted him to get a good look.

He then carved into him the way a slaughter would to cattle. It was a massacre. Ten quick and fierce stabs, deep in the chest and stomach. SLASH! RIP! SWOOSH! One after the other, tearing him open in every direction. There was absolutely no mercy.

As his blood poured down from each wound like a waterfall, Carmine and all three-hundred pounds of his body crashed down, back first, on top of Paulie's desk like a stacked pile of bricks. There he laid, choking on the last bit of vital fluids.

The man stood firm, watching Carmine hold his neck with his hands. Yet, they both knew it was no use. It would all be over any second now.

Carmine gasped for air, widening his mouth open and shut continuously as he lost control of every other nerve in his body.

For the crescendo...the overcoat man looked at his blade before he shifted his focus coldly into the eyes of Carmine one more time. He raised the blade high in the hair.

Turning his wrist down, he hammered the razor-sharp point straight to the big guy's heart. Sprays of blood shot out so high, they hit the ceiling and splattered everywhere else like a firework.

The man smiled while he snatched his blade out of Carmine's dead body for the last time. He then let out an evil chuckle as if his master plan was in sync and went in perfect rhythm. The rich resonance of the violins from the record sounded louder as the man reveled in his masterpiece.

Just as his favorite part came on, he shut his eyes and let the music fill him. Waving his hands in the air with the murderous knife like a baton, the man began emulating a conductor orchestrating an opera.

He then pulled out a black handkerchief from his overcoat. As he persisted to hum to the angelic tune, he gradually wiped the mess off the blade. He did so just enough to see the engraved cursive letter "L" once again, shining in the metal.

Part Two

Greener Pastures

CHAPTER NINE

The news anchors covered the devastation that very night into the following day. They could not have asked for three more exciting stories to report like these. Even though Christmas was still a few weeks away, it seemed to come early to them. It was as if they were pulling a string from the top of a present the way they revealed the details, little by little in front of all who were watching, glued to the broadcast.

While the headlines continued to scroll at the bottom of every channel, I settled in at my row home in the Northeast for the first time in roughly a week. After having had the best sleep I had gotten since the night before the Shunk Avenue explosion, I began collecting my thoughts, one by one.

What was next in store for my journey...I had no idea. However, I was ready and willing to find out.

Although my leg was still healing, and my arm was in a sling from taking a gunshot the night prior, I was still in one piece...all things considered. For that, I was grateful. Yet, I wish I had a few more moments of harmony midway through the afternoon when I got a phone call.

It was Tony Boy ringing me, not wanting to delay the unfortunate news about the murder of Carmine. He wanted me to know.

Cut to pieces like strips of steak you would find in fajitas, Big Carmine was discovered in the bottom of a dumpster near Paulie's suit shop. It was made known that the big guy was maliciously murdered in cold blood.

If that wasn't bad enough, Tony was worried. He was hysterical, telling me he wasn't able to get a hold of Caz all day.

I tried to calm him down. I knew I had to keep him focused. I didn't have the answers either. Yet, I knew we were in this together...we'd retaliate. He then asked me to meet him at a bar called *The Dive* in South Philly.

Once we hung up with each other, I went back to watching the television, hoping to get more information than what Tony was giving. The same reporter was on-screen from earlier in the day. At first, he was highlighting an "unknown" ambush and how The Connor Brothers of K&E met their demise at Alan's Café. *We all know what happened there.*

All in the same breath, he began telling the second story...the one of Pretty Paulie's fate and its aftermath.

"For the big story on Action News tonight...after a Federal informant in the Badlands section of North Philly leaked major details about an ecstasy manufacturing plant, the FBI handed an indictment to Paul Muchetta, a.k.a. Pretty Paul...the alleged boss of the notorious Philly Mob. Video and audio recordings were exchanged for this particular informant's cooperation during the upcoming trial."

Paul was taken in by the Feds long before Carmine arrived at his suit store. The poor guy had no idea what he was getting into. His fate was long-determined.

Paul was now going up against a hand-picked Grand Jury. He was facing twenty-five to thirty years for the accusations against him. This would practically be a life sentence.

They even had a clip of that fast-talking Agent Martinez and his crew on TV giving a press conference about the big arrest. Funny! He also threw my name randomly into his discussion as an honorable mention...just for kicks! That fuckin' guy...a real pisser! They dared to label me as a "Muchetta Family associate," *whatever that meant*.

If that wasn't enough...the third story was even crazier. In retaliation to the rat, a surprise attack from an unknown source was ordered to the Badlands as a message from the Muchetta Family the same day.

"Thirty-two people shot. Twenty-seven killed. Three of the five survivors remain in critical condition. One of those critical three is a twelve-year-old boy," said the reporter in the field.

They did not give out names...but this broke my heart more than anything. It was never pleasant to hear about children getting caught in cross-fire.

Nevertheless, even with the leak and the community being smoked, the recordings and video footage both rested in the hands of the FBI. It seemed to me that Paulie's was an open and shut case in the making without the testimony.

It was all becoming more evident. Tony Boy heard it first before it made headlines the night prior. He tried to contact Carmine after it happened, but he never answered his phone. If he had, he would not have needed to show up at the suit store. He'd still be with us.

Wrapped with guilt, I wished there was more I could have done. We were so busy in the Northeast, we never had a chance to make sure things were clear in the south.

Yet, I knew this situation had to move forward. There was still so much to be done. Red Alan was gone, and I had control of the Northeast. We lived to fight another day.

It was a dark December night. As the moon was shining vividly upon each house and building, I made my entrance to The Dive around nine o'clock. This bar, however, didn't need any extra sparkle. It was known for its hundred-foot neon sign.

It was 9 PM. The place was already packed to the gills with people like sardines in a can. For a Friday night, perhaps I shouldn't have been too surprised. Yet, it was early. All kinds of guests were there. All ages and all races…many different faces.

I left my cane at home for this occasion. That being said, my limp was more than evident. With caution, I held my sling so I wouldn't bump into anyone with it, making my way through the crowds.

Jangles of voices bounced from wall to wall like tennis balls, pitching at all different types of decibels. Through the various sounds, I lurched my way over to Tony in the only corner of the bar that was dim.

The old mope was sulking away in his lonesome. He sat on his stool, counting the drips of condensation from around his Gin and Tonic as they slid down his glass onto his cocktail napkin.

When I approached him, he didn't even say hello. Instead, he looked at me as if his world had ended and I was responsible for it. "I can't believe this happened," he wept, staring intently at his drink.

I tried to stay positive. In times like these, it was more important to focus on the good than the bad. "Tony, I know you're upset...but, we got the Connor Brothers. We blew them away one by one! We have to celebrate *something* here!" I replied.

He turned to me, but he was in no hurry doing it. With unbearable pain in his voice, he kept his response brief. "Yes...but Pretty Paulie is still alive. Don't forget that."

Unfortunately, that was true. Without letting me get a word in, Tony kept going with his dark-as-Hell misery. "And Carmine isn't."

I knew I had to calm him down to keep the conversation moving. I put my hand on his back, trying to bring the old sulk some type of relief. "Tony, I know. I'm sorry he had to go. I certainly didn't plan it this way...none of us did."

Inhaling deeply, Tony said after he let his breath of anger out, "I called and texted him all day.

If only he had just picked up his fuckin' phone, this whole thing could've been avoided."

"You know how bad Carmine wanted to take out Paulie. It could've been any one of us that got whacked, Tony," I reminded him.

He kept chugging each drink while simultaneously asking the bartender for a refill once he emptied the glass. This behavior concerned me. We had a lot to discuss. At this rate, he wasn't going to make it much past us mourning Carmine. It was going to be a long night.

"This was all a fuckin' mistake, kid. This entire thing…from the start. I can't live with it. I just can't."

Finally, I had the chance to speak once he started sipping his next glass. "We will have to live with this, Tony…I've lost a lot of people during this fuckin' madness too. Okay? The war may not be over with whoever is still out there…but this battle, we were absolutely able to win!"

It didn't matter what I had to say. Tony Boy kept shaking his head sideways, bothering the bartender for replenishment. I knew he hated to look at me, let alone hear me. However, I persisted in speaking my mind.

"Plus, the executive game is coming up. I will have the biggest high rollers I've ever had coming in. I'm talking major players looking to spend a lot of cash. The stakes have never been higher!" I said.

It still didn't seem like I was getting through to him…even when it came to money on the table. I wasn't sure where our disconnection was…but frankly, I was getting tired of the static.

"That's all fine and dandy. Meanwhile, I have no idea where the fuck Caz is," said Tony, now looking at his phone in distress.

"I know. Me either."

He glanced back at me once more. Crystal clearly, he spoke for the first time without a glass in his hand, "Fuckin' Lou Gorgeous…he's out there, kid. I'm tellin' ya! He is real. He's going to strike back."

"I'll be ready, waiting for him…wherever the fuck he is!" I replied.

Before I had the chance to get into more detail about this ridiculous "Lou Gorgeous" with Tony Boy, there was something else taking my breath away.

I looked across the bar, still not able to believe what I was seeing. I even double and triple looked just to make sure.

I couldn't believe it. There sat the girl from the night at McCluskey's, the one with the bright green eyes. This time, she wasn't alone…she was with a group of her friends.

She was sizzling hot…just as I remembered her. Yet, the refresh was nice. She might as well have been on fire the way she was radiating heat all the way across the bar to where I stood. She was one of the sexiest girls I had ever seen.

Once I set my eyes on her, I started wondering when it was she arrived. Had it taken me this long to realize she was there? I continued to watch her chat with her friends, smiling and laughing. It brought me back to the first time I saw her.

The way her black-as-night hair would zephyr as she moved her head, looking around to see if anyone was staring at her. The way she bit her cherry-red, bottom lip. The way she mixed her Mojito with the cocktail straw…slowly and in rotation with the ice.

Most importantly…this all brought me back to the look in her eye when I left McCluskey's. Oh, those green eyes. There they were once again…as fresh as spring grass, sparkling like dew in the morning sun.

Yet, she was more stunning this night than she was before. Something was different. This was the kind of girl who unpretentiously grew prettier each time you saw her. I had to go up to her. I needed to know more.

Without warning, I put my drink down next to Tony's. "I'll be back," I assured him. There was only one thing on my mind now.

I couldn't let an opportunity like this slip away. Staggering in my stride towards this bombshell of a beauty, I kept wishing there was a way to hide the fact I had a bad arm and a gimpy leg. No matter how hard I tried, it was impossible to cover up.

It didn't matter at this point. The closer I came in her direction, the less she seemed to notice me. However, the more I saw her…the more excited and nervous I became. I felt a knot in my stomach that only a sailor would dream to tie.

My entire body felt like waves of electricity were surging through it at the speed of light. I was even short of breath, especially now getting a full glimpse of her figure.

With her flawless desert-sand colored skin and shimmering ocean eyes, it led me to believe she was the perfect combination of Mediterranean and Middle East. Just a guess.

She had an olive-colored crisscross front tee shirt on, flawlessly capturing the shape of her perky breasts. Her jet-black leggings did a great job of highlighting every alluring curve of her toned, Rockette legs.

As I came close enough to speak hello, she crossed them naturally. Inside, I thought I was going to faint as I ogled at her perfectly toned thighs move in rhythm. Yet, I kept my composure on the outside...still cool, calm, and collected.

Well, here goes nothing...

"You may not recognize me...but I saw you recently. It was at another bar around here," I said, as smooth as one could be in a moment like this. She widened her eyes as big as they could get. She stared at me like I was the Grim Reaper, coming to collect her soul. Immediately, she turned away.

Her friends were no help, scoffing as they avoided looking in my direction to keep whatever conversation they had alive before I showed up.

I wasn't giving up. I placed my hand next to hers in hopes of getting her attention once more. "It was late the last time, so I understand if you don't remember me," I continued.

My head was getting lighter with each breath…but I couldn't stop. Her aroma was intoxicating…celestial with every whiff. I was hooked. I wasn't sure if it was a secret of Victoria or just her natural essence.

She gently turned her head towards me at that moment. "Is this your *big opener*? The best you can do? The old 'I have seen you before in another place at another time.' Sorry *dude*, not working," she said, whipping her hair around and waving me away.

"It was McCluskey's on 17th Street to be exact," I replied.

"I'm there all the time. Don't remember you. Nice try though, sir!"

"Alright, well…just wanted to come over and tell you that I think you are gorgeous. If you want to have a drink and talk, I'll be over there with that grumpy old guy," I spoke as I pointed to Tony Boy. "If not…that's fine. But I would've kicked myself if I hadn't at least told you how I felt."

"Hmm. Maybe I'll see you around," she replied, dismissing me once again.

It was short and to the point. Her voice was confident. There was no denying that. It had the kind of direct tone you would expect from a girl who knew what she wanted. For her, it was independence. At the same time, it was sweet sounding…like a mandolin. The shell she held was tough…yet beneath it, I knew there was more to her.

The silence of the group thickened. "Ladies, a pleasure," I concluded as I began to walk away.

It was a long shot. A bold move. Yet, I could see this was the kind of girl that did not want to be wooed in front of her gals. She had too much prestige.

As I walked back in the direction towards Tony, I heard her utter behind me, "Thanks! Have a good one! Hope your arm gets better!"

I grinned. My instincts were right about her good nature. I limped my way back to Tony, holding my lousy arm with the good one, thinking, "What a voice…what a girl."

Looking down, I knew that no matter what was next in the madness that was becoming my life, it was nice to have moments like these. To hear the voice of a pretty woman and to tell her all about the beauty she held…even if the time was brief.

It was the same way I felt when I saw her at McCluskey's…or when I met the nurse at the hospital…or at the view of nature's splendor in South Jersey…or the simple laugh of a child. It was all these…the finer things that I appreciated.

This was an excellent contrast given the shit I had to see in my youth and my time overseas in Afghanistan. I still felt the pain, more and more, as these old visions would pop into my mind. I knew they'd never go away…I'd just have to replace it with better. I was working to do so each day.

For a short moment, Vinny's initial offer to go to Maine seemed more enticing than ever. Yet, there was no going back now. I knew what had to be done. I wanted to leave my mark on the streets before it all came to an end.

Tony was in no mood for me acting smitten once I had come back over to him. "Can you get your head out of your ass for a few minutes and put your hard-on away?" he asked.

"Relax, old man…I had to show you how it is done," I replied, shrugging my shoulders a few times and patting him on the back.

Sarcastically, he replied, "Seems like you did really well, kid. She looked into you." He even rolled his eyes during his comment. I remained silent, looking around the bar once more, ignoring his affront.

"She looks kind of familiar though, I must say," he added.

I didn't bother to acknowledge the discussion any longer. It was then I responded, "Okay, okay. Let's get back to what the Hell we were talking about, Tony."

He took a deep breath and pulled out his iPhone, texting away hastily. "Where the fuck is Caz already?" asked Tony Boy, panicking more than a drunk driver trying to pass a sobriety test.

"I haven't heard from him all day either," I replied. "He's fine though, Tony." I began to do the same, sending a few texts to Caz, wondering where he was. *Where are you? Come to The Dive!*

Given the events of the past twenty-four hours, I knew none of us were safe. The real evil was out there…lurking, plotting, scheming.

"I just think if Caz had been taken out, you and I would also have been by now, just as easily. We wouldn't be standing here, able to speak about it, Tone," I retorted.

"God forbid!! Shut the fuck up...don't even talk like that," said Tony. "We just gotta find out what the Hell he is doing."

Nodding my head, I turned over to the bartender for another glass of Jameson neat. As he took my order, I noticed the pack of girls across the bar were gone. Chuckling, I spoke to myself. *Hey...at least you tried, Black!*

All of a sudden, I heard a voice reverberating in my left ear. It was that sharp, sweet tone from earlier...the one I couldn't forget.

"Let me guess...skiing accident?" said the shimmering-eyed princess, winking at me as she made an attempt to turn around and leave after merely asking one question.

I smiled in return, grabbing her hand once more before she could get away, responding, "Something like that. I'll tell you about it if you give me the time," as I looked at my arm sling.

"No thanks. Good effort all-around tonight, though. Thanks for the drink offer. You were smooth. You'll do well tonight." Again, she tried to turn around.

But, I wanted to keep the conversation going. I stopped her once again. "Forgive me...I never even introduced myself. I'm Jack McCool."

"Nina."

Oh, *Nina*. What a name. I wanted to keep saying it over and over. It made me smile that much brighter. "It's a pleasure, Nina."

"Yeah, Jack…it was!" she said, tucking her chin.

I stood up before she had another chance to escape. As quickly as I could, trying not to scare her, I grabbed her by the arm. Wanting to keep her close, I softly murmured, "Hey, listen, do you come here often?"

"Guess you'll see if you hang around, Jack." She smiled with grace as she tried to turn around once more. I slowly relaxed my hand, still not wanting to see her go.

I couldn't stop myself. So, I continued, "Again…this may be a little forward of me, but I'd love to get to know you. I'm not just saying it. I mean it."

I was afraid she was going to vanish at a moment's notice.

"I bet you would, Jack. I am just not available."

"Boyfriend?"

"No."

Man, this Nina knew how to entice…and how to do it with style. She was high class. Quickly, I realized she was not going to be won over easily.

"Well then, let me take you out sometime. One drink."

"You don't have my number, Jack-o."

"Well, may I have it?"

"Mmmmm…I don't think so."

"That's alright, I want you to have mine. You can put it right into your phone."

Her friends were at the entrance, yelling to her that their Uber driver had just arrived. Flipping her hair, she started waving to the door, signaling to her crew.

"I really need to go, my girls are waiting for me. Sorry."

Quickly, I grabbed a cocktail napkin from the counter and asked the bartender if I could see his pen. I then scribbled my digits on it as fast as I could. "Here you go."

"I like to leave things up to fate," she told me, taking the written-on napkin and crumbling it up in her hands like it was a piece of trash. This time, she walked away from me for good.

The sillage she trailed in her stride left me mesmerized as I kept my eyes on her every step she made, departing the bar. If nothing else, I had to know what her fragrance was. Of course…that would be if we ever had the chance to speak again.

My spirits were blue once she left. Yet, moments after her exit, I felt uplifted again. This time, in a different way. In walked the AWOL man…Skinny Caz! "There he is!" I yelled, jovial as ever as he came towards our direction.

"Caz! Perfect timing…we missed you! And *you* missed McCool strike out twice in a row!" exclaimed Tony, loud enough for the entire bar to hear.

At least he was smiling. Yet, so was I. Meeting an attractive girl and seeing that Caz was still breathing in less than a half an hour was rejuvenating.

However, I noticed he was wearing a puss on his face when he came to hug us both. It was a scowl, one deeper than I had ever seen him put on. I knew we had a casualty in the battle…but he looked like he lost it all. His clothes were hanging off him, and his neck was looking like a stack of dimes.

"It is awful about Carmine. May God rest his soul," I said, paying my respects to their old friend while giving myself the sign of the cross. I reminded him that we were all going to get through it together.

Tony concurred with me. "It's a fuckin' shame…but this war has only just begun. We are gonna find who was behind it," he said to Caz, signaling to the bartender for another drink.

Caz sat down and told the same bartender, "Sambuca." The skinny one looked more disturbed as the seconds passed. There was a lot on his mind. "It's gonna be a long night, boys," he told us, giving a weary stare.

Something had happened over the past day. We wanted to know more. I wanted him to tell us…every detail. He looked rattled. It was just a matter of him catching his thoughts while they bounced around his head before he let it out of his mouth.

"Lou Gorgeous…he called me personally today from an unknown number."

Caz told us this as if the IRS spoke to him, coming to collect old taxes. Silence had spread. Neither of us knew what to say. I wasn't quite sure how to respond. Yet, Caz continued on.

"Not only did he admit to taking out Carmine personally…but he knows all three of us, what we are doing and where we are at this very moment."

Tony Boy then asked, finally finding his words, "Jesus Christ. So, now what?"

"He sent for us to see him within the next few days," replied Caz.

"Where?" I chimed in.

"He didn't specify. He said he will call me and we will all be picked up and brought to him."

Puzzling. Yet, as ambiguous as it all appeared…I was ready for it. I wasn't afraid. "How did that asshole end the call?" I asked.

After taking the first sip of his Sambuca, Caz told Tony Boy and I what Lou's final words were. "You and your boys hold on to your pistols…this way you all have a chance."

CHAPTER TEN

The following day was going to be a long one by the way I planned it. This was the kind of morning I wished I didn't toss and turn in bed all night. However, I had a ton on my mind. There were so many questions and very few answers.

Yet, once I got up and at it…I thought of the perfect place to start asking away. Saint Isaac's Children's Hospital, the primary care for children and adolescents of the North and Northeast sections of Philadelphia.

It was time. I needed my injured leg looked at again anyway. Plus, this was an excellent opportunity to investigate the terrible news Monsignor O'Brien gave me about the hospital's imminent danger. Either way, it had been too long since I paid a friendly visit to the many I cared about there.

Once I arrived, everything the old priest told me suddenly made sense. The place was losing its luster. The lingering underfunding was nowhere more apparent than in the hallways. They were crammed with children on various types of makeshift hospital beds. Some were tended by strained relatives and some alone. The naked fluorescent tubes above all flickered continuously as if all the electric was going to shut off at a moment's notice.

In the brief gaps between these unattended unfortunates, the pale blue walls could tell their own stories. Deeply scored by the metal framed trollies, the drywall showed through like white scars.

The cheap prints on the walls were insipid. They lacked in vibrancy so severely, they appeared sun-bleached, even in the windowless strip.

The confined space magnified the groans and yelps to no avail. All the Christmas decorations in the world couldn't conceal this type of sadness. Something had to change. This place needed a makeover more than it ever did in its seventy-year history.

Although for as shoddy as the hospital looked, some of the most exceptional staff in the world worked there. The tenure was immense across the board. They were quality in their talents.

As I strolled down the deserted corridor, out came my old physician...one of the legends, Dr. Dan, to greet me. Not only was he the best doctor in the city, but he was also a great friend as well.

He had perfectly-combed silver hair with a face of one you'd ask directions from in the street...very non-threatening. In a suit, he could have been a news anchor. He was clean cut but with that loveable smile that was only ever removed from his features when he needed to be serious.

His movements were unhurried, choreographed and deliberate. He courted the opinions of the nurses and listened to what they had to say. His voice was deep, and he spoke without the technical jargon. That being said, he always gave it to me straight.

I don't think I had ever seen him without a white lab coat on. He always held a stethoscope around his neck and a clipboard never left his other hand.

"John McCool! Happy Holidays! How have you been, young man?" asked Dr. Dan, shaking my hand firmly. He was grinning ear to ear as he told me to follow him into the examination room.

"I am doing very well, Dr. Dan...all things considered, of course. Happy Holidays to you too...how are you?"

"Oh, just great. Haven't seen you in a few years. Now, where the heck have you been, young man?"

"Ya know...around...haha!" I answered, brushing the hair out of my face.

He had a warm feeling about him, the old doc. He was the kind of man you could call in the middle of the night and ask for support. I felt like I could tell him anything, much like Monsignor. However, with the current madness I was front and center of, I wasn't quite ready to share it...even with him.

"What happened with your leg here?" he questioned, looking around at the dressing I had on as if I were a mummy. I chuckled, scrambling to find the best answer to give him at that moment. I certainly didn't want to give him *all* the details. "Let's just say I was in the wrong place, wrong time," I replied.

He smiled back, shaking his head sideways as he reached for his big thick glasses in his front coat pocket. He put them on and asked me to sit up a bit.

Leaning in towards my leg, he then began removing the bandage wrap that circled around my stem for so long. "You always were, my boy...you always were. How about that arm you have in a sling there?"

"This old thing?" I asked. "No need to worry...I fell out of a tree. It should be fine in a few days." I even winked at him. All he could do was smile, chuckle and pretend like he had no idea what I was talking about.

Dr. Dan peeked out the room to call towards one of his nurses walking by for fresh bandages and some gauze for my leg. A few of them were together. They remembered me too. They were all older black ladies who had been working there as long as the doc. They spent many years working with many patients. They were all class.

It was lovely to see familiar faces still here, giving me the same attention as if I were five-years-old again.

The doc paid came back towards my leg. "It looks like it is healing...whatever it was. How do you feel, John?" he asked me, jotting some sort of notes onto his clipboard. I responded, "Better than I did...but I'm sure I am still far from being one hundred percent, Doctor. It has been one Hell of a week, and I wouldn't even know where to begin."

"Well...it will help if you try and stay off it more. You don't want to keep applying pressure. That's what opens the wounds back up," the doc detailed.

While he continued taking more notes, I looked around at the examination room we were in. It was so outdated, I felt as if I were traveling through time.

The faded paint on the walls and washed-out posters on top of it were from the 1980's at the very latest. The seat I was in had the same tear in its cloth that it did thirty years back.

I was tempted to ask Dr. Dan about the status of the hospital's economic state. It wasn't that I wanted to pry, I was merely curious. I hated to hear that they were in trouble. I needed to know more. This was one of my favorite places.

Glancing around at the room, I asked, "Hey, Doc...word on the street is there have been some financial challenges here, some unresolved dangers."

The doctor's mood changed quickly. His face dropped as if he just witnessed me fall over and croak. "Oh, John," he said, looking down to the floor to relieve the strain. It was the first time I ever saw him in such a state. He removed his glasses and took a deep breath. "It's more than that," he continued.

It was apparent he didn't want to go on in detail. The glooming black cloud above the hospital had been darkening for years. The storm was well on its way now.

"John, we are closing our doors in July of this coming year. They made this decision at the board meeting last week. A lot of people are being affected."

My mouth dropped to the floor. Perhaps the thunder was already striking, tearing into the entire building. I couldn't believe what I was hearing. Yet, from what I was seeing…I had to.

Nonetheless, were they really throwing in the towel, just like that? I used to sit on the board of planning and development after I came home from Afghanistan. This hospital used to have more fight in them. I couldn't live with the fact they'd be backing down to a fiscal deficit…they've pulled themselves out of it before.

"Dr. Dan…I'm speechless. I don't know what to say." Trying to refocus his mind, the doc began taking the wrap to freshen up my leg.

"There is not much to say, John. They brought back that old CFO, Tim Bryce. He's been here the past eighteen months. It's a tight ship he's been running since his return. Now, it's all hands on deck. People will lose their jobs and many of kids in the area will be without care."

Infuriating. Tim Bryce was a guy who was about as exciting as dishwater. He had no empathy. Talking to him was like being alone. You had to have an appointment. But on this day, I knew he was booked hour to hour. I wasn't going to go through the secretary. I was going straight for the walk-in.

"Where is *Mr. Bryce*, Dr. Dan?"

"Third floor with Finance and HR."

Up I stood. There was no time to waste. "C'mon!" I told the doc, now instructing him to follow me. He was reluctant. He didn't like making many waves. However, I knew this hospital in and out. I wasn't going to be shy about the message I would be delivering.

"I need you with me to get up there. There is no way security will let me pass by. I just want to have a word with him."

"Forget it, John. You'd be wasting your breath anyway. There is no point."

I wasn't backing down like the board did. This closure had to be reconsidered. I wasn't standing for a decision like this.

I charged for the door. I left Doc no choice but to follow me to the third floor, if for nothing else but try and stop me the whole way. However, once we made it towards the elevator, he gave in. He saw that I was as restless as a caged tiger looking to escape.

He knew I was right. I was the voice this hospital needed. Being away for too long, I needed to let them know I was back.

When we got to the stale-as-old-bread finance department's floor, I could sense a different feel than the rest of the building. It was much more elegant. The hallways were freshly painted and cleaned to a sparkle. The waiting rooms had comfortable sofas and a Keurig next to them. The smell was of fresh pine instead of mixed chemicals and urine. There was indeed no evidence of financial burden in this wing…or they chose to just not recognize it.

Even Bryce's door was one that seemed fit for a pretentious douche. The mahogany wood and steel nameplate resting in the center as if he were some big shot. Like two battle rams, Dr. Dan and I barged through, flinging the fancy door open with a *WHISH* sound. "Mr. Bryce!!" We were ready for war.

There he sat in his big leather chair, spinning around on its swivel. He was tall, skinny and had a taper fade haircut. I don't know what bothered me more…his five-and-ten glasses, his red suspenders or the bad attitude he wore on his face.

"I'm sorry…do we have an appointment, sir? How did you get in here?" he asked, looking everywhere except directly at me. He even glanced at my arm cast and bandaged leg, squinting his eyes. He probably thought I was some escaped convict.

The closer I walked to his desk, the more intimidated I could see Bryce became. Dr. Dan stood firmly behind me, ready to support whatever I had to say next.

"Mr. Bryce, I am distraught to hear that the hospital is planning to close in July. Are you telling me there is nothing more that can be done to save the place?"

Finally settling, "Who are you again?" asked Bryce. He took off his glasses and tossed whatever papers he had in his hand onto the desk in front of him. He was determined to find more ways to be condescending.

"Jack McCool. You know who I am. I used to be on the volunteer and planning board of this hospital years ago after I left the service."

His haughtiness was his most distinguishing trait. I know this guy remembered me, he just didn't want to. The voice I carried was a loud one. Not only that, it brought the truth.

Relaxing back in his chair, "Ah, McCool…I remember now," replied Bryce, trying his hardest to fake a smile. As he turned his head to Dr. Dan, I looked back to Bryce and simply told him, "Good," with a soft tone and a grin.

Although what he said next made me feel anything but good. "A little more than a discharge from the service, wouldn't you say? And I don't quite remember you stepping down from the board. I think it was a little more than that. I think you had to go away for a long while *somewhere*, didn't you?"

I leaned on the front of his desk with my one good arm and remained speaking as civil as I could. "I'm going to pretend like I didn't hear you say that."

If he were anyone else, I would have jumped across the desk and strangled him blue, one-handed. However, he was the bridge I needed to pass that would keep the hospital open or it shut it down completely. So, I let him continue.

"I don't mean to insult you, Mr. McCool. I just think you're out of line coming in here unannounced, questioning my financial judgment. By the end of this quarter, we will be solidifying the decision. My secretary will see you and Dr. Dan out."

Now that I was a few feet from him, I noticed he smelled like the twenty-dollar knockoff cologne from CVS.

Before he even had the chance to dial in his secretary on his large VOIP conference-call phone, I replied, "Do you know how many jobs are at stake? More importantly, do you know how many families depend on this hospital? You may have options, Mr. Bryce…but others don't."

"There are plenty of hospitals in the municipality…ones close…" he replied before I interrupted him.

"None in this area. None like the service that is given here and that has been given for decades on end."

"Take it up with the committee…I'm sure they'd be glad to have you again," he smirked.

Now, Bryce was on to something. He made the first good point since I walked in his door. *To see the change, you got to be the change.* "Maybe I will," I told him, looking back to Dr. Dan, seeking his nod of approval.

"If you think it is so easy, why don't you try funding the place yourself?" stated the arrogant CFO, sneering as he folded his hands in front of him.

"You're on!" I confirmed.

Bryce cackled before he leaned forward on his desk, looking deeper into my eyes. "How about 20 million at the end of the second quarter in this coming year? Then another 35 million after that by the end of the year? Not a dime less. That's just to keep the lights on…even with that, we're still at a net loss," he detailed. He then waved some of the papers he had on his desk at me as if he was trying to prove a point, showing me the numbers.

I didn't care. I simply responded as I leaned in even closer towards him, "Tell your friends they'll have the money." It was then we saw another first.

Bryce laughed, shaking his head as he unfolded his hands.

"Dr. Dan, as this man's good friend and mentor, could you explain to him the hard financial facts of running a private hospital in a struggling borough?" he asked.

I wasn't going to let him patronize me towards the doc once more. "I know what this city needs. Privileged districts shouldn't be the only ones with good hospitals!" I yelled, walking away from him. I then began to pace back and forth around his office as if it were my own.

"Mr. McCool..."

That was it for me. I knew this guy's only purpose was to sit there in his extravagant suit and pretend like he knew what he was doing. The real work was going to be done by those who really cared.

"I will see you at the next board meeting," I said, walking towards the door with the doc. Just as I made my way to leave, I turned around to make a final statement.

"Here's a thought. Maybe you'll do your part before then and start making cuts in your own department, Bryce."

Alright...maybe one more. I couldn't help it.

"Or you can continue to sit there in that big fat fancy leather chair of yours and let me do your job for you."

I didn't look back. In my last stride out of Bryce's office and down the elegant hallway, I looked around in disgust. Priorities need to be shifted. Reform was on its way.

I was now on a mission. The second quarter of the New Year would be here before I knew it. I had to get things moving.

Dr. Dan and I flew down the elevator. He tried giving me some expensive advice on our way out the door. Yet, he knew I wouldn't buy it as soon as he said it. "Listen, John…do yourself a favor. Try and avoid this. There is no money. If the hospital can't afford it, neither can you."

I smiled wide, rubbing my hands together before putting my left arm around his back. "The hospital doesn't know where to look for money," I replied, winking at him. He didn't want to know more. He rolled his eyes at me and chuckled at the same time.

I noticed something very awry once we stepped out into the main hallway. There were a lot of people who grinned at me. Many who knew me, many who did not. However, there was one face I certainly didn't expect to see. He was far from smiling.

It was the legendary Desmond "King" Carter standing from a distance in front of the water fountain by the men's bathroom. He was eyeing me down as if I were a walking disease, ready to mutate and spread. This was another figure I had heard about for years. The guy ran the black gangs in North Philly since I was born.

He didn't look the way I remembered him. He had a gray sweatsuit on with a black beanie on top of his head. His beard covered his neck, telling me he had been at this hospital for quite some time without a shave. The only thing in his hand was a pair of forearm grips.

We stared at each other for a few seconds. No nods, no words…just acknowledgment of one another's existence.

I then leaned over to Dr. Dan and whispered to him, "Doctor…that's Desmond Carter over there, isn't it? What is his story?"

The doc glanced down towards the proclaimed king. However, at this point, he had already begun venturing away from the water fountain and down another corridor.

Dr. Dan opened his mouth, thinking hard and trying to remember why Desmond was there. Just as he was about to tell me all about it, my phone went off. It was Caz!

"Excuse me," I told Dr. Dan as I walked away for privacy with my phone call.

"What is it, Caz?" I asked, heading towards the water fountain that Desmond was just at.

"Lou wants to see us tomorrow morning! His guys are picking us up 8:00 AM sharp."

"Isn't that lovely? Right after gym time…that's where I'll be instead, baby. Looking forward!" I said, rolling my eyes at the phone. *Yeah, right.*

"Also, McCool…my guy who works in the Federal prison called me. Vinny sent for you, and you alone…he has a message to deliver," Caz baited.

"What would that be?"

"He ain't happy…he wants to see ya at the joint. Make sure you get over there today!"

- 136 -

CHAPTER ELEVEN

Saint Isaac's Children's Hospital offered their services to much of the youth in the area who were in need. Various cases and all sorts of problems. There were always tough days at SICH. Yet today, aside from their financial difficulties, their focus was on one distraught patient. He was going to need all of the prayers in the world.

Twelve-year-old Nathan Carter. A kid who felt the worst of the wrath in the Badlands Massacre just a week and a half prior. The youngest in the crossfire. He was hanging on...barely.

Day to day, his body's fight was more intense than what the usual ten rounds in the ring would deliver. How it would be won, nobody knew.

The only thought running through the mind of his father, forty-one-year-old Desmond Carter was finding a way to bring him some type of relief. He would have stood in front of each punch if he could.

To see his son laid out in a hospital bed with wires and machines hooked up through him and coming out of every which way was dreadful. It was tearing his heart apart every time he looked at it. The beeps that went off on his monitor were a constant reminder to Desmond that the days are precious and they could be taken from any of us at any moment. Now more than ever, there was no denying it.

After locking eyes with McCool just minutes prior, he stood in the doorway of his son's room, squeezing his forearm grip devices harder with each rep. He could not remain still. He was like a machine, waiting for the foam to fall off. His frustration was out the roof.

Looking into the room, he watched his son in his comatose state, struggling to hang on. The rest was in God's hands at this point. All he could do was pray.

While the once-named King Carter stood squeezing away, he was reflecting…deep and hard. He was thinking about his entire life and what he could have done differently. "This is payback…everything I ever did, I'm paying for it through my son," he kept thinking.

That was until, of course, he had a guest interrupt him. One of his very own from the old block came walking down the corridor to pay his respects.

He was a real "hood guy." His name was Jerome. He was a bit younger than Carter, but he spent a lot of time with him years ago when they were involved in *other things*. These days, he did his best to try and keep it as low key as Carter. But for some people, change just doesn't come that easily.

Jerome still hung around the streets late, merely to flash his status as a 'veteran thug' in the game. Everyone knew him. Yet, he did not have the same type of prestige Carter once had. He was viewed differently.

People saw him more like a hostile force, demanding respect. On the contrary, Carter always seemed to receive it naturally.

Nonetheless, Jerome was outside on the old block in North Philly during the early morning of the shooting. Fortunately for him, he was able to find cover when the SUV's came bum rushing in. He found an alleyway with the nearest dumpster to hide behind for protection. It was the only thing that saved his life.

As he walked down towards his friend in the hospital, he smiled wide with his blue Roberto Cavalli leather coat on and a backward 76ers snap-back hat on his head. Carter stepped out of the doorway and over to greet his friend. They hugged each other tightly. "I told him to stay off the corners and away from that crowd, D," said Jerome, whispering into Desmond's ear.

In all truth, Nathan wasn't the worst kid in the neighborhood. He was actually a sweet young man. He was known for helping old ladies cross the streets and giving them a hand with their grocery bags. Everyone around the Badlands' blocks knew he was a stand-up guy.

Yet, one is only as good as the company he keeps. The friends he had were young drug runners for the dealers. He hung around these guys to keep his name alive, to stay cool. He grew up with these kids on the block, they were all he knew.

No matter how many times his dad told him to stay off the street corners with these young rascals, he kept choosing to do the opposite.

"He should've stayed on his stoop, man. Especially on a school night," continued Jerome. He kept his hands in his coat pockets. The two went over to sit down in the chairs in the waiting room.

Carter nodded his head and persisted to squeeze the grips. He was upset enough, he did not need any reminders. Even from those closest to him telling him how it really was.

"Shit ain't right, man. This whole thing is fucked up," went on Jerome, trying to get his friend to see it his way. He moved his hands around in his pockets some more.

All Jerome wanted to know was that his he was being heard out. Desmond, however, forcefully exhaled, remaining speechless.

Yet after a few seconds, he placed the forearm grips down on the table and stretched his hands out, finger by finger.

"I told him too," said the king, looking down on his hand. "I guess he was too worried about being like his old man was back in the day, know what I mean?" The two nervously snickered.

Jerome thought the world of Desmond. Many did. During the golden years, he always looked out for him. They had good synergy...a profound appreciation for one another.

"I say we give it back to those Guinea mothafuckas. Whoever was involved...let's send a message, D. This shit is real out here, homie!!!" exclaimed Jerome, pulling his pistol out from his coat pocket to show him how serious he was.

Desmond's eyes widened. "The fuck you doin' bringin' that into a hospital, nigga?" he replied, pushing the gun away from him. He looked around, panicking, hoping nobody saw the weapon in his friend's hands.

It was then Jerome placed it back in his jacket to appease Desmond. "I lost my brother in this shooting bullshit. Twenty-two years old. Smoked, my nigga…just like that!"

"I know, Jerome. I'm with ya," said Desmond, gesturing to Nathan's room.

"I may not have been close to my brother…but he was still my blood. I gotta do what I gotta do here."

"Ain't gonna solve nothin', J!"

"Then what will, D?"

Desmond continued to remain silent. He grabbed his forearm grips that sat on the table once again, locking his eyes through the window of his son's room.

"Man, I saw one of them in here tonight," said Desmond, referring to McCool.

"Who?" asked Jerome.

"Some young kid…I don't know. He was on the news though when they were talkin' about everything the other day. They tied him to Muchetta somehow. I don't know…but, I don't trust him. Just by looking at him, I don't like him."

"So let's do what we gotta do then, D…we gotta start *somewhere*. Who the fuck is he?"

"Calm down, Jerome…why you so trigger happy? Is it gonna bring your brother back? Is it gonna make my boy pull through?"

With a glooming stare, Jerome looked to Desmond and shook his head sideways. He couldn't believe what he was hearing.

"Your son is in a coma, D. Where is the King Carter I knew way back when? The one who'd make sure he'd let em' know who rules this mothafuckin' city?"

Jerome stood up, hoping as he ascended, Desmond would rise to the occasion with him. He wanted justice. There was more to do than sitting back, hoping things took their course.

Carter played it safe these days. But, how safe could he play the game with his neighborhood in jeopardy and son's life on the line?

Was there something more to prove? Perhaps he had to show everyone he was still a vital part of the community. Whatever it would be, it overwhelmingly troubled his mind. "Maybe Jerome had a point," he pondered. He didn't know what to do….but for now, he was going to squeeze his forearm grips. It always helped him think.

CHAPTER TWELVE

Once I left the hospital, I continued my journey, reluctantly making it to my next stop of the day. Much like where I came from, I knew I'd be discussing some disheartening news with some more unsatisfied people. This was a visit I was not looking forward to.

Good old Fairton, New Jersey where a massive white-bricked building stood grand smack in the middle of town. It was the deserted mystique at the end of the Pine Barrens. Inside the dark, unforgiving quarters of the Federal prison held one of the most dangerous men alive restrained from society.

Dark, empty, cold…the visitation room stood silently at the end of the passageway I walked down. On my way into the chamber, the fluorescent lights flickered, signaling I was going in the right direction.

I walked into the room and plopped down on a seat. I wasn't feeling sure of this visit from how Caz explained it. The last time I was here, it was under unnerving circumstances. From the knot in my stomach, I knew this one wouldn't be much better.

Two rookie guards brought Little Vinny into the room. He carelessly dragged his feet across the floor on his way over to the booth as if *I* was the one summoning him to see *me*. The old man was dominated by a profound sadness, a fatigue engraved on his worn, beaten down face.

You could see how the sorrow grew more profound each day he spent in his quiet, lonely cell. The solemn walls provided an empty canvas, reviving the memory of the losses he encountered along the way.

Not only that, Vinny had been losing many privileges at the prison since the recent chaos. The Feds were on an all-time prowl since capturing Paulie. His white collar treatment and private connections were becoming more limited by the day.

Most importantly, all conversations Vinny was having with the outside world were now being recorded again. They hadn't kept an eye on what he was doing since he first went away. Yet now, Agent Martinez was making an initiative to find what he could anywhere and anyway.

"Watch what you say…theses motherless fucks have been listening to everything lately," said Vinny as his opening statement once he picked up the receiver. I held the phone on my end to my ear, looking directly at him. In a soft tone, I replied, "I heard."

All of a sudden, Vinny let out a violent barking cough. In the end, it had that whistling sound you get when the airways close up. It was unlike him. It made me curious about where the status of his health truly was.

"How's your arm?" he asked, once he had the chance to catch his breath, glancing in my direction. He took out a handkerchief to wipe his mouth as he awaited my reply.

"It's been better," I told him. I noticed how disappointed he was by the way he kept avoiding looking at me. It was as if I was one of his children who let him down.

He didn't waste any time to tell me how he felt, especially with the loss of Carmine in the recent war. "I was sad to hear about the big guy the other night. I had hoped things would have gone a different way. That's very careless planning if you ask me."

Quickly, I fired back. I wasn't going to let him put me on a guilt trip. Not when there was so much that was out of my control. "The best of measures were taken, Vinny."

"There was room for fewer errors."

Perhaps he should've been the one out there. I would have loved to see him do better. Lots of talking one can do behind a glass wall when there is no chance of ever crossing it.

"I'm upset about it too, Vinny…nobody is taking this lightly," I told him.

"He should've been done first earlier in that day…the pretty one," he began. Vinny then looked back at the guards who brought him in. They were unwavering, steady as a statue. No longer did he have the power to nod them away. These guys were there for the duration of our visit.

Vinny went on. "This is what I was fuckin' explainin' to you, kid. You-know-who is ten steps ahead of everybody. There's no gettin' past him," he said, referring to the one, Lou Gorgeous.

"I know how to handle it…and him," I replied. I could get the sense he was losing trust in me.

"Oh really?" he smugly said as he cackled. "I understand that there is a meeting coming up between all of yas. Do you know what this meeting needs to entail on your end...or do I need to fuckin' spell it out?"

His attitude was wearing thin on me. For as much as I did to avenge his son and the honor of the Veccuto crew, he should've been kissing the glass in front of me.

"What do you want, notes and slideshows when I'm done?" I asked.

"Don't be smart. Keep it fuckin' simple."

I wanted to leave, right then and there. Why was I listening to this guy? How was he actually going to help me out? Did he really have the power he once did? Or was he just washed up now, looking for a bag to punch?

"Let me take care of it, Vinny...my way. Everything before went to plan except one mishap that was unavoidable. Don't take your frustrations out on me," I explained, doing my best to avoid detail now that we were keenly being watched.

It was then he continued to laugh at me. Again, I felt like I was there for amusement...much like when I was there prior. This time, he didn't have Caz for an audience. It was just him and I, two guards and a bunch of blank stares.

The evil grin he wore became more baleful by the minute. His wide eyes were dark wells of inky pools with dark shadows underneath. His skin was paler than the full moon.

"You end it when you're in front of him, no fuckin' around…take care of this shit, you little bastard." He pointed at me while he raised his eyebrows, implying much more than what he meant on the surface.

"Are we finished, Vinny?"

I was tired of him thinking he could tell me what to do. As much as I respected the man historically, he needed to know I wasn't going to sit there and listen to him berate me.

The coldness between us was getting chillier. Every word over-pronounced, slicing rather than tumbling through the dry air.

"Next time I see you, it better be done. Tell the others tonight," concluded Vinny, standing up before I was even finished.

And just like that, he hung up. Abrupt, yes…but he didn't hear what he wanted on my end. I wasn't going to be his puppet. He held the strings long enough…it was somebody else's turn.

From there, he walked away and back into this cell without even a notion of a goodbye. I rose from my seat, slamming the phone on the hook.

There was an uncertain feeling I had when I left the prison. I wasn't quite sure about Vinny's intentions anymore. He was terribly eager to take out Lou when before it seemed too taboo to even consider.

Yet, in the moments before I got into my car, all was better. The entire day became a blur. For in that minute, I pulled out my phone. As the sun was setting, a new light was dawning right in front of me.

Feasting my eyes on a text message, it was from the only person who could make me smile genuinely.

"Hey, it's Nina. The girl you gave your number to on a cocktail napkin at The Dive. Do you remember me?" It ended with a smiley face emoji. I was back in the game!

CHAPTER THIRTEEN

One excellent piece of news was that Mighty Mack's Gym was still open in the Northeast. The bad news: my workout routine the following week was anything but mighty.

Traditional pushups and my usual bench press routine became more difficult than trying to move a mountain. Although pain had been a considerable part of my life, I was feeling it even more with these workouts.

I pushed through, however. Utilizing every square inch of my 185-pound, five-foot-six frame, I wasted no time in the old iron cellar that started my mornings for so long in my life. I did away with my arm sling and began taking layers off of my leg cast, little by little.

My beard may have been messier, hair a bit shaggier and Irish knot tattoos up and down my arms a bit more faded, but my heart was bigger than ever. It was the most resilient muscle I had.

In fact, it was beating so hard, you could see it through my sweat-stained gray hoodie. It pounded with each hit I gave the punching bag.

I was sore in every fiber of my body. It felt like my knee was still being stabbed with flying metal inside the deli. My arm kept recalling the piercing shot of Red Alan's bodyguard's gunfire. But that's what living is…one has to be beaten down to the ground in order to rise up to glory once again.

Additionally, there was still so much on my mind. The most prominent thing perhaps being how to restructure…how to reform. Where to go from here with the daunting shadows of Lou Gorgeous in the midst of every place we went, watching…waiting.

I still did not fear Lou. Not one bit. Not the way others did…even though it was confirmed the guy was real. Then again, I worried very little.

Yet, the real thing that kept my juices flowing was the thought of Nina. She agreed to hang out with me after Christmas. Hearing this, I was amped up. There was more fire in my blood than ever. That's why it was perfect timing when Caz texted me at the end of my workout saying, "Come outside. We're going to see *him* now." I grabbed my gym bag on the way out.

I hadn't caught up with the skinny one since before I went over to the prison to see Vinny the day prior. I neglected to say anything. To be quite frank, it slipped my mind once Nina texted me. We had no plan…no course of action. We would have to play it by ear once we got in front of him.

I walked outside. With much stealth and little appeal, a long black stretch limousine came to the entrance of the gym. This happened within sixty seconds of me replying to Caz that I was ready.

As soon as I stepped off the stairs that entered the gym, a large guy came out from the back seat of the limo. He stood on the curb with a black blindfold, tossing it to me and yelling, "Put this over your eyes, McCool."

"Put it over your penis and have your wife jerk you off with it. Who the fuck are you?" I replied as I approached the limo without taking his instruction.

The man stopped me in my tracks with the great palm of his monstrous right hand. It was then I had an enhanced feeling of déjà vu. He looked way too familiar. Furthermore, he held a smile...but not the same way he held out a Smith and Wesson 38-special in his left hand to make it clear this was no time for smart remarks.

Unwillingly, I tied the blindfold around my eyes. I took my time though, just to be a smart ass. What did I have to lose? *Besides my life.* I wanted to make these possible final moments last.

As I was tightening up the blindfold, I could feel the man's right hand all over me, frisking around for whatever I had in my possession. They even took my gym bag from my side. "Whoa, what the fuck?" I asked.

"Keep them up!" bellowed the guy, trying to sound louder than the traffic before us while he finished his search. He took my cell phone, my keys, my wallet and even the headphones I had for my workout. "I'll give this all back to you later."

"I thought we could come to this meeting carrying?" I asked. Unfortunately, he didn't give me back my gym bag which held my only weapon for this occasion.

"You could've," replied the guy. "But only for us to take it away," he concluded. After that, he led me to the back seat of the extended vehicle, ready to chariot me to our next unknown destination. *Oh, joy!*

On the way over, I could hear the familiar sniffles and grunts of Caz and Tony Boy alongside me as the nervousness lingered on in our silence. I even recognized their musk, especially Tony Boy. That grease ball. He smelled worse doing nothing than I did after an hour on the treadmill.

Eventually, I hummed Irish tunes the rest of the way to let the duo know I was there. *La, la, la! My four green fields...each one was a jewel...*

"Pipe down," I kept hearing from the driver.

Finally, the ride stopped. The engine shut off and the doors were being opened from the outside. Perhaps these jerks figured there was a chance we'd want to remain still in the wary seats we sweated sitting in? Who knows? We were instructed to exit the limo, being pushed and shoved out like we were in front of oncoming traffic.

Once the goons removed the blindfolds from our eyes, my instinctive judgment became clearer. It was all coming into focus. I knew something wasn't right. The guys still holding us at gunpoint were the ones from the night of the explosion, guarding the deli. Immediately, the flashbacks I was having gave me all types of violent thoughts from the night; the blast, the blood, the gore. Now, I was as uneasy as ever. My heart was racing like Secretariat at the Belmont.

What exact street we were on, I had no idea. We were somewhere in South Philly. They guided us into the back of an old garage. As we descended down a stairwell inside, things grew more unsettling. All we heard was opera music playing.

A small, murky and bleak basement was our destination. We had arrived. The music grew louder the further we went down.

The room appeared to be some sort of wine cellar at one point. The most elegant vintages shelved in wooden crates all around them. They were trusted to the natural preservation of the cooling soil beneath the stone walls.

Every few feet, brass brackets for candles would shine with what little sparkle they had left. They hadn't been used in ages. There wasn't even any waxy residue on them anymore.

It smelled musty, as most basements do. Yet, this was a pungent mold. A single dangling, dimly lit bulb provided the sole gleam for the entire floor.

There was one wooden table that rested near the stone wall and acted as a desk. An old glass ashtray was the only object on the surface. The three of us sat down in old rickety chairs in front of the table, led by the same two punks from the limo.

Before I had the chance to lean over and ask Caz where the man of the hour was, another brash noise resonated from the top of the stairs. The wooden creeks of the steps were roaring louder than the voices in my head, telling me this meeting was terrible news.

We turned around to see him more clearly. At first, the only things visible were his eyes. They were piercing with venomous light shining right in our faces.

His voice was smooth like olive oil as he spoke to his men in Italian, thick and slow…but the message was clear. To me though, there was something obscure about his dialogue and body language. Then again, it could have just been his greased back hair, his piercing dark skin or his false smile.

He stared at you the way a wolf would stare at their prey. You could tell that the only things he cared about were money and bloodshed…sometimes together.

"Here we are. We all finally meet. Face to face," said the mysterious figure, giving a smirk, looking around the dark and desolate basement. He took off his black fedora and put it on the desk. He then pulled out a thin Montecristo Joyitas cigar, holding it in between his two fingers. "Don't everyone speak at once," he continued sarcastically, chuckling just enough to crack the silence.

I bobbed my head in impatience. I wasn't happy about any of this. Caz and Tony Boy said hello, very quietly but loud enough for all to hear. Tony seemed the most frightened with the way he was biting his nails.

"I take it you sweethearts all know who I am," he continued, confidently. He took off his overcoat and handed it to one of his men. After that, he sat down in the seat behind the desk.

Leaning in towards the table, Caz whispered to him, giving his regards. "Lou, Lou…Mr. Muchetta, we are honored."

The one they called 'Gorgeous' didn't even look back at him. Instead, he lit his Montecristo, responding as clearly as he could that he was not messing around. "Good. I am glad. Hopefully, this helps us all see eye to eye."

The dubious duo that walked us in came over to Lou. They stood on either side of him, keeping their eyes on the two Wops and one dirty Irishman in front of them. They were like guards watching the Parliament gate, not moving a muscle.

Lou went on. "Your friend...Big Carmine. I am sorry you had to see him similar in a way I tore apart Chris Veccuto."

There it was! Everything was out in the open. Nobody could deny it anymore. Lou was the mastermind the entire time, orchestrating Paulie and the Connor Brothers to carry out his course of action. Vinny was right with what he told Caz and I. As much as I didn't like to admit the little one saw this one from miles away, he did.

"But he had it coming. Much like that stupid kid. Wrong place, wrong time. I'd do it all again if he came back from the dead and tried to finish the job," he continued, blowing his cigar smoke in perfect circles above him.

My knuckles grew white, and my mind was racing at a mile per second. This was our real enemy, the one right in front of us. Even more so, he had no problem showing us his iniquitous demeanor.

"I implore you all to see where I am coming from here. Paulie is my cousin. The Connor Brothers worked for me, they were business partners of mine.

What you did...it had very little discretion. I am not sure what you sweethearts were thinking."

Nobody said anything. There were probably many answers to give, but not quite the one Lou was looking for.

"I need you all to learn from your mistakes...like Carmine." He finally gave a full smile, ear to ear as he prepared his next statement.

I had enough. Out of nowhere, I spoke up. I was tired of remaining silent. "Mistakes are the portal of discovery."

Now all eyes were on me. However my statement was interpreted, it didn't seem to fulfill the Caz or Tony by the way they widened their eyes. It most certainly gave no appeasement to Mr. Muchetta.

"Smart mouth," he replied, leaning in close towards my direction for the first time during the whole sit. "Next time, keep your James Joyce quotes at home...or I will find a place for you to put them."

Surprised that he even knew I was referencing the Irish author, I replied quickly. "You bring us here to kill us?" I looked right and left at his boys then back to the gorgeous one. I just wanted to hear him say it. Caz and Tony couldn't believe the way I was talking to him.

"I'm not gonna kill any of you. I would have done that by now." In an attempt to be even flashier, he pulled out a switchblade, twisting it back and forth in the light. It was like a mirror reflecting in the sun, it shined so painfully. As it burned its beam into our eyes, I noticed the letter L engraved on it as he continued to ramble. "However, that can all change in a moment's time," he continued.

The way his men remained silent and stern gave me even more reason to believe Lou ran a tight ship. He was the kind of guy who people did not only fear...but their heart fluttered just hearing the name. The biggest question was how was I going to take him down? What was next after this meeting? How were we going to pull this off? Not for Vinny...but for us.

"What I'm offering today is as good as it is going to get. Believe me...it won't get this good again."

I couldn't wait to hear what he had in store. This guy was full of himself. What could he possibly give us other than our deaths?

"I am going to tax each of you...one by one," said Lou.

I cackled, shaking my head sideways. That was the best he could do? What was he, the DMV charging us for a late car inspection?

"How much you talking?" asked Caz, sitting as still as I had ever seen him.

"Fifty Grand each in three weeks. You call Umberto when you all have it...he and Frankie here will collect."

As Lou looked to Frankie, the guy on his right, the realization of the proposal was sinking in. Along with it came a moment of silence. Lou was a guy who was a few steps ahead of the rest. I assumed that nothing he did was ever just 'cut and dry' like he was advising. For as much as this seemed appealing,

I knew there was more to what was simply a 'tax' paid to clear us of any wrongdoing. We had to make sure we took him out and did it quickly.

"Are we clear?" asked the gorgeous one.

"Lou, I mean...Lou...," a nervous Tony went on again, unable to figure out what his next sentence would be after saying the man's name twice. He was ridiculous.

All of a sudden, I had a revelation. Just as my thoughts of strangling Lou across the desk passed by, I started discerning rationally. Tony's stuttering brought me back to the previous week, right before I put that last shotgun shell into Red Alan's skull. Before that pathetic ginger-headed scumbag roared his final 'FUCK YOU' to me, he mumbled what seemed like gibberish when I asked him about the alleged Caribbean Connection. I knew there was more to it, even when he first spoke it.

"Ooo...ooo....ooo," was what I thought he was saying. The more I crossed the T's and dotted the I's...or should I say assembled the L-O-U's, he was saying, "Lou...Lou...Lou."

Now, I really had to speak about something. *Ask away, McCool.* I needed to be in on what I had been yearning for. Something that could have changed all of our lives...and the future of the kids at SICH. "I have a question!" I stated.

Lou barely looked at me, but I knew he was all ears. He continued to sit and play with his switchblade on the wooden table, spinning it around on its side like a propeller. "How about I do you one better than taxing us all?" I asked.

Assuming his silence for curiosity, I continued. The other two had a slight sense of where I was going with this. I could tell they wanted no parts. However, I could not resist.

"This Caribbean Connection...if it even really exists...and if you are even in on it, I know people who can help. I counted cards for five years down in Atlantic City. Not only did I learn a thing or two but I have bookies down there who can open the door and expand this thing further than you can imagine: Boston, New York, Baltimore, Miami, and more. Even across the country: Chicago, Vegas, LA...the possibilities are endless."

Still, he wasn't looking in my direction. He didn't appreciate me bringing the topic up. He sat still, counting the bottles of wine around the room as if he didn't know how many were there already. He was stalling.

I leaned on the table in front of me to show him how serious I was. "Let us help you. On the front lines, I know we can spearhead this for you, Lou," I continued, being the most polite I had been the entire time we were there. I kept showing him my open hands as a true inviting gesture.

Finally, he uttered, quietly and with caution, "I can't go there. I don't know what you're talking about, sweetheart." Yet, his condescending tone told me differently. He knew *exactly* what I was talking about.

"I'm just saying, Lou, you want to turn a nickel-and-dime operation into millions..."

That was when he interrupted me. All of a sudden, he was louder than he had been the whole time. His voice echoed like a shout through a tunnel.

"In case you're in the dark about all this, kid…let me shed some light…."

SLAM! Lou grabbed his switchblade, jamming it into the table. He cut deep down through like it was made of paper. Right in front of my hands! We all jumped. Yet, I was far from backing away.

His mood shifted. "We're done here!" he concluded, widening his eyes and signaling to Frankie to guide us out. Caz and Tony Boy stood up as Lou yanked the blade from the table, only to clean it with his cloth of any wood dust it accumulated.

I arose as well. I was still fixed on my offer. Based on Lou's reaction, I was sure he wasn't in the dark to what I was asking. I wasn't giving up yet. I was going to have my hands on this venture, one way or the other. We couldn't kill him just yet.

There was no shot I'd let him get away without bringing me in on it when Fitzy assured to me, the asset I'd be to the project.

Frankie led us out of the basement and back on our way. Meanwhile, Umberto began pouring Lou a shot of Limoncello from a bottle he kept under the desk. Before we reached the stairs, the gorgeous one spoke once more. As he was doing so, he continued playing with his knife.

"Three weeks, my sweethearts. If I have to see you guys here again, I won't be holding this blade in my hand without your blood on it."

CHAPTER FOURTEEN

Time was flying. The clock was ticking. It was Christmas Night in the Northeast. The decorative lights on the neighborhood houses weren't the only things shining brightly. My eyes were smiling radiantly, ready for what was to come that evening.

This was the most festive time of the year. People were gathering together to join in the yuletide merriments. However, for me, I was coming along and celebrating differently.

It was the night of the executive poker game!

Place your bets!

All kinds of gamblers came together for this kind of thing. Doctors, lawyers, bankers, politicians, drug dealers, priests, Indian chiefs…you name it. I didn't care who they were or where they traveled from; as long as they brought their ten grand minimum buy-ins onto the table to play.

We held the big game in the back of the AOH Hall on Tulip Street, known merely as "Hibernian." It was an old Irish-Catholic fraternal organization's clubhouse that held functions and parties during the week. Yet, during every few weeks on the weekend, it contained a different type of occasion…mine.

My parents were members when I was a tiny tot, as well as Fitzy. The folks who ran the hall knew me through and through. They were fine with me conducting business. In exchange, of course, I took care of them as well with a little piece of the action. Everyone made out!

The back room wasn't much, but it was just enough for a poker game. There was a buffet table on the rear wall for coffee, snacks, drinks, and cigars. Next to it was a big orange couch with a long coffee table in front of it. Caz and Tony Boy sat there, guarding the stack of money as if it were going to fly away at a moment's notice.

In the middle, there laid the big green poker table with cards and chips scattered all over. Around it, every kind of character in the city sat, ready to win. The light above them, hanging from the ceiling, shined upon every lucky and not-so-lucky hand.

I would never rest my feet on a night like this. Especially with now having a healed arm and leg, I walked around and made sure everyone was having a good time and that each was accommodated to their liking. Once the games began, I'd circle the perimeters of the room, methodically. Although I enjoyed playing the game myself, I enjoyed watching the money work for me rather than me work for it.

Everybody was in for the big score. There was a councilman from the 15th District playing, one of my favorite guys. He was the youngest member of the city council. He was always campaigning, talking about his role. I liked him mostly because I could always depend on him to lose the game early and cough up a few more dollars to raise his chances. Yet, having him in the room was a plus. I was able to learn what was going on in city hall and get some of the latest political gossip.

My handy dandy lawyer, Eliot Rivishowitz, made his way over. He was an older Jewish gentleman with a lot of class. It was great to review some of the legal battles he was dealing with. One never knew what to expect in an uncertain future, so it was good to be educated on the law and how I could make it work for me.

'Flying Hawk' was a Native American casino owner from the west coast. He'd come in every holiday to meet with some of his old pals on the east coast. He was very close with Fitz over the years. They worked on many different business projects together. He never missed out on a game when the opportunity would present itself.

Then, there were a few half-wiseguys who would show up once in a while. Sometimes, they got lucky. Then again, I was a firm believer that you made your own luck in this world. Nothing is given to you, you gotta take it!

There was one wannabe I always got a kick out of talking to. His name was 'Crazy' Terry Green. He was from the old neighborhood. He was a nice guy, but he always had a story. He reminded you of the kind of kid continually trying to impress the cool crowd in the school playground.

As the night started to wrap up, he came up to me with an immense smile. I was refilling the coffee and restacking the cigars at the buffet table when I heard his voice, screechy like a tire being braked on the road.

"Hey, Jackie! What a game, man!" he tried whispering in an excited tone as if he actually won. Even when he was attempting to be quiet, he was loud.

"Oooo! Terry…sorry you got beat so early. But, hey…we are all used to it by now," I said, straightening the buffet tablecloths up as he continued on.

Terry laughed…mainly because it was true. He rarely made it out of the first forty-five minutes. Afterward, he would hang around for many hours after just to tell me a few stories or corny jokes. Out of the four or five tales, one of them I'd choose to believe.

"Haha, fuck you ya little shit!" he said to me, slapping my lousy arm.

With a smile, trying to hold back the pain from it still trying to fully heal, I asked, "How's the family?"

"Not bad, I must say. We did Christmas at the wife's side this year…so, you know I was looking forward to tonight."

"I hear you, buddy."

The crazy one then grabbed a Styrofoam cup to pour himself another round of coffee. This time, he looked like he was preparing me for another one of his grand narratives to tell. I could see it with how jittery he was. It was either that or his nickel-a-day cocaine habit kicking in.

"How about you, everything good?" he asked, patting me on the back.

"Always good, brother…always."

Then, he looked around at the room before he glanced back to me, lowering his voice. "Say...can I talk to you for a minute, Jackie? In private?" he asked.

"Yeah. What's up, Ter?"

We then sauntered over to the entrance door, away from the buffet table, cigar smoke, clinking of poker chips and anybody or thing which could hear what he had to say next.

"Listen, I got something for ya...something real nice. A big job...BIG money involved," he told me, talking with his hands as if he was holding an imaginary box.

"Oh yeah? What kind of job?" I asked, rolling my eyes.

"Rich guy. Cherry Hill, New Jersey kind of yuppie...he screwed me over with some blue-chip stuff in the stock market this past year. I'm looking to get back at him."

"I'm listening."

He was over the moon to tell me what he had in store next. So excited, he was spilling his hot coffee on his hand, and it wasn't fazing him.

"Do you know anyone who can crack safes?" asked Terry.

"I may," I replied. Immediately, one name came to mind. Yet, I wasn't entirely buying this proposal as quickly as he was presenting it.

"I know where this fuckin' whale keeps a safe in his house. All cash. I'm talkin' about one-fourth of a rock in there he keeps!" Terry told me, implying a quarter million dollars.

"How would one get inside to get the safe?"

"The guy is away until after the New Year. He's taking his new girlfriend down to Puerto Vallarta. It's all clear. I can give you the security codes to his garage and the entrance door to the house, the code to turn off the alarm...I just need someone in who can crack the safe and get the fuck out of there STAT!"

I nodded my head. Thinking about the opportunity at stake, I was reflecting on the hospital and what I was going to have to do to save it. This was a crucial time where I needed all I could get. If I wasn't going to do business with Lou and the Caribbean Connection right away, I couldn't turn down a score. Then again, I had to consider the source.

"What's in it for you?"

"Hah! Besides revenge? I don't know...finder's fee...twenty percent? You and the others whack it up three ways?"

"Will you do fifteen if I can find the power?"

"I'm not going to tussle with you, Black. You're doing the legwork, my man!"

"I'll talk with the guys. I'll see if I can sell it to them."

"You're the man, dude!"

"I'll call ya!"

Terry walked away and out of the back room with a cheesy grin. I then went over to the couch where Caz and Tony Boy sat to join them. First, I took a sip of my Jameson. Secondly, I looked at each of them. They were as quiet as church mice, itching for the night to be over. Then, I looked out the window. The sun was finally creeping up. The poker game was coming to an end.

The three of us thanked the players for coming, hoping they all had a good time. We walked them out of the AOH and made sure they were okay to get where they were going next.

After cleaning up and putting everything where it belonged, we sat down at the poker table and counted the cash in our Cassida money counter, trying to speed things up so we could get to breakfast at the diner down the street.

While we were meticulously stacking the twenties, fifties and hundreds, Tony Boy pulled his phone out of his pocket as if it were burning his leg off. His eyes widened extensively at whatever message came through. It was as if his phone cracked to pieces and he just realized it.

"Holy shit!" he uttered.

"What?" asked Caz, dropping a few bills to the surface of the floor.

Tony Boy continued. "Paulie's case ended this morning...it didn't even go into a RICO trial. They settled."

That was quick. For a guy with as much pull as he had though, I wasn't surprised. I then asked, "What did they give him?"

"Seven years instead of twenty-five!" said Tony Boy, still shocked. He tossed his phone on the table after reading a bit more. After that, he went back to totaling the dollars with us as the discussion continued.

"Wow, that's a hell of a deal!" I replied.

Caz then asked one of the most ultimate questions we all wanted to know the answer to. "What did *he* give *them*?"

"An allocution!" said Tony Boy.

Our jaws dropped to the floor. "Get the fuck out of here!" yelled Caz, losing even more bills to the floor this time. It started to look like a parade down there.

We couldn't believe it. For a guy like Paulie who preached about the old school, here he was breaking the one principal thing he stood by: his oath and allegiance to the family.

Tony went on with the details. "He admitted to running the show for the past twenty-five years. Took the heat and everything."

"What a pussy!" Caz exclaimed. "He couldn't stand trial like a man...threw in the fuckin' towel just like that?"

Tony reminded us all, "You never admit to *this thing*. I don't give a fuck who you are or what you're doin'!"

Loyalty meant everything, especially with these Italians. The old traditions that were diminishing in the new era was the saddest thing to see.

Caz then asked the next critical question. It was probably the most important one...especially for us. "What's that mean for Lou Gorgeous?"

"Who knows?" said Tony.

"Speaking of...fellas, we're coming up short with him over here! It ain't good!" I yelled, pointing to the dollar bills.

They both looked at the stack of money in awe as I cross-referenced the cash counting machine with my own calculations. Since I was good with numbers, I wanted to make sure every penny was accounted for.

"We are splitting this three ways evenly. Calculating what we all had saved up before tonight...looks like we aren't quite where we need to be yet. That's not good considering there is only one fuckin' week left to pay Lou."

This was not nearly the amount of cash the usual card game brought in. I was bummed. I wasn't sure where the disconnection was. It seemed to me like the players were spending abundantly...maybe I had more on my mind than I realized, who knew? Either way, it wasn't going to keep us alive.

Although it was far from the worst I had seen over my time running the game, the revenue left me far from content with the night's outcome.

"What are we gonna do?" asked Tony.

Caz replied, "Beats me. This doesn't leave us many other options....we gotta take Lou out!"

I stopped both of them before their idea grew into a plan. "Not yet. I want in on the Caribbean thing...I really do. I know he has his hands in it. Once we get that, then we can take him out," I reminded them.

Sitting back in his chair, Tony Boy tried to tell me, "Hah! Keep dreamin'! We won't make it that long!" They were both disappointed, I could sense it. I promised this night was going to be the Super Bowl of money making. I had to find another cash cow while justifying keeping Lou alive long enough to get a piece of the Caribbean Connection.

It was at that very moment I remembered my conversation earlier in the night with Terry Green. How could I have forgotten so quickly? I proceeded to share the information with the fellas.

"Whatever we do...in the meantime, we still gotta pay Lou. He still has more power over us, now especially with Paulie out of the equation. Lou knows every step we're taking. He's not going to be an easy slain," I started. I looked to Caz considering he was the first I thought of when presented the offer. He had a history of working safes.

I asked, "Say, Caz...I got a safe-crackin' job. Would you guys be in?"

"What do you mean?" questioned the skinny one, leaning up in his chair.

"Terry Green. He was in here last night telling me about this big score that's paying up to a quarter of a million."

"That fuck. You sure it was him...or was it the lines of blow talking?" asked Tony, always the pessimist. He sat back in his chair and looked at me, eager to hear what I'd say next.

"He's talkin' 250 large...it's worth the risk. At this rate, we need to pay Lou, and we will starve without it after this game bleeding us dry over here," I reminded them.

"When?" Caz asked.

"The second day of the new year."

They both looked down and then back up. Tony shook his head, disagreeing as usual. It was okay...I had my hopes set that Caz wouldn't be able to resist such a score.

Before Tony even had the chance to express his concerns to either Caz or myself out of it, the skinny one replied, "I am in."

I opened a smile. Tony shook his head sideways. Reluctantly, he uttered, "Fuck it...it's Christmas. I guess we all don't have much a choice!"

"Merry fuckin' Christmas indeed, boys," Caz said, toasting with the last bit of Sambuca in his glass. Tony Boy and I joined in with the Jameson poured neat in front of us.

"Well, it's Saint Stephen's Day now," I reminded them, downing my shot before slamming it on the table.

"What the fuck is that?" asked Caz.

"An Irish celebration!" I shouted. I figured this was something better shown then it was explained. So, I decided to take them to my favorite bar in the Northeast following breakfast...the place where Fitzy, Duffy, O'Hara and myself spent many good and bad nights...The Trinity Bar.

"Not much to celebrate," said Tony.

"Alright Tone, relax. I'll call Terry on the way and get the wheels in motion with this thing for New Years' week," I said. Not only was the bar nostalgic to me, I knew it would offer a sense of inspiration to give the story justice.

In Gaelic, St. Stephen's Day is called Lá Fhéile Stiofáin or Lá an Dreoilín, meaning the Wren Day. Christmas in Ireland lasts not just for Christmas Eve and Christmas, but days into January with special celebrations and observations extending the festive season.

On St. Stephen's Day, the day after Christmas, the wren bird is cheered. Why? The story goes that during Penal Times when there was once a plot against local soldiers in an Irish village.

They were surrounded and were about to be ambushed when a group of wrens pecked on their drums and awakened the sleeping soldiers. The plot failed, and the wren became known as "The Devil's bird."

In Ireland, a procession takes place where a pole with a holly bush is carried from house to house and families dress up in old clothes and with blackened faces. In olden times, an actual wren would be killed and placed on top of the pole. Here in the Northeast, we drank.

No matter how good or how bad your holiday was, all still showed up at Trinity to partake in the night. They even had the Clancy Brothers playing on the jukebox when we arrived.

The wren, the wren, the king of all birds
St. Stephen's Day was caught in the furze.
Although he was little, his honor was great
Jump up me lads and give him a treat.

I convinced the two Italians with me to join in a shot of Jameson to start the night. It wasn't their usual glass of Gin, Anisette or Sambuca, but I think they enjoyed the whiskey as it rolled down their throats.

"Top o' the mornin' to ya!" I said. Although at this point, it was the late afternoon. "A salu," was their response. They chugged down the shots. I ordered us some Irish Coffees to sip on for the evening. I had a big night ahead and I was excited for more than just Saint Stephen's Day.

As I was going to Killenaule
I met a wren upon the wall.
I took me stick and knocked him down
And brought him in to Carrick Town.

Up with the kettle and down with the pan
And give us a penny to bury the wren.

Before I got the chance to enlighten the fellas on what the night had in store, Caz leaned over and inquired, "Jackie...how come you never mentioned what Vinny asked you to do with our friend, the gorgeous one, the other week?"

I hesitated as he asked the question. I didn't necessarily know where to begin either. Instead, I responded with my first thought that came to mind about the little one. "Fuck him!"

Tony Boy eyed me down while Caz scoffed. "He wants me to see him after the New Year. He's not happy with Lou still alive. You were supposed to plan with us, Jack…not be in the fuckin' gym and neglect us before we went in. He ain't happy with ya," Skinny told me.

Quickly, I replied. "I got to say, Caz…I don't like Vinny's fuckin' attitude lately. The way he was talkin' to me when I saw him last…I was insulted."

"He's a dying man, Jackie…spending his life in prison. How would you feel?" asked Tony Boy, giving his two cents.

I jeered before shaking my head side to side. Whether or not I empathized with the man, I didn't like how he was trying to control me from behind a glass wall.

"Cowards die many times before their death…but the valiant only taste of death but once!" I said, looking directly at Tony Boy and putting my pointer finger up to signify the number one. He turned away from me.

"If it's still the Caribbean Connection you're after, McCool…forget it…it's not gonna happen," said Caz, putting his hand on top of mine.

"You think it's for me? It's not…it's for SICH, the children's hospital in my old neighborhood."

"Huh? What about SICH? What are you talkin' about?"

"I'm trying to save it. They want to close the place…I'm not gonna let it happen. However, this is a way to find the cash for them…it's with this Caribbean thing. Listen, I'm not hot on Lou either…but if he's the bridge to the most money around here, I'm gonna kiss his ass to cross it."

"Jackie...I mean...," Caz went on just before I turned away from him. Something was distracting me from his banter.

All of a sudden, I felt a tap on my shoulder. Could it be? In a place like this? Amid the Irish drunkards singing and dancing to Celtic classic tunes, such a rare beauty in my presence? The one, the only...Nina?

Indeed. There she was. She actually showed up when I invited her! I was thrilled as could be. A smile lit up my face.

As her eyes gleamed across the room, she had a beam of joy dashing inside of her come out for all to witness. She took her finger and brushed her shiny brunette hair aside. When she did, I was able to see the bright red lipstick on her lips matching the red jacket she wore. Additionally, her invigorating aroma had me dizzy where I stood, once again.

"I didn't think you'd show up," I admitted. I was so glad she proved me wrong.

"I wasn't going to," she responded, giving me a hug and carefully placing down her purse on the bar stool next to me.

"What changed your mind?"

"I guess it was the Christmas spirit, McCool."

"As am I."

I snapped out of my daze for a moment. I almost forgot to introduce her to Caz and Tony Boy. After I did, they immediately began talking amongst themselves. For me, my focus was now on Nina. She was the belle of the ball this evening, to me...for sure.

"Did you have a good holiday?" she asked me.

"Well, it just got a Hell of a lot better," I replied.

"Oh, Christ…don't start your shit."

"What? I'm just saying…," I began just as she cut me off.

"Yeah, I bet."

I decided to change the subject. She wasn't quite ready for me to dive in head-first with the charm this early in the night. I figured I'd ask her about the Irish holiday instead.

"Now, Nina…I know you don't celebrate St. Stephen's Day. You're Italian aren't you?"

"And Lebanese…how did you guess?"

"You have a Mediterranean aura to you…what can I say?"

"Okay…I'll give you a few points for that."

"Thank you. What's your last name, dear?"

"It is *Constancia*!"

"Beautiful."

"Yeah, there's a small fire of Latin in me too!" she mentioned, winking at me.

I knew it. There was something about her that radiated a foreign heat…an enigmatic allure. I also got the sense that she still had reservations. Although she showed up, I'm sure it wasn't an easy decision.

I could sense this with her off-balance posture, resting on the bar next to her purse. She was keeping her distance. Although she was seeking the sense of companionship the way she interlocked her left hand with her right, she was cautious.

It was time to order a beverage. "What do you like to drink, love?" I asked her.

"Hmm…a Mojito sounds good."

"On its way!"

I signaled to the bartender to get us our drinks. They were indeed taking their time to bring them back. It was a busy night.

I figured this was an opportune time to ask her to the dance floor. I didn't want to waste any time…not in a moment like this!

"Come dance with me!"

"No, no, no!"

I began to pull her by her arm she had rested on her hip. As much as she fought the urge, I kept at it, trying to loosen her tenseness.

"C'mon, everyone knows how to dance!"

"McCool…get out of here, you crazy man!" she responded, smiling. I knew she wanted to. Her mind was telling her no, but her body was saying yes.

"We can stop when you've had enough, trust me," I promised.

Finally, she gave in. I took her hand and we swept over towards the dance floor. It was as if I was in a dream. This beautiful woman was actually joining me to move with the music for merely one song. That was what we agreed to. Man, I was the luckiest guy in the bar that night.

I positioned my hand on the small of her back. From there, she put her hand on my shoulder. Our free hands met. Together, we danced to the song while our feet stepped in a perfect pattern to the beating of my heart. As the tune progressed, I felt more relaxed, being in her company. I didn't even know what the song was…but we just kept moving.

She preserved her eyes on me, widening that gorgeous smile she wore so well. From there, I knew exactly where to take her. It happened naturally. Every moment, every angle seemed to be planned in advance. It did not feel forced at all. It was as if we were floating.

Both of our bodies swayed with the music. She moved so effortlessly and with such elegance. Yet, there was a sort of harshness to her, I could tell. She was indeed someone who shouldn't have been underestimated. She came from a dark place. Then again, so did I…in many ways.

I didn't quite care at the moment. Perhaps it was because I was falling for her already. The space between us grew more enchanting, causing more of a warming sensation by the second.

My heartbeat was growing steadily along with it. Our dance felt perfect; everything from our breathing to how our feet paced in rhythm.

Right here, right now in these very moments with Nina, I was truly living. Nothing else seemed to matter. I then allowed her to lead…to take me anywhere on the dancefloor she'd pleased.

She went left, I went left. She slowed down, I slowed down. We joined in tempo with the melody, with the dance and with each other.

Each second that passed, my breath seemed to be taken away a bit more. We continued like that until the song ended.

In my eyes, after that dance, I could see more of how perfect she truly was. I did not want this night to end.

I could tell she was ready to go by the way she hurried to finish up her drink. She wasn't going to change her course of the night, she made a promise to herself. My time with her was so real. It was time to let her know I was serious. "Go on a date with me, Nina…on an actual date. Not this bar shit…a place you'd like."

Smiling, she turned to me and said, "I like this bar shit."

"I do too…but I would like to get to know you as well. Somewhere private."

"I don't do dates."

"Why not?"

"Not my thing. I don't trust guys. It never ends well."

"Jesus…I'm not just any guy. And this won't be just any date."

Rolling her eyes, she put back whatever was left in the Mojito. Slamming the glass down, she got the attention of all around her before she started. "Thanks for the drink!" she told me as she rummaged to get her belongings together.

"Wait, wait…just hold on half a second!" I spoke up.

She kept moving, of course. "I'll see you around. This was fun…really," she yelled back, darting towards the door.

In true McCool fashion, I kept going after her. "You're killing me. One night, Nina. I want to take you somewhere nice, sit down and have a nice conversation. That's all." I was hoping to not be too pushy, but I couldn't resist.

With a sigh, she stopped suddenly and turned around. Tilting her head, she said with a smirk, "I haven't been on a date in a very long time. There hasn't been a reason…hasn't been an occasion."

"You're the occasion," I replied.

She was quiet. She knew I was honing in on her and I would do nothing to stop. I had to have more of her time…I had to see her again.

"I just want you to try something different. I want to show you a good time," I continued.

Still nothing, no response. I knew she knew I was right. The more she was holding herself back from having a good time, the more her mind was telling her to take a chance.

"A girl like you deserves that," I finalized.

She rolled her eyes again, letting out a soft chuckle. Following a deep breath, she gave in. "After the New Year. You pick the place, McCool. You got one shot. Let me know. I got to go."

After that, she stormed out. No goodbyes, no notion of when or if we would talk before that. The ball was in my court.

I went over to Caz and Tony Boy who were sitting there, silent and still. I couldn't tell if they were rooting for me or if they were upset I was neglecting them. The only thing I could tell them was, "Fellas…I think I'm in love."

CHAPTER FIFTEEN

In prison, one is continuously surrounded by four walls. There is nothing to do but stare at them…to look at the paint that continued to chip off as the minutes, the hours and eventually the days would blur into each other.

During such a stay, while a prisoner could have no idea of what was happening on the outside, they could have even less an idea of what was going on inside. One could also forget their own name.

The isolation was total. The stimulation was zero. All an inmate could do was feel the cold walls that held them confined.

Vinny was doing anything to pass the time, slowly going mad, theorizing absurd meanings from the wall's blank stare.

Not only was McCool becoming number one on his shit list…but he was losing faith. His plan was beginning to crumble.

It had been a Hell of a year. Even as the new one approached, there was still nothing to look forward to…nothing to feel joy towards. That was, of course…until he heard the news of Pretty Paul now joining the same confined life he had been rotting away in for two and a half decades.

This gave him hope. Weirdly, it gave him something to smile about. Perhaps Paulie didn't quite meet his fate on the outside…but he would undoubtedly meet it on the inside, one way or another.

Vinny had this top of mind that very afternoon he was in line to get lunch. The cafeteria was a discord of loud chatter. Each table was a confined huddle of people raising their voices to be heard above one another.

The food was secondary to the information that was exchanged here. Over the over-salted fries, alliances were formed and gossip was traded like poker chips.

As Vinny stood in the queue for his plate of nothing fresh, he shifted his eyes onto the big black man in front of him in line.

He was a massive fellow, nearly two heads higher than Vinny. However, he was far from lanky. There was a bulk to him. His muscles showed beneath the prison scrubs.

He was the kind of guy who received daily jokes about his stature...ones about "the air being thin up there." Though his legs moved slowly, he was still walking just as fast. Each stride carried him to the next position in line.

Nobody messed with this guy. He was the one you called if you needed somebody beat up over an inmate struggle or an issue between two gangs.

For no reason, Vinny deliberately reached over and grabbed the last sloppy Joe in front of the big black man before he had the chance to. It was fresh on the counter.

Like a massive bear in the woods, the guy turned around slowly and stared down at Vinny as if he stole his bee's nest, full of honey. One was said to even hear him growl.

"What the fuck is your problem, old man?" asked the guy with a storming voice that echoed. He towered over Veccuto with a deathly look in his eyes.

"Who said I had one?" replied Vinny, looking so far up, his neck began to hurt. The big black guy chuckled, smiling and shaking his head sideways as he turned back around, carrying onward in the line to the next section of food. "It ain't worth it," he said, out loud. He was looking forward to the desserts too much anyway. He had no time to waste on a washed-up seventy-year-old man.

As the big guy turned around, the little one felt a fire rush quickly through his veins...the way poison would enter the body through a snake bite. There was no taking it back. His rage was already in effect. The wrath consumed him, submerging any morality he had left.

It was then Vinny tapped the big black man on the shoulder. Once he spun back around, Vinny hit him under the jaw with his right fist, BOOM! The punch sent him to the floor like a ton of bricks. Nobody knew what to do or say. Here was this old man with a power nobody thought he still had. The highest power of all he still possessed...a mind he wasn't quite ready to lose yet.

He then climbed on top of him, smashing his knuckles into the big guy's face six times consecutively...three lefts and three right hits, deadly delivered. The black man cried in reply while blood gushed from his nose and pouring down his jaw.

There was a myriad of prisoners, watching in awe. They were too astounded to move. They stood, looking over their shoulder to the person to their left...then to their right. Nobody had a clue.

After a minute, the elderly Mafioso backed off as he rose to his feet. Just as the big black guy looked up at him, he thought it was over. He shook his head sideways, holding his hands in the air in surrender.

Out of nowhere, Vinny kicked the big black guy so hard in the face, it seemed his head would fly off. He wasn't finished yet.

The little one stood over him, watching him like a hawk. The big man spat out blood and teeth. He struggled to get to his feet.

Yet once he did, the little one immediately knocked him down again and then grounded his face into the cold concrete floor with his boot.

Security then started rushing down the stairs and across the cafeteria, pushing everyone in sight that stood in their way. It was time to put to this menace down and get him out of the building.

Vinny jumped back on top of the guy. He continued to beat him down to a bloody pulp. Just when everyone thought he was finished, he pulled out a carved piece of wood from his shirt. Holding it tightly in his left fist, he clenched onto it firm until his entire arm shook.

SHANK! Vinny shoved the shank right into the big guy's stomach.

"YOU EVER LOOK AT ME LIKE THAT AGAIN, YOU BLACK MOTHERFUCKER…I'LL KILL YOU!!!" yelled Vinny as he took his thumbs and pushed them into the eyes of the man, attempting to gouge his sight from their sockets.

"WHO ELSE WANTS SOME?!?!?!?"

A squad of prison guards came rushing to the scene, pulling Vinny off the big guy before he nearly killed him. Thankfully, the man survived. It was if they were trying to pull a pit bull off biting through his toy. It was vicious to see.

The rest of the prisoners continued to stand around and watch. Nobody honestly knew what to do…or why Vinny did what he did. They figured there was something up his sleeve. Only time would tell.

CHAPTER SIXTEEN

It was the second day of the New Year. The three of us were well-prepared for the big night of the safe heist. Finally, it was time to make some real money. I was more than ready, considering how lousy the Christmas poker game's revenue yielded. Plus, the following night, the entire sum of money was due to Lou. We had to make it happen! We didn't have a choice!

The wealthy target we were plotting to steal from was Gerald E. Jones. He was a hugely successful financial planner who resided in one of the most beautiful domiciles of Cherry Hill, New Jersey. He was away on vacation until the end of the week.

Mr. Jones lived in an affluent community. It wasn't quite gated...but it probably should have been with the way it was laid out. Lavish homes, luxurious cars, and an eerie quietness filled the peaceful street. Police were nearby, even when there wasn't a reason to be.

That being said, we needed to be in and out of this house to retrieve the money before any neighborly suspicions would arise.

We parked about a block away from the house in one of Caz's secondary cars. He didn't want to "dirty the Cadillac" or be recognized during this score. The cold rain was falling down onto the windshield steadily like an endless bucket of water being poured out from the blackened sky.

Caz sat restlessly in the driver seat, studying the house's blueprints while Tony Boy remained silent next to him on the passenger's side. I was in the back, continuously looking at the garage codes on the small sheet of loose-leaf paper I had, making sure that Crazy Terry wrote them down legibly.

Between Caz's fidgeting and foot tapping along with Tony Boy's uncanny quietness…they both looked ready to get in and to start safe-cracking. At that moment, I figured that I had to be too. It was now or never.

The manor in front of us was three stories, red-bricked and not nearly as old as one would assume. There must have been many wings to this abode. Additionally, there were more windows than a casual glance could count.

Everything about it said expensively built. This was a great indicator that the safe it held was full of what we exactly wanted and ready for the taking.

Yet still, the source was Crazy Terry. I had to remain apprehensive. I knew that what we were getting into may not have been as prodigious as it seemed.

With one last glance at my watch, I confirmed, "It's time. Let's do this!" I then took a deep breath before we put our ski masks and gloves on. We gathered our items before we departed. The leather sacks and flashlights. Lastly, we all packed our heat just in case the night would get heavy.

For me – it was the classic Springfield XD handgun, one of my favorite shots of all time that I trusted in. I kept it hidden in the basement of Hibernian for a long time. We finally rejoined after such a length of separation. I kept petting it like a kitten, I was so happy to have it back in my hands.

In due time, the three of us hopped out of the car. Once we got out, the rain pounded down on us like shooting bullets.

With the stitched brown leather sacks thrown over our backs, we broke for Jones' travertine pathway and up towards the garage, crouched low in a stealth-like stride. The bags were empty, but they were soon to be collectively heavy with a quarter a million in cash.

Trotting along towards the mansion, our socks were already drenched from the chaotic heavy rain. The sudden torrent flooding seeped into the soles of our shoes. You could hear it with every squeak.

A startling rumble rang loud in the crisp winter air. Violently, the rain turned from bullets into canon fires, barricading everything in its path. The winds grew even more potent as we came closer to the garage door of the house, trying to blow us off course. Yet, the Sconce lights below the roof led the way; we knew where we needed to go.

I took my hand and felt the gun at my side with my fingers…just to make sure it was there. I had to remind myself I was protected.

For the first hurdle, we had to get into the house. Quickly with the other hand, I punched in the codes as the wet paper began crumbling in front of me. Alas, the garage door went up. After that, we jetted inside.

I put on my flashlight before turning around to make sure Caz and Tony Boy were still backing me up. I proceeded with the entrance code to the house on the wall of the garage. As I finished with punching in the last number, the keypad lit up one more time saying, "Unlocked!"

All three of us were in! My mind raced quickly, asking the same question. *Yet, will we make it out?*

The foyer smelled of rich mahogany. It was indeed new money looking to appear old. Wooden panels along the corridors, ornate chandeliers, and oil paintings of old bearded men in tunics and ruffs.

The stairs ahead were twisted in a perfect spiral like a child's Slinky toy pulled from each end. The staircase led up from a tall galleried room with a rug spread out over flagstones and a fireplace big enough to park a car in. A long, polished wooden table had been set for four.

"We better get out of here before dinner is served," joked Caz, pointing his flashlight towards the perfectly placed settings on our way to the next level.

We made it to the second story and into Jones' office, right where I was told it rested. Dead center at the end of the hallway. It wasn't anything too special. The room was painted grey, and it had only one floor-to-ceiling window, which faced the front of the house.

Tony Boy went right while Caz went left. I stayed straight and went immediately towards the wooden desk. On its surface sat a desktop computer monitor, a yellow-page notebook lying open, and a stack of printed papers seated under a turtle-shaped paperweight. There was a swivel leather chair behind the desk.

A tall bookshelf, bursting with leather-bound financial planning books in each of its rows stood in the right corner.

In the left corner of the room was a brass statue of Lady Justice. Behind that was an interruption in the wall. My eyes stared at what appeared to be a small door, seeming to lead to a passageway of some sort. It looked like where we needed to go! This was to be the gateway to our golden ticket, the heart of the home's wealth.

It was time to get to work!

I signaled for Tony Boy. We got our weight underneath the hefty pile of brass, inching it away from the door little by little. Caz came over and kneeled on the floor, preparing to get his hands dirty. Gently, he ran his fingers along the outline of the door, trying to find its entry point.

We made it this far. In those moments, we were hoping the prize inside matched the one on the outside.

"Bingo!" he yelled. There it was....right in front of us all...the big box of treasure. Long, steel and strong...the safe was holding the highest prize for which would give us a grand payday!

Caz wasted no time. He shined his flashlight on the safe and began his methodical cracking process. Tony Boy and I decided to keep watch. He went over and looked out the front window while I inched my way closer to the office door.

The face of the combination lock was a circular, rotatable dial. Caz knew precisely how the spindle inside worked...every single part of it. From the drive cam to the rod. Visualizing the small shaft resting gently atop the wheels inside, Caz understood more than anyone how the notches came into play and how to make them move in the right direction.

I glanced over at Tony Boy to make sure he was still keeping watch and to get a thumbs up that we were good on time.

Putting his ear to the steel, Caz turned the dial several full revolutions clockwise. He then rotated the dial counterclockwise and listened carefully for two clicks near each other. After that, he returned to the lock again only to repeat. Both Tony Boy and I were eager to see how skinny one was going to complete this.

Caz was still listening for clicks. This sounded easy...but nobody could do it like him, especially without a stethoscope or any tools. All he needed were his ears. It was amazing!

"Open sesame!" he whispered.

Before our very eyes, there it was...staring right back at us. Piles and piles of Jackson, Grant, and Franklin stacked neat and clean. It was as if it was all just sent over by the U.S. Mint the way it was wrapped in bank straps.

Tony opened his sack first on the floor in front of the safe. He reached, shoulder deep with both arms. He began hauling as much as he could into his possession. I came over to assist, picking up the stacks that didn't make it into his bag. Time was of the essence. I was fervent to get the money and fly out of there as if it never happened.

Everything was fine and dandy. It looked like this was going to go as smoothly as we anticipated. The cash just kept coming. Oh boy, oh joy! We were all smiles. If I can remember it right, I think Tony Boy even told me he loved me, distracted by all the money. That was the first time he was kind to me, I guess some things just tend to work out with the right timing. *Don't they?*

Maybe not always. Just when we thought we were home free and before Tony Boy could have let us know, lights other than what we were holding began beaming inside. They were rhythmed, blue and red lights, flashing into the big window in front of us only to burn our eyes as we were packing the money up.

Three police cars came rolling up Jones' driveway. No sirens…just the blinding indicator that they knew someone was in this house who shouldn't have been. *Oh shit!*

How could this have happened? What neighbor spilled the beans in the short moment's time we were heisting? The fuckin' police were looking right at us, coming out of their cars and packing more heat than we had on us! Unbelievable!

"Fuck! Must have been a silent alarm or something!" yelled Caz, looking out the window, instructing us all to hurry up and get as much loot into the bags as we could.

"What the fuck? Who set us up, McCool?" screamed Tony in my ear, now exuding the nervousness he wore so well. That didn't take much.

However, I did not want to waste time worrying about who did what. I was more concerned about getting the fuck out of there. Our time was up.

We didn't get all the money out of the safe. Yet, we got as much as we could in those last few seconds. Bolting out of the office and down the stairs, our destination was the back door of the house on the first floor. Cash was spilling out of our bags in our tracks. Tony even slipped on a few hundred dollar bills. He didn't fall down...but he was close.

The sliding-glass back door was at arm-reaching distance just as we heard police breaking down the front entrance and storming inside Jones' domicile. When they did, the loud-sounding alarm went off, and they screamed at us to halt and drop the bags immediately.

In the pursuit to slide it open and get to the back porch, we made it out altogether in one piece. We dropped our flashlights. However, as we ran on and off the back porch and into the yard, shots began firing at us. We weren't going to remain intact too long unless we sped it up. The sliding glass door was shattering behind us.

"Through the bushes! We'll sneak through the other house to get to my car!" yelled Caz, pointing at a row of hedges dividing Jones and his neighbor. "If it's even there still," commented Tony Boy.

"FREEZE!" we heard in the back. More of the boys in blue came rushing towards us from both side entrances to the yard. We continued to run for it as they opened fire and demanded us to stop! We chose not to listen.

Caz, Tony Boy, and I flew into the shrubs like birds towards a nest. My heart was racing. I could barely see between the ski mask moving all over my face, the torrential rain pouring down, and the branches of the hedges poking at us in every direction.

The police were getting closer as we made it into the neighbors' lawn. We were breathing furiously, doing our best to get across and out front to the street.

"There, the gate!" yelled Caz, pointing towards the vinyl exit of the lawn. We looked back quickly, shooting back at those coming closer. With opening fire back at the law, I knew we were on the brink of disaster.

However, we were already in the middle of a catastrophe. If it meant death or prison…I'd always choose death. I'll never go back…not even for a second! I'd rather them kill me.

"Are we all here?" I yelled asking, running towards Caz's car, which was now in plain sight. More police covered the entire street ahead of us. Quickly, I looked behind me. It was only Caz and I together. From about five yards back, we could see that Tony Boy kneeling on the ground. He was just starting to scream. He had been shot. They got him with a bullet in the back of his leg. "Ah, no…Tony!" yelled Caz. He attempted to run back and help him. I stopped the skinny one right away. There was no time. The fuzz was already swarming in on him like lions, about to pounce on fresh meat. Luckily, Caz and I were carrying all the cash.

"We need to go now, or we're going down with him…come on, let's get in the car!" I shouted.

I felt sick about it. Yet, we had to keep going. We continued shooting back as we hopped in the car. The engine had started. Our chests were pounding. Caz stepped on the gas as if he were stomping it to its very metal core.

By the grace of God, we made it out of the neighborhood. The car's windows were shattered on the way out. Bullet holes now consumed the vehicle's body in our hot pursuit. We were on the chase. Within seconds, the police were on our tail as we flew out onto the road at laser speed. There was no guessing how this was going to end. Either way, probably horrible.

In no time, we were weaving in and out of traffic on the nearest highway as the rain intensified. We were blinded by both the onslaught of gumball-sized raindrops and blinding glares of light coming in from every direction.

"You have unmarked license plates, right?" I asked Caz, packing more bullets into my gun. I just wanted to be sure.

"You know I don't take any chances, kid," he told me, trying to focus on the road yet still smirking about it.

The wipers were frantically moving over the never-ending sheet of water. It was the only glass in the car still in one piece. "The nearest exit…we will get off there!" said Caz.

All of a sudden, we noticed the blue and red lights again. The last few police on the chase were still on our tail as we skidded out tightly next to and around each car on the highway we could have. The tires were squealing. The engine was pushed to the limit, over 100 miles per hour.

Finally, we saw salvation…an exit. Where it would go…we didn't know. "Take it!" I yelled at the top of my lungs. At the last possible second, we swerved over and made it around the bend of this exit. Barely though…I was convinced the car was going to flip over and we'd tumble down the hill!

To say the least, my nerves were wrecked, and adrenaline was to the roof. Yet, we were still able to lose the cop cars behind us. It was exhilarating

All we heard next was the ear-splitting screech of metal on metal. They must have gotten in a crash. We didn't know for sure! Either way, we escaped…by the skin of our teeth!

After a few minutes of turning left and right into different parts of nowhere, Caz and I went down a dark dirt road, leading to nowhere. There was nothing but a long road and trees. "We have to burn the car," he said, slowing down on the path. We could now hear every part struggling to work. The tires were blown, the belts were loose…who knew what else? This vehicle wasn't going to go much further.

"In this rain?" I asked.

It was then he parked under a large willow tree for shelter. "This should keep it dry for a bit," he replied, snickering at me.

"You said there were no plates on here. Why do we have to burn it? Why can't we just leave it how it is?" I questioned.

He looked at me intently, "Again, not taking any chances at all here, McCool." He hopped out of the car and walked behind it, towards the trunk.

I took off my ski mask, sitting in silence. I was continuing to try and catch my breath for a moment. Everything was happening so quickly. Putting it all into perspective was hard. I heard the trunk open and close.

Within seconds, Caz came over to my side of the car, dripping wet from head to toe. He held in his possession; the sacks of money we took, a red plastic can of fuel, and a bag of old rags. I hope he kept them dry if we were planning to do what he said. "It's a good thing I have a full tank. But...I don't have any matches. I looked," he told me.

Just as he was about to suggest we go to a convenience store, I smiled. Into my pocket and out into my hand, I showed him my wallet. All this time later, I still had one of the few things I survived the deli explosion with...a matchbook from good old McCluskey's Bar. It was still right next to Duffy's carpet cleaner business card.

"I saved these for a rainy day!" I said, winking at him and tossing the matchbook in his direction. He just about caught it at the last second.

"You're an ace, kid!" he told me, laughing and shaking his head sideways.

I was trying to save as much time as I could, speeding through the process of pouring gasoline in and on every part of the car. The seats, the hood, the trunk...wherever! Caz lost the extra time, however, trying to blaze the fire. He attempted to strike a few, but he failed. The brimstone was breaking off with each fling. Three matches were left before I grabbed it from his hands to show him how it was done.

The first one I struck burned. Phew! The light flared up. So did the car. The rag in the gas tank was just dry enough and the fuel spread with a blazing inferno. We ran away as quickly as we could.

An explosion lit my eyes followed by an incredibly loud noise. Along with it, a shockwave blew away everything in its path.

The cloud of fire rose from the ground! It looked like the gates of hell were opening in front of me. From there, we walked back on to the road and tried to figure out where the fuck we actually were!

CHAPTER SEVENTEEN

It turned out that it was a silent alarm at the Jones house that McCool and the boys robbed. Crazy Terry didn't do *all* his homework like he claimed to have done. *Go figure – one can never trust a guy who puts cocaine above everything...especially himself!* Now it was time to pay the piper!

The local police brought Tony Boy in that night, charging him with his unregistered weapon. Considering he crossed state lines from Philadelphia to Cherry Hill, the case escalated. Right as they contacted the state, the Feds got involved. Within days, they picked up the charge and brought him into Philly headquarters, putting him through the ringer before they'd send him away.

The interrogation room was as intimidating as it looked in the movies. It had one steel table in the center with a bright circular lamp dangling from the ceiling, shining down on the soon-to-be condemned.

Sitting solemnly at that table, Tony stared at the far corner of the room, wishing he could dig a hole and disappear into it.

Then, just as his visions overwhelmed his senses, in barged Agent Martinez and Agent Davey with a whole list of questions for the captive. They were smiling away, walking towards him.

"Anthony Tomasello. We meet again. Weren't you just here about a month ago or so?" remarked

Jay. He stood there, finishing his coffee in a Styrofoam cup in one hand and holding a manila folder in the other. Davey ambled over to Tony Boy, smug with the notion that there was something dirty he had on him.

"Kiss my ass!" yelled the troubled wiseguy. He even spit on the floor.

Davey responded, "Maybe I'll have someone in the joint kiss it for ya, Douche-bag!"

"Fuck off!"

Jay then demanded the room. "Listen up!" he yelled, throwing the coffee cup in the trash can forcefully as if he were making a slam dunk. "You want to stay in here or do you want to rot away like the others such as your pal, Vinny Veccuto?"

Tony Boy sat back in his metal fold-up chair, profoundly sighing and remaining quiet. Although his wrapped up hamstring was still in pain from the gunshot, he restrained from showing any emotion. He looked up to the light, hoping the ceiling had more answers for him to the questions these boys had.

"That man will never see the light of day. Do you want that to be you?" asked Davey, now with his hands on the table.

Jay spoke up. "Help us out. Then, we can talk about helping you," he commented. He then placed the manila folder on the table and asked Tony to take a look at what was inside.

The pictures were from the day they met Lou Gorgeous. It was the limousine that picked them up.

The shot was outside of Mighty Mack's Gym in the Northeast.

"What were you doing in that limousine?" Jay questioned in a much softer tone.

"I was on a date," remarked Tony, tossing the pictures as they slid along the table, almost falling to the floor.

Jay looked at his partner then back to Tony Boy. "That's cute. I'm sure you gave it up easily the way you did at your little heist the other day." He walked around, back and forth, kicking the floor with his shoe.

Tony rose up from his seat a bit as if he were going to jump out of it, planting his feet firmly on the cold tiled floor beneath him. He about had it with these Federal agents at this point….and they weren't even in there two minutes.

"We had a camera outside your buddy McCool's gym. It picked up this limousine. We thought it was weird, so we followed it all the way down to its destination. This was of course, at a one…'Lou's Auto' where you, Mr. Tomasello were seen stepping out of."

Tony then started paying attention. The wine cellar was the only place he remembered from that day. He didn't remember making a stop at any auto shop. Then again, all three had their eyes concealed before they entered Lou's, blind as a bat.

"I ask you…what went down there at the auto shop?" whispered Jay.

Even though he was shocked, Tony Boy remained silent. However, it didn't seem certain to the agents if it was because he didn't know much or if he knew *too* much.

Martinez cracked his neck and looked away "That's good. Nothing to say. Just like the rest of them!" he stated profoundly.

All of a sudden, Tony leaned in on the table in front of him. He opened his eyes wide and took a deep breath, staring at Martinez and Davey as if he was about to reveal all the secrets they were looking to discover.

"I'll tell you what was goin' on there if you'll promise you'll make sure I get out of here," he boldly claimed.

The two agents looked at each other, then once around the room. They then finished with a nod. "We can work something out...depends on what you give us," Davey said.

Tony leaned back in his chair again and exhaled. He picked up the pictures that were leaning off the edge of the table and stared at them for a few more seconds before he began talking.

"I don't know what's up with this old Lou's Auto here..."

Martinez then slid another chair in the room over to the table. Davey continued to stand, crossing his arms in front of him.

"But the reason I got in the limo..."

Every word, every predicate...they were listening. All ears were tuned in to the voice of Tomasello, who was teeing this up as if it were the grand story of all time.

"I heard your mothers were in the back seat, taking turns giving hand jobs."

Abruptly laughing, Tony Boy flung both pictures across the table again. This time, they hit the floor. Jay rose from his seat to stand with Davey. Together, they stormed out of the room right away. "See you in court, asshole!" yelled Davey on his way out.

There was no talking to Tony. The only thing on his mind was the way McCool left him to rot in the beating nightly rain as police scooped him up from that lawn like dog waste.

The two agents began walking quickly down the hallway after their exit. They weren't going to deal with it anymore. Enough was enough. "What a waste of time," said Jay. There was no getting through this brick wall this way.

"Piece of shit, that guy...just like the rest of them!" Davey chimed in.

They got to the end of the hallway when all of a sudden, they heard a loud thudding noise echoing. It was the big, brawn, heavy presence of the young go-getter, Agent Rock. He was sprinting in their direction like he was playing hot potato with the papers he held in his hands.

Once he caught up, he was smiling, sweating and shuffling all at the same time. "Martinez, Davey...can I see you quick?" asked Rock, gasping for breath. He was waving the papers in front of them while doing so.

"Not now, Rock!" replied Jay. He and Davey continued walking straight and quickly as if they were on an official mission from the president.

"It's about your photos of the limousine and the Lou's Auto place!" yelled Rock. *Screech*! They came to a halt. Martinez and Davey turned around and asked Rock to go on.

"My team and I looked some stuff up...Paul Muchetta is the owner of Lou's Auto, the place where the limo was."

They both rolled their eyes. He was the king of obvious information...there was no keys to the castle for that. "What else did he have?" they were both wondering.

"So what?" Davey blurted out.

Rock continued. "His name is on everything! It's on the title to the place, the deed, the insurance..."

"This isn't helping, Rock," interrupted Jay. He was itching to turn back around and to get on with what it is he wanted to do.

"Except," led Rock.

Davey couldn't take it. "Jesus Christ, just fuckin' say it already!" he yelled.

"The invoices," replied Rock. Martinez grabbed the papers from the big guy's hands as if they were on fire. He began looking over them one by one as Rock continued to explain.

"They are signed by a one *Luigi* Muchetta....all of them, to each customer."

As puzzling as it sounded, it was true. Each invoice was the name he was claiming. This was quite the discovery. Yet, where was it leading to?

"It turns out Paul had a distant cousin from the other side nobody knew about all these years," detailed Rock. That was when he pulled out the last piece of paper in the stack of sheets Jay held in his hand.

On this photocopy was Lou's passport picture and information below it. As the boys looked closer at the print, they saw that it detailed when he came into the country into New York in 1987 at the age of twenty-nine.

Sighing, Jay gave the papers back to Rock, holding onto only the passport photo. "You got nothing, Rock…no arrest sheet, no evidence pointing Paul to his cousin. Just another stand-in relative to another one of Paul's rackets. A family fuckin' reunion!"

Rock smirked. "That's what I thought too," he said. The suspense was becoming grueling. They were tired of the build-up. "Out with it already!" Martinez yelled at him as his loud voice ricocheted throughout the hall.

"Until we went back and investigated the murder scene of Carmine Copetelli again at Paul's suit shop."

After he said that, Rock pulled out a birthday card. It was not the usual document the FBI was used to looking at. Then again, this was not the standard case. "It was recently Paulie's birthday…check this out," continued Rock. All three began intently reading the card that rested in both hands of Rock, holding it out for all to see.

Paul, mio cugino,

I am here for you no matter what happens, my big cousin. Together, you and I will run this city the way we have been doing for many years!

Buon fortuna,
Lou Gorgeous

"Your mystery guy!" yelled Rock.

Davey was rolling his eyes, looking down the Federal hallway for any other kind of answer. He wasn't entirely buying what Rock was trying to sell here. To him, it just did not add up.

"Who else has the balls to write something like that to the don of the family?" asked Rock, tapping his hand on the picture that Martinez was holding.

Before Davey had the chance to open his mouth and reply, Martinez interrupted him. "The *real* don of the family," he said.

Rock was all smiles. It was as if a light went off over Martinez's head and he was the one who lit it. He let out a chuckle along with a sigh of relief.

"My motherfucking mystery guy!!!! Rock, you God damn genius…you're getting a raise!!!!"

"Really?"

"No."

Martinez finally turned back around and headed towards his office. Davey and Rock followed behind him, matching every step.

"They figure as far as we are concerned, we have the boss of the family in jail and that they're in a weakened state. When now…they're stronger than ever!" said Martinez, starting to think out loud.

Rock kept smiling. He knew he had something juicy. Now it was all coming together. The challenge for the three was finding a link to make an arrest!

"Davey…go get the team in the conference room now. Then, I want you to gather everything you can on this 'Lou Gorgeous.' If we can bring him down, all the cards will fall with him."

"Roger that," replied Davey, even though he didn't like the way Martinez was speaking with him lately. He talked to him more like a subordinate these days than a partner. Just as he was about to rally the troops, he asked Jay one more question. "What's the word over in Allenwood?"

What Davey was referring to was the latest news in the maximum security prison in Pennsylvania, the same place Tony Boy was headed.

That same night, Little Vinny was transferred there after his incident in the minimally protected Fairton facility. Luckily and to his ultimate wishes, he exchanged a look for the first time in over twenty years with the one, the only…Pretty Paul Muchetta. Although it was from afar, it was still an acknowledgment. No words were spoken…yet they weren't needed. They both knew how they felt about each other.

CHAPTER EIGHTEEN

Finally, it came…the night I had been thinking about since I planned it. It could not have arrived quicker. As a matter of fact…if I had to wait any longer, I probably would have lost whatever was left of my crazy mind.

I picked the fanciest place in town for the occasion with Nina…Del Frisco's Steakhouse in Center City. It was sophisticated in every sense of the word…the imported food, the sparkling drinks, the warm ambiance. Very soon…the fine company.

Located inside a notable landmark that was once the First Pennsylvania Bank, it offered an extraordinary dining experience. There were magnificent, tall balconies draped in plush red fabric overlooking the sweeping main dining room. Then, a breathtaking three-story wine tower served as the centerpiece of the entire restaurant for all to see a vintage bottle brought in from each part of the world.

Bobby Darrin's unforgettable hit "Mack the Knife" set the tone as the melody for the evening, echoing from ceiling to floor with grace. With a setup like this, Scarlett Billows were certainly soon to spread.

Downstairs, different outlets boasted private reception areas. This included what was affectionately called "the Vault"…literally an old bank vault turned into a dining room.

Del Frisco's was the kind of place you could sit down, relax, enjoy your meal, have a pleasant conversation with someone, look around the room and say, "This is class."

I found my finest black suit and gray collared shirt. Everything from head to toe was tailored and pressed, seam to crease. Needless to say, I was more than ready. I was prepared for anything.

Although I was excited, there was more on my mind. On my drive over to the restaurant, I kept thinking about the talk Caz and I had earlier on in the day. We were upset to lose Tony Boy to the police a few nights prior. To have him take the heat for us was not in the plan.

We scored enough money during the heist to make it worthwhile. Most importantly, we'd be able to pay Mr. Gorgeous. Yet, without Tone...it wasn't the same. As much as we quarreled, a part of me missed him. Yet, that's how it goes. Unfortunately, this life doesn't always ensure a happy ending.

In due time, we'd find out how long his sentence would be. I was confident that when he would be released, I'd take care of him personally for making the grand sacrifice for us.

I grew anxious standing in the lobby, waiting for my date. What had me more concerned was the fact that she was far from being on time. I paced back and forth, looking at my watch and thinking if this night was actually going to happen or not. Was she standing me up? Did she change her mind at the last minute? Was the thought of this rendezvous merely too good to be true?

My mind raced as my heart continued to pound. The two couldn't keep up with each other. As I held my right hand close to my chest, I realized my palms were sweating just as quickly too.

Then, it happened. Right as I was convinced this night was over before it started, she marched in through the front door. Every head in the place turned as she beamed a billion-dollar smile, one that was almost blinding! Her black hair was curled to perfection. It frolicked with each stride she made.

The lights in the restaurant seemed to dim as her glowing presence diminished them. The girl was like a living angel, hiding her wings and halo. All this to be said, I somehow forgot how late she was at that very moment.

As her skin-tight dress moved with her hips, I could feel my heart racing once again. The closer she came to me, the harder it pounded. This was unlike any other girl! I was sure of it.

"You look absolutely stunning," I said, smiling at her. I took both of her hands, pulling her in to kiss her cheek in greeting. Ah, the smell of her...I was feeling lightheaded already.

"You don't clean up too bad yourself there, McCool," she replied, tilting her head sideways and smirking back in the sexiest way possible.

"Shall we?" I asked, pointing to our table.

The hostess seated us up the stairs. I reserved for us to dine on the elegant balcony. Up there, the service and vantage point made you feel like royalty.

As expected for a Friday night, the restaurant was full in every capacity. I looked around at the busy tables below. An old couple eating side by side, one glass of wine each, studiously bent over their meals.

There were groups of young gals in their thirties collapsing with helpless giggles as a stern woman dining alone nearby looked on into the distance, frowning. Businessmen in their grey suits, drinking Johnnie Walker at the bar in the far back. A family and their teenage children were quietly conversing about the first semester in college over in the corner.

Yet once we were seated, nothing else mattered. The rest of the room blurred. There was nothing around more stimulating for me to see other than who was sitting across the table.

The waitress came over right away, eager to jot down our order. As Nina picked up the drink menu, she looked through it as if she were studying for a test. Yet, I knew her well enough already. She was just nervous. From the brim to the dregs, her taste buds craved simply one particular drink.

"She'll have a Mojito," I told the waitress, smiling back at Nina. Chuckling, Miss Green Eyes countered, "Jameson neat, two fingers for this proud Irishman here," with a smile back.

The waitress then scurried away to bring our drinks out quickly. From there, I couldn't stop staring at Nina.

"So, you *do* pay attention," she said, raising her eyebrows and glowing with yet another pearly white sneer.

I leaned my body into the table towards her, gently whispering, "Oh, I'm sure your focus is keener than mine!"

She let out a chuckle and said, "Mmm...I don't know."

"But, *I do*."

The way she laughed got me every time. It wasn't just the sound...it was her expression. The way her face scrunched, the way her eyes filled with joy.

"Quite the choice, McCool," commented Nina as she nodded her head in approval. "You probably take *all* the girls here, don't you?" she then asked, batting her eyelids.

"Only the pretty ones," I said, winking one eye.

"Is that so?"

She knew she was beautiful, there was no denying it. Yet, she stayed humble about it. It made her even more enticing.

"Then again, to come across a rose like you is as rare as finding one grow in the concrete," I told her.

"Hah! Nice one."

"It will only get nicer as the night goes on, my dear...especially for this end of the table. Believe me."

"You and your corny one-liners, Mister. Are you finished?"

"I'm just getting started."

"Oh, Good God!"

The snort she gave with her next laugh was adorable. It was then, another unexpected warmth rushed through me like rolling thunder chasing the wind. She brought her hand to her mouth, a bit embarrassed. This girl was great!

"So…what is it you do for a living, Mystery Man McCool?" she asked after regaining composure.

"A little this, a little that."

The drinks came out. "That was quick, thank you," I said. Her Mojito was perfectly put together, assembled with fresh lime and mint leaf. It looked great next to my Jameson. "I made the Mojito strong," said the waitress.

"That's okay, she can handle it!" I commented, smiling at Nina, swirling the whiskey in my hand. I smelled it too, just to make sure it was right. "Ahh!"

I then raised my glass as she did the same.

"What are we toasting to?" she asked.

"To you, my darling."

We then clinked our glasses with an echoing chime. *"Slainte!"* However, as charming as I came off, she persisted in wanting to know what my means of living entailed. Before she even sniffed her Mojito to make sure it had enough white rum, she asked me, "C'mon…what do you do, McCool?"

I responded, "I dabble. I don't put all my eggs in one basket. To depend on one profession is unreliable, especially this day in age."

"Construction, right?"

I couldn't help but chuckle back at the GoodFellas reference she was making. Although, I was no Henry Hill…I was still flattered she thought of me in such an ambiguous way.

"Actually, I am on the planning board over at Saint Isaac's Children's Hospital. Budgeting and finance," I explained.

"Really? Very interesting. How'd ya get involved with that?" she asked, sipping her drink.

"Well, I grew up as an orphan. SICH brought me in after my parents were killed in a car crash. They really looked out and took care of me for the longest time, along with a few others. But, there wasn't anywhere else I felt safer…not even close. I always knew I could come to them for anything. Besides my church, it felt like home."

I had her attention. I continued on with my plan. Considering how excited I was, the ease of my joy came out. She could sense it.

"Now…it looks like the hospital is being threatened to close. The Diocese…they're no help. The C-levels are over it already…looking for an exit strategy. So, I've made it my duty to keep it open. There are still a ton of kids in the city who need its care. The community would be lost without them."

"Wow. Where do you find the money?"

"We've extended every bank loan and line of credit possible. It's my job to research different government funding and ways of aid. Plus, donations are always welcome. We are always open to generous supporters who believe in the spirit of the hospital as much as we do."

She was hanging on my every word now. She was so tuned in, she was sucking her drink down like it was water. I don't think she even realized how quickly it was dissipating until her lips hit nothing but the ice.

I resumed as she listened intently. "Children in the surrounding neighborhoods deserve to have the best care possible. Lots of families depend on SICH. I'm not going to let anything stand in the way of affecting that."

She replied, "I got to say, McCool...I am impressed."

"Thank you. I don't do it for the recognition or the money. This is simply a part of me...has been for a while. I'd die for those kids."

She mixed the remaining ice in her cocktail slowly. As she looked back to me, I could see the shock in her eyes growing wide with every other word I spoke. It was then when I switched to her.

"But now, you...Miss Nina. Tell me more about what's behind those shining emerald eyes?"

"Ah see...you couldn't resist holding back the charm for too long, huh?"

"Well, you bring it out in me."

My feelings were genuine. The shimmering green locked me in, pulled me towards her firmly and took me into a trance.

"*Ah-hem*! My life isn't nearly as exciting as yours. I work in accounts payable for a real estate office," she admitted after clearing her throat.

Yet, I begged to differ. "There can be excitement there. You're the one yelling at people to pay you. Lots of power...shows you can really take charge! Not that I didn't know that about you already," I told her, twirling my whiskey once more.

"Oh? What else do you know then?" she asked.

"Well, there's something about you…not sure what it is exactly. Whether it's from your past or still currently in your life. But, this thing…it's keeping this stone wall up and men out your life for a very long time."

After I asked this, she remained quiet. She looked around the restaurant for a minute. The waiters were running and balancing round trays of hot plates. The bus boys were scattering to clean tables nearby, tossing silverware into buckets. They turned off the crooner music and brought out their piano player and violinists to provide the sweetest symphony. It was beautiful. However, she was the only song I wanted to hear.

"Tell me what it is," I whispered.

"You got me."

With a firm grasp on her fresh drink, she leaned in as if she were about to give me terrible news. I knew whatever she said though, I wouldn't mind hearing it coming out of her mouth.

"I have a son…nine years old."

Then I sat back. *This girl had a kid?* I certainly needed to know more. What were the details? How old?

"His name is Andrew."

"That's a good name choice," I responded.

"Yeah, I thought so. That, *and* the fact that I live with my parents scares most men off."

"These aren't bad things…there is nothing to be ashamed about," I comforted.

"I had him young, I was eighteen. It was a time I thought I was in love, ya know? It caused me to become skeptical, that's all. You are right…I do have some trust issues."

"That's a harsh way to live. But, I get it…"

"I had to grow up fast, McCool…that's all. I had to learn how to be a tough girl. I don't really take much shit."

"I can see that. May I ask…where's his father?"

"Jail. He's been there since Andrew was born. And he ain't ever getting out."

It was then she took a deep breath, pulling her dress down to make sure it wasn't riding up her legs as she kept readjusting her position.

"Now, I have a question…have you been to jail, McCool?" boldly she probed. She even smiled and sighed after, thinking I was going to give her the answer she already knew and didn't want to hear. I knew this was a time to be genuine. However, my silence wasn't helping at all.

She pursed her lips to the side, replying, "That's a yes."

Quickly, I countered. "Not for long. I was in the Army as well. When I came home from being in Afghanistan, I wasn't myself."

"Really? Tell me more."

"We'll save that for another time."

"Maybe another drink will get it out of you."

On the inside, my brain rattled. Inside, I paused, intently reflecting on those years. The memories were still as dark as the cold cells that held me away for many sleepless nights after the dangerous time in the desert.

"So, tell me more about the planning board. The guys with you at the bar…are they with you on this?" she questioned.

"No, they are just friends."

"I see."

I turned to the waitress, putting two fingers out, signaling for a pair of refills. She asked if we were ready to order our entrees. However, neither of us even glanced at the dinner menus yet.

"What else should I know about you, McCool?"

"What else would you like to hear?"

Little did she know my autobiography was complex - not like that of books where words were so plainly written out and flow from page to page…but of books torn, frayed, and indecipherable.

"So, you grew up around here you were saying?" I asked, avoiding her previous question.

"I did. 13ᵗʰ and Porter."

"That neighborhood ain't the same, eh?"

"Nope."

"Same with the Northeast. It's like a silhouette of what it once was when I look around, ya know? Different place, different people…but I still recognize some of the old traditions. They're still there, lingering on."

The waitress came back with fresh drinks. I tipped her a twenty before she even had the chance to place the glasses on the table. After that, I raised my glass once again to the beauty before me to make yet another toast.

"The more things change…"

Nina knew how to finish it. "The more they stay the same."

We rang our glasses together once more. After that, it was time to decide on a meal. With so much to choose from, it brought a silence to the table, making it the first of the night. Yet, there was something peaceful about it. Just in time, the mandolin joined the piano and violin players, adding another layer of excellence to the experience.

With more added laughs and first-rate banter during dinner, it all brought the night inching closer to an end. She got the chicken parm, I got the veal.

After the espresso, I offered to take her home. Nina admitted she did not like guys to know where she lived. However, she'd make an 'exception' for me.

With her ankles crossed, her knees leaned against the center console. I watched her as I slid into the driver's seat, starting the engine of my Acura with the push of a button.

I wanted to reach out and hold her hand. Rubbing my hands together, I forced them into submission.

Observing her movements, a sigh escaped my lips as I put the car into drive. I adored the subtle tilt of her head when she turned it to look outside her window. Watching her, I felt a chill and rubbed my arms.

Although she was allowing me to drive her home, there weren't many concrete signs telling me whether she had a good night or not.

She was still hard to read, the way she continued staring out her window. Whether she was counting stars or trying to avoid my direction all at once was difficult to tell.

She loosened up after a few cocktails at dinner, and I was able to get to know her better. Yet now at the tail end, she was back to being reserved. Did the liquor wear off? Perhaps she was just over this night entirely? It could have just been me she was over.

I figured this was an excellent opportunity to put the radio on. I planned to let the music muddle the silence a bit...maybe it would get her talking again. Who knew? I sure didn't.

Reaching for the volume button, I put my finger out with ease. Whatever the first song that came on would be, I'd take my chances.

My collection of tunes varied. Sinatra to Jay-Z, The Clancy Brothers to Meek Mill, Patsy Cline to Bruce Springsteen. Brucey – the man, of course being my favorite!

To me, various types of rhythm spoke different languages of the soul. Music is a reflection of one's mood... a mental escape from the ordinary!

What was the lucky number going to be? We had a winner: Drake - Hold On, We're Coming Home. *Ah, she may be a bit too classy and reserved for this.* At least, that was my initial thought...until she spoke up.

"Turn it UP, McCool!!!"

Man, she really was something else. I liked it though. As soon as the bass began, the sound ascended. Her head bobbed to the beat. She then brought her hands up to move them in rhythm with the melody.

I got my eyes on you
You're everything that I see
I want your hot love and emotion…endlessly
I can't get over you
You left your mark on me
I want your hot love and emotion…endlessly

I loved watching her get excited…even if it was the smallest thing that would do so. It reassured the fact that she was comfortable to be around me.

'Cause you're a good girl and you know it
You act so different around me
'Cause you're a good girl and you know it
I know exactly who you could be

Just hold on, we're going home…

And that's where we ended up…right in front of her home on 13th and Porter. It was your average South Philly row house.

Red bricks with a peaked roof of slate. The blocks swirled with other hues giving the two-story dwelling a mottled look. Against the midnight blue sky, the house blended in like any other in her district. Yet, I knew it was different…especially those who dwelled in it. There was something about this girl that made her just as much a mystery as me. But, I liked it.

"I had a nice night," she said as we pulled up. She reached for her door to leave. Turning the music down, I smiled and grabbed my door handle. Slowly, I walked out of the car and towards her direction. I looked inside the car and could see her puzzled face, not sure how to feel about what was next.

I came over to let her out of the car. "Ah, what a gentleman. I guess chivalry isn't dead," she commented.

After she thanked me once more, I came in for a hug. Subtle with my timing, I did not want her to think I was hasty. However, I had a good time…I had to show that.

She hugged back like she was hugging her kid brother. When I leaned in for the kiss, she turned her head. My mind started running again. *So, that's where she sees this going…nowhere. The friend zone.*

That was okay. Every defeat is a stepping stone…bringing you closer to victory. I'd take this night for what it was. I was gracious just to be in her company. That was all.

As she let go of hugging me, her hands clamped onto mine on our way apart. She stood still for half a second. Yet, I was getting mixed signals. It was as if she was giving me another shot.

I pulled her back in close to me like a boomerang. No, no…I wasn't messing around here. She couldn't get away that easily. She was just too damn sexy!

The way the moon was shining on every part of her, she beamed in brilliance. I couldn't let a chance and a girl like this slip away.

I closed my eyes and went in for the kill just as the Drake song in the car was ending.

You're the girl...you're the one.
Gave you every...thing I love.
I think there's something...I think there's something.

Brushing my lips onto hers, I nearly knocked the wind out of both of us. Yet in that passionate moment, a lightning bolt rushed through us and all the way to the blood in our veins. Our bodies were on fire, forging together. I felt like we were both going to explode with hot, burning desire.

For as much energy that was charging inside of me, it was exhilarating in ways I never felt before. I rested my hand below her ear, caressing my thumb across her cheek's smooth skin. Our breaths mingled. Strands of her hair came down the back of her neck, wrapping around the rest of my fingers.

I felt her tingling touch run along the center of my back, pulling me closer until there was no space left between us. We were pressed against the car. Her heart was beating against my chest.

Her spring rain scent, her sweet taste. It was all so overwhelming. Delectable. I did not want this to end. I needed every part of her. She was so intoxicating. Although we were both lost in the moment, reality was right around the corner. She giggled like a schoolgirl, knowing it was time to part ways. Pulling away from me, she looked deep into my eyes. "Wow! That was nice," she replied, smiling, looking at the ground. "But I got to go."

I embraced my fingers to her chin, slowly bringing her head back up. My lips were ready for another peck before I let her go. "I'll see you soon," I told her after. She beamed ear to ear, kissing me once more, and holding on to the edges of my leather coat. Once she let go, she turned towards her house.

"Later, McCool." Man, she had a hell of way evoking that luster in her face when she said goodbye. She was so tantalizing.

I watched her walk until she made it inside. Every step. I couldn't resist but smirk, shaking my head as I walked back to the driver's seat of my car. I'd do anything to see her again. Whatever it took!

I jumped into my ride, thinking about the night. What a time! More importantly…that kiss. The smile on my face was one nobody could take away. Then again…that all changed in a moment's time.

Stealing my thunder, Caz called my cell. I put him on Bluetooth. Yet, when I asked if he took care of the "thing," he gave me the news. "Hey, Cazzy baby…did our friend get the vig?"

"Jackie, I reached out to Frankie and Umberto to make it happen. Turns out, that guy we robbed in Jersey…he knows Lou Gorgeous."

I clenched my fist, frustrated, looking at Fitzy's Claddagh ring on my finger. Just as I was about to ask what the next course of action was, he replied.

"Lou wants to see you and I again…tomorrow."
Dynamite!

CHAPTER NINETEEN

Waves of fury were running through my veins, but I never let it entirely come to the surface. It shot deep down like an inferno waiting to explode from the core of me. I needed to extinguish the flames before they would spread. The ultimate question was how. Perhaps the answers were coming.

Bright and early the following morning, Caz and I found ourselves back at the uncanny wine cellar we initially met Lou Gorgeous.

It was the same process as before. Frankie and Umberto arrived at our location in the long black limousine, making sure we were blindfolded until we reached our target. Once we set foot in the basement where Lou sat, he stared us as if he were a parent waiting for their child. With his fedora on his head, he smiled at his desk. Also, he was finishing another shot of Limoncello, puffing a Montecristo cigar.

This visit was a little more unusual than the first one. I wasn't sure if it was the recent events clouding my judgment or the way Frankie was acting on the way over. He was very aloof and quiet. It looked like he didn't want to be a part of anything that was going on that day. Something wasn't matching up.

There was one thing we could depend on though. The undoubtable lure Lou gave. It was as if he was trying to put you to ease even though it was known he could kill you at a moment's notice.

They say the most villainous of monsters come with smiles. With Lou, he brought the charm and friendly welcome too.

"Nice to see ya again, sweethearts," he spoke softly, greeting us with his arms open. Coming off the staircase, Caz and I looked at each other to see who was going to respond first.

"How are you, Lou?" I asked. Frankie and Umberto walked past us to stand on either side of Lou like they did before. With their hands folded in front of them, they remained quiet as the gorgeous one continued.

"I've been better."

I had the perfect counter…a vital response. I inhaled a deep breath, exhaled, opened my mouth and prepared my statement. Yet, Caz stole the stage as he spoke right before the words came dripping off my tongue's tip.

"Look, Lou…let me be the first to say it. Jack and I apologize about your friend. Had we known he was with you…we wouldn't have taken the score!"

That wasn't where I was going with this. I wished he had the chance to take it back. I wasn't sorry for any of it. In fact, I'd do it all again if I could.

"As much as that upsets me…it's pale in comparison to what brings you two back into my office," voiced Lou.

"What do you mean?" I asked.

"Sure, Mr. Jones is a friend. But, I already settled it my way."

Umberto then walked over to Lou's desk. He reached into the top drawer and pulled it out slowly. Inside, there was a manila folder that he picked up. From there, he showed us what it held, two pictures that were taken recently.

It was the shore of the Delaware River under the Ben Franklin Bridge. It appeared to have been captured at a crime scene given the yellow caution tape bordering the perimeters. Police cars were in abundance. In the center were Federal agents dragging out a dead body from the water. How Lou got a hold of these photos were a mystery to me.

"The guy who gave you the tip, Mr. Green...he met his demise. He was found taking a swim in the Delaware River this morning."

Unbelievable. There was Crazy Terry, floating to river's edge on the glossy prints. Not that he was an A-class citizen, but he didn't deserve this. He was harmless. I sat there, defeated. I felt like I was responsible in a way. I didn't even want to look at the photos, I shoved them away.

Lou went on to describe Terry's drowning. "I watched him go too. I watched as the icy cold water from the dirty river thrust up into his nostrils. I could see his face become numb while Umberto's hands sucked away every last piece of life left in him. From the way his body thrashed in the water, I could tell he was in a great deal of pain."

Instead of the warm adrenaline boiling inside of me, I felt a new feeling of hatred burning. You could see it smoldering in my eyes as Lou went on. What a madman…if you could even call him a man. I wanted to kill him!

"The good news for you two is that I spoke with somebody I know on the inside of the Federal department. Your boy won't do much time in the joint. That is, granted he keeps his mouth shut."

"He will," Caz replied.

I stood up and inched my way closer towards Lou's desk. With every step, I wanted him to feel my wrath. I thought about what Vinny tried to coerce me to do when I visited him last. Maybe he was right…maybe this was the time to finish the job and forget the possibility of the Caribbean Connection.

I placed my hands on the desk, looked down and then brought my head up to look directly into his eyes. "So, what is it you want, Lou? Another fuckin' tax or something?"

"Not quite," he replied, looking intently at the placing of my hands. He couldn't stop staring at them. "I want to know more about these Atlantic City connections, McCool. How are they going to benefit me with the Costa Rican?"

All of a sudden, my mood changed. There it was. Salvation! The only thing that brought me back to level ground. I couldn't believe it. Finally, he was ready to talk about the only thing that mattered to me. Well, as far as business was concerned. I pulled myself away from the desk and sat back down.

"I'm glad you asked. How much support do you need, Lou?" I asked him, smiling intently in a way he would.

Lou stood up and responded, turning his head towards Frankie, "Well, I've never talked to the Costa Rican directly…only Frankie here has! What a fucking mistake!"

All of a sudden, Frankie leaned in on Lou's desk. He put his hands on the surface in a similar way I just did moments prior. "Get your fuckin' hands off my desk!" yelled Lou, standing up and widening his eyes while striking the fear of God into one of his top guys.

"Unfortunately, gentlemen…Frankie's connects did not come into fruition the way I anticipated. His judgment stinks much like the way he stinks!" he continued, now looking to Caz and I who were sitting a few feet in front of him.

Frankie turned his eyes to Lou and remained silent. You could see the frustration within him, waiting to be released.

"What can you guarantee me?" asked Lou, ashing the Montecristo.

I knew just how to handle this. I was taking over the conversation. "A guarantee for you to make more money than you're making now. Isn't that why I am here?" I questioned.

Lou scoffed, scratching his head. He was probably wondering why he was allowing me to talk to him this way.

"If I pull Frankie off the project and put you on, McCool…what kind of strength do you have? Can you bring it nationwide?"

"I can."

"How so?"

It was time to get down to business. This is what it would all come down to. Before showing all my cards, I had to make sure the right amount of money was on the table. I was going to make sure I came out of that room with nothing but the upper hand.

"Before I dive into details, we need to discuss what is of the utmost importance, Lou…numbers. I need to know how this is going to split. If I'm extending and exhausting my resources to you, you need to deliver me a pretty bow."

Lou smiled. He was the one now leaning on his own desk, tapping his fingers on the surface. He nodded his head, knowing he had to choose his words wisely. With his other hand, he put out his cigar into the ashtray in front of him. When he did, he slid his hand down his hip, keeping it there.

"Cute," he told me.

The room stayed silent for a bit. I could see Frankie leaning over on Lou's desk again…even after he told him not to. As he looked over to his boss, he spoke to him, continuing to look back at me as well.

He whispered, "Lou, with all due respect…do you really trust this kid? Who is to say he won't fuck the connection up worse than I have?"

BAM! Out of nowhere, Lou battered his signature knife kept at the side of his hip through Frankie's hand. It was as if he was hammering a nail. "AHHHHH!!!" wept Frankie, falling to his knees in agony. "LOU, PLEASE!!! LOU!!" he continued to yell, grabbing onto Lou's suit coat with his free hand.

Caz and I nearly jumped out of our seats. We sat and stared while the sounds of Frankie's cries carried on, ringing throughout the basement. This guy, Lou…he was insane! It was becoming more evident with every word and action he delivered.

Smiling, Lou continued to press the knife down with his deathly grip, deep into the palm of his consigliere. Frankie looked up, begging to be spared of the torture while blood spilled out onto the desk.

WHIP! Lou then pulled the knife out of Frankie's hand and stood there, looking down at the man on the floor, persisting to scream and cry.

Holding his bloody hand with the other, Frank gazed up in terror. All he saw were deep, dark eyes staring back, suggesting he ought to rise to his feet before things got worse.

"GET UP, YOU FUCKIN' PUSSY!!!" yelled Lou, inches from his face.

Slowly, Frankie assembled himself enough to stand. His mouth quivered as he brought one foot in front of the other, catching a towel Umberto tossed over to wipe his blood off.

"Don't get any more of your mess on my desk or I'll be wiping it up with your face, you cocksucka!!!!" screamed Lou.

Frankie kept the towel wrapped around his hand. He kept looking at it then back to his boss. He was astonished. While he was still trying to figure out why Lou reacted the way he did, he continued to worry about what his next move would be.

Caz and I sat still...quiet as church mice. "Did you boys learn a valuable lesson?" asked Lou, looking to the two of us. He continued to hold his knife at his side. He did not wipe the blood off. Turning his back away from Frankie, he looked around the room while taking a deep breath.

"Rule number one: never have me ask you to do something twice," he said. Turning back around, he looked directly into the eyes of Frankie while uttering his second rule inches away from him. "Rule number two: never cry like a little bitch in front of me...it only makes me nauseated. I have no empathy!"

"Lou...for real, come on?" inquired Frankie, now leaning back on Lou's desk with both hands...one of which now making a mess

The gorgeous one's eyes grew wider. The room was even more silent. He looked at his knife then back at Frankie. Then, over he glanced at us. What happened next, nobody expected. It had us all in shock. We didn't know what to do.

That was when Lou let out an uncontrollable belly laugh. To laugh back or to be scared...that was the question.

So, we let out in merriment. We exhaled for the first time in the meeting. It was a bit relieving given the frightening scene we just witnessed. Perhaps there was a bit of joy behind the darkness that overshadowed him.

Lou went over and gave Frankie a hug, continuing to laugh. "I'm so sorry...is your hand alright, pal?"

Frankie, still in pain, told Lou he had to go to the hospital. Even though he was smiling, he was far from feeling great.

Lou, with a grin, cheek to cheek looked at his right-hand man and said, "Maybe this will take the pain away!" *Slash! Slice! Shink...SPLAT!*

He didn't stop stabbing Frankie in the back, figuratively and literally. The yells Frankie let out were just as fearsome. After what seemed like twenty-plus stabs, Lou let Frankie's red, torn-apart body fall to the floor. "Rule number three: never talk back to me!" he said, pointing the knife at Caz and myself.

Umberto came over to retrieve Frankie's body and take it out of the room. It was as routine as if he was hauling bags of garden seed to bring to the lawn.

We sat there with our mouths wide open. I knew I was up against a crazy guy, but the Caribbean Connection was something I needed. Not for me...for the kids at SICH. That's what this was all about...nothing else!

"Like I was saying...you bring your AC connects on and make this thing come alive. I'll make sure you deal directly with the Costa Rican and myself on this. We will all reap the benefits. There is no one of us with the upper hand...we are partners on this, kid," explained Lou, making it clear he wasn't messing around.

He spoke with conviction. I was intently listening as he made his way towards me. This is the closest we'd ever come to one another. I could see his face fully in the light for the first time. The long white scar that ran from his left eye to the corner of his mouth was evident as could be. I didn't know what they were from…but they indeed highlighted that he was well-traveled. As Lou continued holding the bloody blade in his hand, we locked eyes.

He then looked at Frankie's body being towed away. "There's a man who worked for me for years…dead, right in front of you. Now, I've taken ones you love away from you…and you have taken some whom I trust away from me. However, I am hoping we can put that behind us. I am hoping this can bring us together, this Caribbean Connection," said Lou, pointing over to the carcass Umberto was tugging out of the room and up the stairs.

I countered, "Again…what are you looking for as a split, Mr. Muchetta?"

"70/30 in my favor," he said, putting down the blade and removing the fedora from his head.

"I was thinking 55/45…you take the latter."

"Ya crazy, sweetheart. I'm not goin' that low. My fuckin' name ain't Red Alan Connor."

"I'm not comfortable at thirty, Lou."

"Eighteen to twenty-million a month in total revenue. Half of that is our share. If that doesn't make you comfortable, I don't know what does."

"Forty-two percent does. You need me on this!"

"Meet me at forty," he said. I stared at his hand he lent out. This was the time to make it happen, I told myself. It was now or never. "Do we have a deal or what?" Lou asked.

So, I sold my soul to the devil. *Was I making the right choice?* I wasn't sure. This guy was pure evil…a psychopath! This was the same menace who was behind killing Chris Veccuto, Fitzy, Duffy, O'Hara…and almost me. *What was I getting myself into?* This brought *sleeping with the enemy* to a new context.

In the end, I didn't care…even with the dirty looks Caz gave me. I had one thing on my mind, and it was the children of SICH…they needed me. In turn, I needed this.

"Fuckin' dynamite," I told Lou, shaking his hand back. I looked down at the Claddagh ring on my hand, still shining after all this time. I laughed to myself. *Finally, it was my time to shine.*

Part Three

Caribbean Blue

CHAPTER TWENTY

What's a life worth living if its not on the edge?
In several ways, Black McCool was finally able to go the distance. Things were lining up rather well going into the heart of the year. At least, it seemed that way for awhile.

First and foremost, his relationship with Nina was skyrocketing to prominence. By late February, the two were going steady. He could not have imagined it coming together any better.

Nina was merely the highlight of Jack's days. In her embrace, his world would stop on its axis. There were no sounds or any stimulus quite as high as when they were with one another. All else stood still effortlessly in these times.

This was the kind of affection that one would pray and waited a lifetime for. He'd inwardly thank God whenever he could. The feelings Jack had for Nina were those to be cherished for life. He felt himself falling for her, more each day.

Secondly, business was great. The operation with Lou Gorgeous and the Caribbean Connection had become more lucrative than anybody could have ever predicted.

Thanks to the hands-on approach they had on the sportsbook website, *Clubroyalflush.org,* Jack and Lou saw a ton of money come in from the result of it. The sky was the limit.

Known only as "The Costa Rican," the overseas mastermind was the one who administered and controlled millions of these bets in a wireroom in San Jose.

Jack remained to be the only direct contact to the Caribbean Connection in the states. He led the bookies in AC and their networks nationally as well. As long as Lou saw his share, everything stayed copacetic.

Overall, it was genius. The operation opened a new charter for the entire gambling world to explore. They were attracting an increasingly diverse customer base.

Clubroyalflush.org was a "price-per-head" bookmaking site. These websites typically used agent-bookmakers, who gave customers user-names and passwords to access the site and place bets.

No financial transactions were made online. Instead, details of bets were stored and tracked on the site, while collections and payouts were made in person, by the "agents."

If customers were unable or unwilling to their pay debts, they would be met with threats and intimidation, forced to pay interest on top of the original sum owed. That was where the real money was made…the vigs. It was the dawn of a new era for a new-age kind of racket.

By the end of each month, the venture would yield anywhere between eighteen to twenty million dollars in total revenue from more than eight-thousand participating gamblers.

For Jack, that meant about three to five million a month going into his pocket, give or take. The majority of what he made he planned to give to Saint Isaac's Children Hospital by the end of the quarter to keep them from closing. Of course, it was all that mattered to him with this project.

Nonetheless, he also allocated the time to take care of himself...which meant Nina too. There was no doubt about it. He made sure he wined and dined her in every possible way like the princess he saw her as.

He purchased an elegant three-story home in Radnor, Pennsylvania; a town right outside Philadelphia on what was called the Main Line. This was an excellent and affluent stretch of municipalities.

On the other hand, Caz wanted no parts in the gambling operation...too risky. Then again, he had his strip club taking care of him. That is where he felt safe, both physically and financially. This setup was quite alright with Black, he felt; more for him.

Yet, he knew it was just more than that. Ever since the last meeting with Lou at the beginning of the year, Jack could feel the tension between him and Caz escalating. It wasn't something he was happy about. As much as he tried to keep the relationship alive, he felt as if Caz was pushing him away further as the days passed.

Inside SICH, Desmond's son remained in a comatose state. He was praying the doctors would tell him that something would change any day. They were more than lenient keeping him on life support considering his insurance provider was telling them he was out of options. He was praying, hanging on to the only thing he had left…faith. A guardian angel was needed.

Tony Boy was still behind bars. Thanks to Lou's connections inside the Federal department, he'd be released that year. For him, it wasn't quick enough. He was chomping at the bit to get out.

Vinny was still waiting for his opportune time to get in front of Paulie. Now that he was relocated to the same maximum security facility as the pretty one, he was doing his best to get face to face with the pretty one. He needed to speak his mind, at the very least.

Meanwhile, the FBI's quest for learning Lou's history was giving them anything except what they were looking for. He came up clean in every category. No felonies, no misdemeanors…not even a parking ticket!

They were losing patience and were almost out of options. It was time to get creative and to get inside the family in a unique type of way.

It took a few months to get the wheels in motion, but it finally happened. It was very long overdue.

The first time Jack met Nina's family, he was a bit nervous. As a matter of fact, his body was shaking on the way into her house. It had been a long time since he felt this way about a girl.

Meeting her folks was extremely important to him. He wanted to make a good impression in any way possible.

Jack and Nina were outside of her parents' front door. Cold sweat glistened on his furrowed brows. With his hands clasped tightly in front of his stomach, he continuously fiddled with his knuckles, weaving his fingers in and out of each other just before entering inside.

"Relax! Don't be afraid...my family won't bite ya, McCool," said Nina, smiling and being giddy with Jack, holding onto his trembling arm. "I know, I know," he replied. She then opened the door.

Once they walked in, Jack was taken back. Nina's parents' embrace was that of what he'd never seen with family; warm and welcoming.

Her mother was the taskmaster, mission maker and decider of the direction of the home. She organized the chores, the school work and the fun like any good co-head of the household would.

Her father lived to work, you could tell by looking at him; work at his job, work at fixing up the house and work at getting enough sleep so that he didn't doze off on the way to the factory the next day. Once in a while he would smile or laugh - and when he did the world brightened for those precious moments - then he would sink back down into his chair to watch his 'programs.'

Jack felt something endearing about Nina's mother. Perhaps it was the way she loved everything her daughter did, praising her and makes a jovial conversation out of anything.

Then again, it could have been the way she catered to Jack when he came in to meet them. They had the kind of instant bond one hopes to have with a parent. This was something he lacked in his youth. It was a change for him to see.

Her parents were wonderful. However, Jack was excited the most to meet someone else in the household. For him, this would be the biggest test, the pass or fail…what would decide whether he'd make it with Nina or not.

Her son, nine-year-old Andrew.

He was a shy boy. When Jack first saw him on Nina's couch, he was hesitant to say anything to him. The kid was content on his IPad, quiet as a church mouse.

He had a red Phillies hat with the letter P on the front in the color blue. To match that, he had a blue Phillies shirt with the name of famous pitcher Roy Halladay and his number 34 on the back.

Jack took his time. He gradually made his way to her son, looking back to Nina. She nudged, signaling him to introduce himself.

"You must be Andrew," said Jack as he bent over forward towards the boy, trying to get eye level with him. Andrew looked up at the Irishman quickly then went back to playing a video game on the IPad in front of him.

"My name is Jack."

Still, the kid remained dazed to the screen. Nina came over and gave him a scowl, suggesting to him to show a little more manners towards their company. "Be polite, Andrew," she said in a soothing tone only a mother would possess.

"Hi," he uttered quietly with his eyes wide open. Smiling, Jack looked towards Nina and then walked over to take a seat on the couch next to her son.

"I see you are a Phillies' fan," he said, grabbing the brim of his hat, trying to get his attention. Immobile. The kid still paid no mind to Jack. Whatever he was playing on his IPad was undoubtedly consuming every part of his concentration.

Andrew nodded his head, murmuring, "Yeah."

Jack replied, "That's crazy. So am I," pointing at himself as if it were rarer than it actually was they were both fans of the same team.

Nina smiled at Jack before walking out of the room for a minute. She went back into the kitchen to sit with her parents. She wanted to see how her son would react without her in the room.

Jack went on as Andrew continued to stay glued to the IPad. "You know, buddy...the '93 Series when the Phils played the Blue Jays...I was there. I met Curt Schilling. He autographed a baseball personally for me."

Still nothing. He half-smiled, but it was far from genuine. He didn't look in Jack's direction. It was almost as if he was doing his best to avoid him by any means. The shyness was a curse.

Jack was persistent. He kept trying to connect with him. He was devoted to it, even if it would take him all day. "You know...he is still tied for the most

300-strikeout seasons. Many have tried to come close, but they simply haven't."

"Yeah," responded Andrew, looking up momentarily. Then all of a sudden, something great happened. He had a few more words in him. "Roy Halladay pitched a perfect game though."

Jack laughed, looking up and shaking his head at the ceiling. "Ah, yes!! You remember that huh? 2010, two years after they won it all. Wish they played against the Yanks in the '09 Series the way they did with the Rays in '08."

"Yeah. I just want the Phillies to be good again," said Andrew, looking down at his lap and putting the IPad aside for the first time. It was so sad the way he reacted to the team and how they were currently playing. He took it personally.

"They will, buddy. The right leadership and a good bullpen are all they need. They'll be on top soon enough!"

Andrew nodded his head. You could see the blues pouring out from his face. It was something Jack wanted to understand. He knew there was more to the kid than what he led on. Considering he came from a ton of sadness himself, he yearned to find a way to empathize…both for Andrew, and him.

"Hey…have you ever scored a game by hand?" asked Jack.

"No."

"I'll show you some time. It's fun. It gives you a personal feel for the game…it makes you think about every pitch, every hit…even every error. It's a whole different perspective."

Finally, there was a smile. For the first time, he looked openly happy. Jack put his arm around the kid. "Would you like that?" he asked him. Looking up, Andrew nodded his head 'yes.'

Nina came back into the room. She couldn't take her eyes off Jack. It was as if she was falling more for him by the second.

The way he mingled with her son simply showed another side of his affection...his warming and compassionate nature. His love for SICH was starting to make more sense. It was all such a turn on for her.

After some quality time spent with Nina's family, Jack wanted to take the night in a different direction...as did Nina. It was *his* turn to show her where he called home. Not only that, he wanted to make sure she felt just as comfortable there as he did.

They arrived close to midnight. The full moon, sitting high in the sky, was bright enough to lend its glow into all windows, leading the way...right into the master bedroom.

The lights were turned down low, dimmed to an easy and tranquil mood for both of them. To fill the air, Jack put some slow music on from his stereo to make it even more soothing.

The room was elegant. Gentle beige hues gave it a timeless and sophisticated warmth. With a color scheme so versatile, the pairing of the fabrics and furniture brought a visual serenity.

The Japanese screen above the bed established scale and theme consistent throughout the space. A spherical pendant light lent soft dimension. The linen-upholstered headboard had a graphic boost from the Greek-key patterned pillow in the center.

They both sat at the foot of the bed. Neither of them said a word. Smoothly, Jack reached out his hand to caress the back of Nina's head to kiss her passionately and tenderly. Sparks of electricity danced over his skin. It was a magical feeling, causing him to shiver in complete excitement.

"You're so beautiful," he whispered. She felt his warm breath in her ear. She wrinkled her nose in protest.

"Just keep kissing me," she whispered in return. It was then Jack leaned over and took Nina's hand, kissing the edges of her fingers. As he could see her closing her eyes, he knew they were both ready.

He came even closer, bringing his lips to hers before opening her mouth with his tongue. She grabbed his shirt and pulled him tightly towards her. While he ran his fingers slowly through her hair, he was distracting Nina by sucking her lower lip, biting it gently. He then slid his hand all the way down along the smoothness of her back until he felt the hook and eye of her bra, pinching it to release its closure.

After that, she stopped him. Standing up for a moment, she pulled her shirt off and threw it to the floor like it was on fire. She was burning up. McCool proceeded to do the same.

Jack pulled Nina in tight, span her around and pounced on top of her like a lion. The speed at which they continued kissing was just as rapid as their hips moving against one another in sensual friction. They could barely keep up with the rate their desire was growing. They couldn't take the rest of each other's clothes off fast enough.

From there, Jack slowly progressed his lips to her neck…down to her chest…around her stomach, all the while trying to remove one last piece of clothing…her jeans.

He then wasted no time traveling down her smooth, perfectly-toned legs. From her hips to her thighs. He brought his face up to her panties. That was when he pulled them off…with his teeth. Slowly with style, he moved his hands down her legs again.

She put her arms behind her head as he continued to kiss the erogenous zone around her vagina. It was relaxing and exciting all at the same time. "Oh my God…I want you so bad!" she panted, now back to grabbing a fist-full of his brown hair.

He thrust his tongue inside her, sounding off another resonating moan. It was music to his ears, more so than the slow tunes coming from his stereo. She was quite the instrument to play.

Without even thinking twice, she held onto him for dear life, pulling him in closer. Getting the sense she wanted him in deeper, Jack put one of his fingers inside. Long and deep, he knew he hit *the spot*. It was confirmed when she exhaled even louder.

Her legs were shivering. Her gasping grew longer and louder. She latched onto his shoulders, pulling him up from down under and whispering, "I want you in me…all of you."

He let his tongue do a little more work until Nina's eyes rolled to the back of her head. At the same time, her face was glowing.

After that, he came up on the bed only to sink himself to his knees. She began to arch her back, looking at his face with her mouth wide open. She was dripping…waiting! The strength of what was building was staggering.

She closed her eyes in a moment of ecstasy, catching her breath, anticipating the feeling of what was coming next. She couldn't wait.

Suddenly, she felt Jack hard against her stomach. He settled himself in-between her legs. Slowly, he moved up and down, timing his thrusts with her sighs and wails. She cradled his hips with her thighs.

"You like that?" he softly spoke.

She answered him by latching her arms tighter around his neck and plastering her mouth onto his. She was kissing him in a way she never kissed anyone before. Nothing felt as good as the sensation of him gently sliding in and out of her.

It was then Jack picked up the speed. Nina arched a bit more, stretching beneath him. These movements sent him even deeper. As he continued to pulsate much more profoundly, he came up and reached around for both her ankles to hold in his hands and above her head.

Now at a steady tempo, Nina placed her hands on his chest, his nipples, and then his abdomen. Within a few more minutes, she trembled. Her entire body was shaking. She muffled her own orgasmic wails by putting both of her hands over her mouth. He then removed her hands, grabbing them with his. He wanted to hear her yell.

Jack was reasonably close to the climax himself. However, not wanting Nina's excitement to be over too soon, he reduced the speed in his thrusts. The enthusiasm from the sounds of Nina's pinnacle was sending a tingling sensation to the pit of his loins.

Once she had the second to capture her composure, she looked up at him and asked, "Let me get on top?"

As if they were wrestling, Jack made a reversal move to send Nina squatting her delectable Thoroughbred thighs on top of his ready-to-go rod, armed to explode in her at any second.

Their sweat-slicked bodies were sliding together. "You dirty girl...ride that cock!" Jack told her. He took the palm of his hand and smacked the right cheek of her bodacious derriere while she bounced up and down on him like a seesaw.

She took both hands and rested them on his stomach, extending her arms until they locked in position. From there, she began to thrust back and forth. He reached up and cupped her perky breasts, rubbing the nipples with his thumbs as she continued to moan.

Now, she was moving quicker. Harder. Sweat was running down the small of her back. Her body was red and furious, full of burning desire to release. She was so close. The suspense was building. In the next moment, another eruption went off inside her.

Jack was barely hanging on. He wanted to keep going…but he too, was at the finish line. Right when he felt his explosion about to burst inside Nina, he reached over to squeeze her buttocks and he squeezed his eyes closed. She continued to rotate on top of him, the ride wasn't quite over just yet.

She then put her hands on her own breasts, rotating her nipples with her fingertips this time. She smiled at him, feeling the last bit of fireworks going off inside her body. Jack grunted in satisfaction. She came down to kiss him once more.

Nina then stopped moving, looking to catch her breath. She slid off his body and laid next to him, smiling and kissing Jack continuously. "That was amazing," she told him.

"You ain't kiddin' there, doll," he replied.

Jack laid there, looking up while Nina cuddled in close to him, closing her eyes in the comfort of his warmth. Once her head hit the pillow, there was no more to think about. All was right in the world.

Typically, for her to fall asleep would start with being caught in a carousel of thoughts. Every idea, notion and event from her day would replay in her mind, demanding analysis before she could be allowed to drift away.

Finally, when that carousel would come to a stop, and her mind was able to meander freely in random thoughts, she'd sail away into a dream.

Tonight seemed a bit different. Her mind was clear. She had more than a typical guy with her. She had the kind of man she wanted.

McCool was indeed one who was separate from the pack. He was tough, loving, funny, and always looking…in her words, "Sexy as all Hell."

Was it possible she was falling for this guy already? This feeling was so strange to her. On the other hand, so many things were telling her not to. It could have been dangerous. However, this attraction she felt towards Jack, she felt throughout her whole body, it overwhelmed her and made her feel complete for the first time. It had no bound nor length nor depth…just absolute.

It felt as though she was in the middle of a treacherous fire, yet completely safe at the same time. Someone had given her peace when so many other men had given her turmoil.

Then again,

Soon after she fell asleep, Jack closed his eyes. Their consciousness ebbed and their minds went into free fall, swirling with the chaos of a new dream.

In the middle of the night, he woke up to pick up the ringing cell phone going off nonstop on his nightstand but not before he checked one last time to see if the noise woke Nina. Her eyes were closed. Jack went to take the call.

Yet, he did not realize that Nina did in fact, roll over moments later to watch him get up and talk in the distance for what must've been an urgent call this time of night.

Who is he talking to? Why so late?

At this moment, Nina's guard went back up as she bent both ears, trying to hear the conversation from afar. An hour had passed before he returned to bed. Still no answers.

CHAPTER TWENTY-ONE

No doors. No windows. No way out. Every minute was hell. Looking around, all one could stare at in solitary confinement of a highly elite maximum-security Federal correction facility was an indefinite expansion of pure white space.

One could run forever and never get anywhere, never make progress. No light. No shadows. Just the color of white.

Vinny spent his days staring into those very white walls of the dreary Allenwood, Pennsylvania's formidable prison, remaining quiet and content. Once in a while, he'd let out a cough or a wheeze during...yet it was *no big deal*, according to him. His health was just fine, in his eyes.

He kept reminding himself of why he was there...the reason why he nearly killed a man in Fairton...to come eighty miles across the country...to settle the score, once and for all.

Paul Muchetta...that was the reason. It was a blind-siding kind of afternoon within the first few months the two were there. The setting was dead center in the main cafeteria.

It was in the middle of two separate lines for food amid the various conversations of the prison chambers when the two crossed paths. The magnitude of the moment was twenty-five years in the making. It was pretty powerful, like two worlds colliding. The old enemies came within talking distance of one another. For some, it could be considered historic. At first, the silence was somewhat surreal. That was, of course, until Vinny broke the ice.

"You're a fuckin' disgrace," he blatantly said to Paulie, looking deep into his eyes, meaning every bit of it. Anyone in line who heard it turned their heads towards the scene. Vinny's reputation was becoming a more violent one these days. Not that it was ever gentle, but it was growing further from it with age. The old man was intimidating, considerably since the incident in Fairton. Word of it in the jailhouses spread like wildfire.

Paulie responded, still in the procession of his line. "Look who is talkin' over here!" The lines continued to move as did the two, further away from one another. Guards from every corner of the room kept an eye on the situation.

"Turn your back on *our thing*? To not go to trial? Who the fuck do you think you are? You ain't a man," continued Vinny, raising his voice a tad…simply to be heard across the room.

"That's fine…I ain't a man like you. I ain't gonna rot away in this place like you're gonna, you miserable motherfucker you!" countered Paul

Vinny then nonchalantly walked out of his line. He inched his way closer to where Paulie was standing. His voice grew quieter while his temper became hotter.

"I should slit your throat right here and now, in front of everyone! I always knew you weren't shit, now you showed it to the whole world! You're no better than my scumbag brother who rots in hell," he said, almost face to face with the pretty one.

The entire time, Paulie continued to smile back while Vinny scowled like a dog. "At least he rots with company. Your two sons and whore ex-wife are there to remind them about how you're joining them all soon!" said Paul, softly yet with conviction.

"You fuck…"

Just as this was said, Vinny brought his arms up, ready to shove Paulie down like a ton of bricks. Before he had the chance, three guards came rushing down to get in-between the two lines. They wanted to break up the potential madness right away. They didn't want to see anything escalate, especially between a pair of old-timers like these two. Too much paperwork, meaning they had to do something.

All of a sudden, Vinny began coughing and wheezing, holding his stomach with one hand and his mouth with the other. He almost lost his balance. The guards asked if he needed help.

"I'm alright, I'm alright," he said. However, his slow walk back to the line said differently. Paulie kept a close eye on what he was seeing. He wasn't sure what to make of it yet, but he smiled more full knowing Vinny was becoming weaker.

Lurking in the shadows along every step Jack took on the sidewalks of Brotherly Love, he was being followed. There weren't many places he could avoid being watched since the start of his involvement in the Caribbean Connection.

His profile went up…the suits he dressed in, the fancy places he'd go to. Yet, as exposed as he was becoming, the good news was that the Feds weren't nearly close enough to finding anything they could pin on him.

Despite coming up short, they weren't giving up yet. Agents Jay, Davey and Rock were all together one night in a white, unmarked van on a South Philly street. To their excitement, they spotted the target. Better yet, he was out with Lou. The three couldn't believe it. The gorgeous one was out for the very first time in public.

None of them ever having seen Lou before, were all eager to get a good look. "Even with this guy out of the gloom he hides in, we can still barely tell who it is," commented Davey, holding the binoculars tight to his eyes while sitting in the passenger seat of the van.

Lou and Jack were walking towards the corner of Wolf Street where there were a few Italian restaurants on opposite ends of one another. Old school joints. Each one, classy.

"Even if we could, it means nothing without a record…which he doesn't have," said Jay, taking the binoculars from his partner to get a better glance at the view himself. Davey didn't like Martinez feeling he could just take what he wanted just like that.

Rock then perked up and asked, "How are we gonna fuckin' get these guys, boss? What do we really gotta do here? I mean, seriously."

Jay took a deep breath, putting down the binoculars and picking up his cell phone. "If we can't tie anything to Lou, what are we gonna do? Go say 'hello'?" he rhetorically asked.

It was going to be a desperate mission. One that wasn't impossible…yet one that was going to take time and specific calculation. Jay continued, "We are gonna have to come heavy on the kid, McCool. That little shit…I want him to feel the worst of our wrath, more so than Lou!"

As he said this, Martinez exuded a hatred like no other. For whatever reason this vendetta against McCool became more prevalent than that of Lou was unknown to the other two agents…but they were bound to find out one way or another.

"What did you have in mind, Jay?" asked Davey, rolling his eyes at him.

"You'll see. I can't quite talk about it yet," their fearless leader told them.

"Ah, c'mon Jay…what is it? What do you have up your sleeve?" Rock inquired, tapping Jay on the shoulder continuously.

However, Martinez remained reluctant. He was holding his cards close to his chest. "Don't you worry. It's something good."

Lou and Jack were conversing inside an old-school restaurant in South Philly. It was called *Esposito's Trattoria*. It had a 19th-century Sicilian feel to it. The warm nights, the stucco homes, the crickets in their silence. It was discreet, stylish, and sophisticated to the bone.

It was the kind of place you booked two months in advance. Nobody got a table on impulse. There were large mullioned windows covered by long embroidered curtains. In the center of all the dark walnut tables held vases of bright, fresh flowers. They changed the arrangements daily.

Most of the food was ordered overseas from the good old boot. There were no faults such as *fugazi* garlic bread or canned gravy. What you were getting here was always top-notch quality.

Delicate live piano music set the tone for a delightful meal. Good conversation accompanied by soothing tunes. Once dinner came out, these two got to *real talk*. Although he was more than aware he was now "sleeping with the enemy," Jack still felt a bit unsettling during dinner.

"This place reminds me of back home in the motherland," Lou was telling McCool, looking around at the restaurant's decor.

"Beautiful country, disgusting fucking people. Coming to the States meant everything to me as a kid. The opportunity is everywhere," said Lou.

Jack nodded his head, listening intently. "There is a ton of it here in America…as you know," he told him.

"What about you? What opportunity here gives you your drive?" asked the gorgeous one.

"Well, every day is a new romance when you fall for the life you're living…but most importantly, my hospital. I mean, it's not really mine…but it's the closest thing I have to home. I'm trying to save it, Lou…every and any which way I can," detailed Jack, with a passion. Lou smiled, nodding his head and telling him, "I didn't realize you were a philanthropist, my boy, that's very commendable."

"Not only that…I'm falling in love with this girl," replied Jack. Lou chuckled for a few seconds, cutting into his eggplant parmesan. As he was doing so, he signaled to the waiter to bring over some more of the fresh minced garlic they kept in-house.

"I'm sure she is wonderful, she must be dealing with you," joked Lou.

"She sure is."

The two chortled. Lou looked around the restaurant, awaiting his garlic. Jack then began to tell him, "It's funny…I think she got mad the other night when you called late about dinner."

He chuckled once more, remaining silent. Jack continued on. "It's as if she doesn't trust me sometimes…I don't know. That's the only caveat, I guess."

It didn't seem to faze Lou. He didn't even acknowledge the statement. He was never serious with anyone nor married…it wasn't his forte. So, he quickly changed the topic.

"I'm a little concerned…anything from Cassimo lately, my boy?" asked Lou, diving into his entrée waiting for the real details. He wanted to know the truth about what was going on with Caz considering the guy wasn't around much anymore.

Jack replied, "Not really. Not sure where he stands with the feeling about you and I in business together, ya know?"

"Money and emotions never go together, Jack. Like oil and water...keep them separate," Lou told him. He then went to grab what was left of his red wine right as McCool did the same, replying, "You're right, Lou. A' salu!" while raising his glass.

The age-worthy wine selection was a personal variety, imported from Lou's hometown in Caccamo.

"Luigi...it is an honor to break bread with you," said McCool, pouring himself and Lou another glass from the bottle. The gorgeous one smiled, nodding his head up and down in agreeance.

Sniffing the glass as he twirled it around, Lou remained silent while Jack continued to speak. "I must ask," he said to him, taking a sip of the red delight.

"What keeps you behind the scenes for so many years? Why hide in the shadows of Veccuto or that fuckin' traitor cousin of yours? You're the real power...you have been all along."

Lou then looked over at the piano player. He closed his eyes and let the tune swim through the air and into his mind like a wakeful dream. The notes indeed were relaxing. It was like relief being delivered most divinely.

"The artist, like the God of the creation, remains within or behind or beyond or above his handiwork, invisible, refined out of existence, indifferent, paring his fingernails," said Lou, softly, keeping his eyes closed until the end of the quote.

Jack's eyes widened. He couldn't believe what he was hearing. "So you have read into James Joyce?" he asked, shocked as ever.

"I didn't want to admit it when we first met...but I have to hand it to the Irishman, he penned some good stuff!"

"I'll cheers to that as well!"

McCool raised his glass again. For this moment, much like the vintage wine from overseas, was something to be savored.

"Jack...the real reason I live in the darkness is because I don't trust anyone. I never have. Not even my older cousin. As you can see, I had good reason. The way he turned his back to the family...I cried that very night I watched it on the news."

"I can respect that."

"That being said, I want us to be successful together for years to come!"

Business was business. They both knew that. Anyone can make the quick hustle or the big score of the week...but very few in the game could make a racket last for a long time to come. To make that kind of commitment, there had to be an unbelievable amount of trust involved on both ends of the bargain. If not, it would never work.

"Do you trust me?" asked Jack.

Lou chuckled. He wiped his mouth with his napkin after taking a few more bites of his eggplant. After that, he replied, "I think it's fate we are doing business together. The obstacles, the challenges…it all aligns for a reason."

There was then a bit of silence after he said this. Jack soaked in the weight of his words, not sure how to respond or if it was a good time to do so. Plus, it looked like Lou wasn't finished with his lecture.

"If I didn't trust you by now…I'd have killed ya," concluded the gorgeous one, leaning into the table carefully and ever so intently.

It was a hard statement…yet true. Lou was a man who held a tiny circle of direct contacts. Coming into the light after hiding in the blackness for over two decades, expanding that circle was a hard thing to do for anybody.

"I'll toast to that!"

Jack raised his glass.

"You're family now, boy!"

Jack toasted with Lou. He then paused. He thought long and hard about what the gorgeous one had just remarked. What was family to McCool? He never had a clear definition of it other than his crew in the old neighborhood, his church or hospital. That being said, he always reflected on Fitzy's view of friends and family. Many times, what resonated most came from his reflections during his time in Afghanistan.

In the midst of Jack's silent pondering, Lou asked him, "What about you? How do you feel about your luck? How fortunate will we be with this venture, McCool? Tell me."

Wanting to be nothing but class and thoughtful, Jack took his time in delivering his best response. "I don't ever wait for luck in this lifetime. Nothing is won by chance. I take the pound of gold as it shines in front of me! It may not be there tomorrow!"

For a line like that, Lou raised his glass. He smiled, knowing the young man was as well-read as he was well-rounded in the gambling sector. "Good form, Jack…good form."

Lou took a sip of his wine…then paused. Just as one of the waiters raised the curtain a bit from the nearest window, the gorgeous one noticed something a bit off as he stared outside.

"Let's skip the espresso, kid."

"What happened, Lou?"

Although it was from a distance, Lue noticed the white van parked across the street. He knew what he was staring at, there was no denying it. Lou came face to face with Agent Martinez.

"We're being watched."

CHAPTER TWENTY-TWO

After dinner, Jack drove himself home. He and Lou weren't going to hang around after being stared at by the Feds all night. There were more important things to look into...such as the past.

He slowly walked up the dark stairs of his house and peeked around the corner. First, he made sure Andrew was tucked into his bed. After that, he stepped into the master to see Nina. She was already asleep, yet he came in to kiss her anyway.

Jack took a deep inhale and exhale. He staggered over to his study across the hallway. Right away, he went to his liquor selection, neatly arranged by title next to his cigar humidor. After pouring two fingers neat of his top-shelf Jameson, he sat to reflect a bit. Looking out his window and into his backyard, he reflected on what Lou said at dinner about *family*. It reminded him of two different times in his life, both before he went to the Middle East and just as he was leaving it.

It was late in the year, 2003. Jack sat on the watchtower, looking out at the heat waves rising off the desert floors of Afghanistan. They were vaporous ghosts of a time forgotten. He sat there and studied the vast landscape intensifying toward the mountains to the south.

Below and all around him, he saw his fellow troops scurried to and from the station in the hot midday sun. As he sat there watching, he thought of the fresh produce and cardboard-boxed-scented basement at Tommy Tiernan's store. It was carved out of an ancient row house that sat on the corner of Kensington Avenue, back home in the Northeast. Completely emerged in his memory, he could see the light from the street up above. It poured in when the cellar doors sat open on the hot summer sidewalk.

Tommy was Fitzy's older cousin on his mother's side. Fitzy would often take Jack there when making his rounds or before a jewel heist. He'd drink cold beers and eat a hoagie from the deli up above, all the while shooting the shit with Tommy.

Jack remembered one time before he went away, the summer after high school, Fitzy taking a massive bite of the hoagie, chomping away. Half-chewed, he barked, "Hey, Tommy, you hear numbnuts here joined the Army? He's leaving next week. Fuckin' eighteen-years-old…he's out to see the world now!"

Tommy shot him a quizzical glance. "Dude, what the fuck?"

"That's what I said, Tommy." Then, swallowing down the last bite with a swig of icy beer, he continued, "Yo, Tommy, you'se remember Dick McCusker? He and you both did 'Nam about the same time, right?"

"Yeah, yeah…Dicky. Works down the airport for TWA. Goes to Hibernian!"

"Right, right. Good guy, that Dicky."

Fitzy took another bite, another swig. He wiped his mouth with his hand, looked at Jack, and pierced him with his cold, steady eyes for what seemed an eternity. Then, he looked at Tommy.

"Yo, cuz, what the fuck did the army ever do for you? For Dicky?" Tommy looked back at him quickly with a cheeky response before Fitzy beat him to it.

"Make you a *man*? Make you *all you could be*? Fuck that! Right, Tommy?"

"Absolutely, absolutely."

Fitzy leaned toward Jack. "They're gonna tell you that you're some kind of band of brothers. That the only people you can count on when times get tough is one another. They're gonna tell you you're family, and all of them, all of them! They're gonna believe that shit."

Jack was hanging on every word…nearly every predicate.

"But know this, kiddo…and know this good. They ain't family. They ain't shit. The only thing you can count on when the going gets tough is your brains, your gut instinct, and that fucking rifle they give you. Ain't no family in this world but the one you eat fucking turkey with on Christmas Day. Ain't no family in this world but me."

Fitzy's intense eyes almost seemed hot, burning something deep inside Jack. "Promise me, promise me right now, you ain't gonna forget that, kid."

Jack sat there in the tower. In his mind's eye, it was as if Fitzy was sitting there right beside him…telling him the truth of the world all over again. He thought about his lieutenant, taking account once more of what a candy-ass piece of West Point shit he was. He thought about the mission coming up in the morning, the long IED laden road from Kabul to Mazar-e-Sharif, the eye of the needle through the deadly Tangi Tashkurgan Gorge.

"Ain't gonna be no family there, especially that prick lieutenant. Family? Hell, he ain't even a friend."

CHAPTER TWENTY-THREE

The summer wind came blowin' in and it wasn't slowing down anytime soon. It was already near the end of June. Everybody around was having a good time...especially me! I mean, how could I not? I was on top of the world! Everything was finally coming together for once.

On my way out into the city one day, I made a few calls to Caz after receiving a leery text message from him. I needed to know more about a particular something. He wasn't picking up, but I didn't plan on letting it deter me. Not on a day like this one. I was overjoyed...more so than usual.

The morning was postcard perfect. Traffic was running on time. Downtown, the skyscrapers were picking up precise beams of light from the bright sun, and the sky was an unbroken backdrop of blue.

This was also the day I brought in the last sum of money that was going to make the quarterly goal for the hospital. Although I'd been bringing in as much as I could on a monthly basis all year, this was the most essential drop-off of them all. The fight wasn't over yet...but it was a Hell of a start. Knowing how much this was going to help the many and positively impact the community, it kept me motivated each day. It even seemed to inspire the entire team!

When I came through the front entrance of SICH, I brought the warmth of the beautiful day in with me. "Keeping these doors open!" I yelled, strutting proudly towards those who awaited my arrival.

One of the old nurses recognized me. "There he is!" she yelled. Everybody gathered around to see the check I was writing. They were all clapping, Dr. Dan, the hospital staff…even Mr. Bryce, the guy I needed to impress the most. This financial relief in sight was certainly a cause for celebration.

All were convening with delight in the corridor. Yet, in the midst of the happiness, I was starting to feel uneasy from where I was standing. Smiles extended towards me, attempting to turn my face away from the one individual I grew keen on focusing towards.

He was merely passing by, looking to get a sip of water from the fountain when I walked up to him and asked, "Let me buy you a cup of coffee." It was a bold move…but he accepted the gesture on the condition it was one cup.

First and foremost, I made sure the money got into Bryce's hands and into the SICH account. After that, I made my way over to the cafeteria to buy coffee for the same man I asked to drink it with moments earlier.

He and I sat down at one of the tables. I could sense that Desmond 'The King' Carter wanted nothing to do with me. He made it clear. His silence towards me told it all. It was louder than everything else going on around us. The nurses, the visitors, the patients.

All of a sudden, Desmond took his first sip of coffee with a slurping sound, uttering to me afterward, "You better make this quick, boy." He looked me dead in the eye when he said it, demanding that I come up with a good case for taking this big-shot gangster's time.

I hesitated at first. The man was a street legend. I mean, he went by "The King" for a reason. I wanted to make sure whatever I said was going to be respectful. I did not want to cross the line one bit. After the news Dr. Dan had shared with me recently, I knew I had to tread lightly.

"I have heard about your son," I began, softly. There was very little for me to empathize with him about in this particular matter. So, I followed with the best thing I thought of...merely the only appropriate line one could say. "I'm very sorry." I leaned in towards him on the table in front of us.

He looked at me with a blank stare. I knew I was far from the first person telling him this. However, I meant every word. I needed him to know that. "Keep the faith...we never know what the future holds," I continued.

Desmond perked up. Perhaps it was the coffee or the fact he thought I was pontificating for a moment. It was as if I awoke the boiling anger inside of him in that very second. "Oh yeah? What the fuck you gonna do about it?" he asked, pointing directly at me.

I paused, knowing there was nothing I could directly do. I responded with the only thing I was able to offer, "I will pray for you and your son, Mr. Carter."

"We got enough of them coming in, kid. We need a miracle here."

"I totally get it. Sometimes we can all use one."

Again, he grew silent to calm himself down. Now guzzling down his coffee without a care in the world as to what the temperature was, I could tell he was more eager to end this chat with me than before.

"I know you very well, Mr. Carter. I don't know if I ever introduced myself…my name is Jack McCool, I am…,"

"What the fuck you want, kid…an autograph?" interrupted Desmond, looking around, shaking his head sideways.

"I understand you're frustrated, Desmond." This was far from the right response. At this moment, he sat up straight and spoke louder to me than he did the entire conversation.

"No, you don't, not at all. This isn't just fuckin' frustration…this is panic, fear, loneliness…mixed with exhaustion. Try your world upside down with the lights off…I'm lost."

I was now speechless. He was right. I couldn't fight him on this. There was no way I could tell him otherwise nor tell him there was any way I'd bring him a remedy of some sort.

I let him continue. I could tell there was more he had to get off his chest. "I'd do anything to have my boy back to the way he was…even if it meant *me* getting smoked."

I sat up straight myself, trying to mirror his posture. "Look…I sit on the board here at the hospital. What if I could help you somehow with medical bills or such? I am sure this has brought a huge financial strain," I offered him. I looked around at the various visitors, hospital staff and patients. At this point, he needed more assistance than what they could provide. Between Desmond and I, we'd have to think of something together.

"I ain't askin' for none of that, motherfucker," he quietly told me.

I tried even more to reason with him. This hospital meant everything to me…especially the people in it. "What can I do? What is there possibly on your plate that I can be of assistance with?"

Again, he became silent. There was very little care given to the fact that I held a seat on the board. So, I pleaded. "Give me something."

Desmond then finished the last bit of his coffee, slamming the cup on the table. He began, "The people you associate with," before he paused. I leaned in again…this time, a bit closer, wondering where he was going with this.

"Wipe them all off the planet. They the reason my boy is in here right now up in this mothafucka, man."

As much as it made sense he was upset, there was only so much I could have done. Those he wanted gone were no longer a factor.

"Desmond, Paulie Muchetta is the one you'd be after. He is in jail…nobody is getting to him there. He's going to die in prison, there is no changing that. Don't worry…he is suffering as the days go on."

Shortly after, The King's coffee cup went flying. His hand smacked it out the way so quickly, I thought it was being shot out of a cannon.

"Man, this wasn't Paulie. Him, I knew well…he wasn't capable of what went down that day in my neighborhood. You know who the fuck it was, motherfucker…don't play dumb with me. I'm too old for that shit."

Now, I was the one sitting in silence. I knew who he was referring to. The one, the only…his master, the Almighty.

"His cousin, Lou…the man you work for," continued Desmond, pointing at me once more.

"I can tell ya, man…he's no saint…but he…," I began before Carter stood up and pushed his seat behind him, causing a screeching noise on the floor.

"He's a fuckin' piece of shit. As is anyone who associates with him," he told me, inching his way towards my face, implying I was no better.

Although he had a point about Lou, I felt there was no biting the hand that fed you in my case. This was the same hand led me to the most fabulous fortune I'd ever seen. However, I needed to level with him.

"You think I like working with him? You think I enjoy being in his company?" I asked, standing up to be eye to eye with him.

"Shiiiit, little nigga! With the money you're making...ain't no way you hate the man as much as I do."

"Listen, Mr. Carter...I'm going to talk the committee here. I want to make sure your insurance and your..."

He stopped me again. "Man, that's my only offer. Nothing else. Don't fuckin' give me the runaround. Any friend of Lou Muchetta is an enemy of mine...we clear?"

He didn't let me answer, not even with my just intentions. Yet, in Desmond's eyes...I was just as bad as the company I kept. I sat back down, slowly, assuring him that I was far like those I did business with.

There was no changing his mind. "Thanks for the coffee. Right now though, I'd rather drink alone." I got up myself, checking my watch. I was ready for the next stop of the day...or as ready as I could have been.

"Here we go again...same person, different prison," I told myself while driving down the deserted interstate highway. This time, Allenwood, Pennsylvania was the destination. If any place had a more eerie feeling to it than Fairton did...this was it.

I couldn't believe I was going through with this again. When I first got the message from Caz I was being *sent for*, I almost wanted to ignore it. This was no the second time I felt such discomfort.

The countryside stretched before me like a great quilt of golden, brown and green squares held together by the thick green stitching of the hedgerows. It soared and fell like giant waves on a gentle ocean. Occasionally there were cows and horses scattering out from a farmhouse.

The penitentiary crept up on me. It was hidden in the final row of trees…vast, curtaining the grand building.

The guards at the gate were anything but friendly. No words, no emotion…just guidance to where I needed to go next. It almost felt as if I was beginning a sentence myself.

I walked into the confinements slowly, dreading every step onto my way inside. Seeing the white walls surrounding were always justification for me that this place had no end…and it was just too easy to forget where you started.

There he was…the man, the miserable, the tremendous morbid. Vinny was already waiting for me when I arrived into the visitation room. I wasted no time in saying my own kind of 'hello' to him. Additionally, I did it with a smile, brushing the last bit of dust off my Armani suit in front of him just to exude my flash.

"We have to stop meeting under such terrible circumstances! Perhaps we should celebrate once in a while. How's your health, Vin?"

He did not look happy, per the usual. However, this time, he looked even less healthy than he did the last visit we had. His eyes were dropping down further, his timing to respond was slower.

"Black, I asked you here today because I was curious to see if you have a death wish?" All of a sudden, a violent eruption of coughs and hacks let out from Vinny's mouth.

"Excuse me?" I questioned, raising my voice just a little. The only one appearing to be dead was him.

"I fuckin' ask you to do something…to make somebody disappear, and this is the result? No movement, no care in the world? Instead, you go into business with this motherless fuck?" he continued.

"The more you think you know, Vinny…the less you understand," I replied, shaking my head sideways. The nerve of this man…I was furious!

His voice was growing hoarser. It was getting harder to hear him, the more he spoke. "You don't even include Caz? You don't even tell me about this? Fuckin' *oogatz*!!"

"I offered Caz a piece of the pie…he declined. So, fuck him!"

"You're makin' a big fuckin' mistake with this guy, Jackie…he owns you now! I am telling ya it's all over," he detailed, referring to Lou Gorgeous.

"Nobody owns me but ME, Vinny…let's get that straight right now!!!"

"Keep thinkin' that. When you're making millions one day and the next, you're lying in a puddle of your own blood…don't call me for me to tell you I told ya so."

I didn't know who I wanted to try and kill first: him or Caz. A better heads-up from the skinny one would have been nice.

"What the fuck are you saying?" I asked Vinny.

"He's not going to let you live, you little fuck. He will let this operation make the most profit it can, reap the benefits and assure with everything in his power…you don't live to retire on it."

"You're out of your fuckin' mind. He wouldn't be able to run this shit if it weren't for me."

"Shhh, kid…you're too damn loud."

"Don't you shush me, Vinny. You started this!!!" I yelled, standing out of my seat. All the guards nearby stood alert, staring at us.

"You're walking down a dangerous path, boy. The best you can do now is run far away," he said.

"I ain't fuckin' runnin'. Not from him, not from Caz…not from you."

"I don't know what to say then."

"You're just mad that I'm doing well. I'm doing better than you ever fuckin' dreamed. Now, you'll rot in here and wither away to a miserable nothing!!"

"You'll just never learn, will you?"

"You can go fuck yourself, Vinny."

I slammed the phone on the hook just as he voiced his last words. I didn't hear him, but I could read his lips. Either way, it meant nothing to me. I smiled back when he said it.

"You're dead to me, kid!"

CHAPTER TWENTY-FOUR

From the glitzy lights of the casino buildings to the gentle winds along the subtle sands, I loved the shore. That bright day in mid-July when Jack and I traveled to explore America's Playground, Atlantic City...that memory replayed in my mind for a long time to come afterward. I could have stayed there with him forever. In my heart, we did.

"Nina, this place is almost as beautiful as you," he told me. God, he was good. Even when he sounded corny, I thought it was cute.

Here, this whole time I kept telling myself not to fall for a guy like Black McCool. He was a bad boy...the kind my parents always told me to avoid. Their advice kept my guard up my whole like. Now, I was letting it down. This was unlike me. I felt vulnerable.

Yet, I could not help myself. It wasn't all the money he was making lately either...that didn't matter to me either. It was his actions.

Whenever he looked into my eyes, it was as if every ounce of breath was taken from my lungs. Every time he kissed me, it felt like the world stopped, leaving just the two of us to dance together.

Every time he held my hand, he became my anchor. He grounded me, steadying me. I was growing accustomed to this feeling.

Is this what falling in love was like? A story you never wanted to end? Ever since I was a little girl, I longed to feel complete like this. Now that I was in love with a man like Jack, I couldn't bear to lose him.

After a long afternoon of him making various stops within the depths of AC, we finally made it to the beach. I wasn't quite sure what he was doing at these numerous *stops*. It made me suspicious…as if there was more to his unknown than I realized.

For as much as I adored him, he truly was an enigma. He was masked with elegance when I knew he was draped in decadence, deep down. Although, I guess there is a little mystery to all of us.

We walked for miles that evening on the beach. The soft sand caved beneath my bare feet with each step.

The sun's rays peacefully floated, resting on the warm waters. Timid clouds rarely exposed themselves. They were allowing the sky to beam blue.

My ears invited in the quiet whisper of waves, sharing the ocean's secrets while the call of the seagulls occasionally broke the silence. The fresh air's salty smell tickled my nose. Light, breezy drafts sent tingling sensations through me.

Suddenly, I stopped. Something caught my eye. Along the sand in front of me sat one of the most exquisite pieces of sea glass I had ever seen. It was the size of a half-dollar. It had a mix of turquoise and pale jade to its reflection. Wavy ripples were running through it, one end to the other.

I picked it up and handed it to Jack. "Would ya look at that," he said, examining both sides of the glass. "It is quite lovely, my dear," he continued.

"I know it is," I replied, taking the glass back and showing him every single coil and curvature to its form. I wanted to make sure he saw and appreciated all the features the glass held. "There is so much to it. A gentle touch, a warmth, a character. Then again, there is a multitude of secrets it hides. There is so much unfamiliar…where it's been, the things it has seen."

I said this to him, looking into his eyes. I wasn't sure if he realized I was making a comparison to him. *Oh well.* I put the sea glass in his pocket just as he pulled me back into his warm embrace. It was then he told me the three words I had been dying to hear.

"I love you," he told me for the very first time. I was smitten…no turning back now.

I couldn't believe it. *Did he say what I think he said?* My goodness…I felt the same way. So much, I could barely stand it. I gasped, replying, "Say it again, McCool."

Chuckling, he smiled, saying, "I love you, Nina." I answered by kissing him. "I love you too, McCool."

We kissed again just as the sun changed its hues from bright orange to almost tangerine. The colors merged with the sky like watercolors on a canvas. The clouds were cotton-candy shaded. They blushed at the warm touch. Silhouettes of birds flew home across the air that was now magenta. As the sun dipped half of its circle into the water, the reflection in the sea made it look complete.

"The way the sun is hitting your face in its final moments, darling…it's sparkling those luminous greens brighter than ever," Jack said, studying my eyes as he did best, long and deeply.

Once again, we joined in a kiss. The mauve of the dusky sky intensified, and in just a while, the high star had finally set, giving way to a thousand others. It was time to enjoy our night at the casino…and of course, the bedroom.

We spent the latter half of the evening at The Borgata, a world-class casino with premium leisure amenities. After finishing up some delectable Japanese cuisine, we walked around for a bit. We played a couple of slot machines. Yet, we quickly realized when the reels gave us cherries and lemons instead of lucky sevens…it was time to up the ante *elsewhere*.

The hotel room on the 42nd floor. It was full of shadows from the moonlight, piercing into the balcony window. From the ocean waves nearby, a refreshing draught of salty air whipped through briskly, bringing a taste of the sea with it.

It was all so intoxicating. However, not as overwhelming as Jack. He was my drug, my fix I needed. One touch and the high would be instant, I just knew it. He was amazing.

Whatever he would want to do to me is what we'd do. There would be nothing I could do to stop him – not that I'd want to for any reason….but maybe just a tease for a little would heat the room up a bit.

We both entered subtly. However, as soon as the door closed, every pretense fell. Any reservation we had melted away and all we wanted to do was fuck each other until we passed out. Every kiss had a raw intensity to it – breathing fast, heart rate accelerating even more swiftly. I was moaning with anticipation already.

He grabbed my hair as he pinned me against the wall, telling me he wanted his lips to run the course of my body. He didn't want to miss a curve…not one crevice! His hands went first to chart the territory, moving from head to toe. *Oh boy!*

Those perfect, strong hands. I felt chills immediately as his fingertips would slide along my edges slowly.

His rugged features were so alluring. His broad shoulders, beautiful dark hair and solemn brows offset by a boyish grin. His eyes shimmered like zircon stones gleaming down onto his soft nose and strong jaw. So sexy! So seductive!

Ah…but I still wanted to tease him. I didn't want him to take me so easily just yet. As hard as he was to stifle, I stopped him in his tracks…I told him there was more to be done before he could have his way with me.

"Strip down and get into bed, sir," I told him, mesmerizing him with my green eyes. I pushed him off a little. He couldn't keep himself away. I assured him, "I'll be right back, McCool."

"You're killin' me, baby…you're killin' me," he whispered, continuing to kiss each square inch of my neck.

I bit my lip and pushed him off me again gently, walking away slowly. "I have a surprise for you," I said, looking behind me, beginning to undress, little by little in my stride towards the bathroom. I grabbed my duffel bag, full of clothing on the way.

He was something mystical in the moonlight, that McCool. His body was that of a Greek Adonis. I was peeking through the cracked-open bathroom door as I was sliding myself into something a little more *comfortable.*

He was great. Those broad shoulders. That smooth tan skin. I could barely wait to get out there. Yet, I took my time. I wanted to look just right.

Just before he peeled the covers back to crawl into bed, he poured himself a glass of water by the mini-bar. It was burning up in the room…I figured it was because of him.

I looked myself over one last time before coming out. I was wearing his favorite green silk dress of mine…skin tight! I went over to my iPhone and played Kings of Leon's song, "Closer" from the playlist. Showtime! I pretended as if I was a stripper in a gentlemen's club. However, at the end of this private dance, we'd both be paying up to each other.

I moved my hips one way and swayed them to the other. The beat was slow, the words were intense, and the electric guitar chords were erotic. The closer I came Jack's way, the more I could see him sweat. I liked it, so I took my time. I wanted this to be extraordinary, hard for either of us to handle.

Driven by the strangle of vein
Showing no mercy I'd do it again
Open up your eyes
You keep on crying
Baby I'll bleed you dry
Skies are blinking at me
I see a storm bubbling up from the sea

And it's coming closer
And it's coming closer

Once the straps of my dress finally fell to my sides, he studied me intently. I moved slowly to the music, making my way even closer towards him. He was on the edge of his seat…in more ways than one.

I came over and put my chest in his face, continuing to move my hips with the slow tempo of the song. Intently, he grabbed at my knees, sliding his hands up evenly up my legs. After that, he put his hands on my ass.

He opened my dress slowly, unzipping it with his thumb and third finger. After that, he began running his finger along my back. "You're sexiness is dangerous, baby...I want to devour you right now. Every fuckin' single part of you," he told me, kissing the erogenous part of my neck. I closed my eyes and slowly breathed in and out. He was definitely the dangerous one...not me. That was for certain.

Before I knew how it happened, I was naked on the bed with him. Our skin was moving softly together like a well-oiled machine. I could feel his hand enter from below moving fast while our tongues entwined in a kiss.

His fingers then went inside, changing my breathing with every thrust. My moans timed to his body movement. "Oh, McCool...you *are* good, too fuckin' good!"

I laid down. Then all at once, he shifted up on top of me, onto all fours. He kissed me from my breasts all the way to my stomach. His hands remained light on me, following the trail of his lips.

After that, he began licking and using his fingers all at once, watching my reaction, feeling how my legs moved. He was watching my body quiver. "You're all mine," he told me, whispering in my ear before nibbling on it a bit.

He put his head between my legs, nuzzling the center at first. His beard was a little rough on the insides of my thighs. Then with his lips, then his tongue, he sparked a fire.

I had to cry out in astonishment, in gratitude, at being eaten and touched in all the right places. It always made me grateful when a man would find it.

I simply couldn't get enough. He made it even harder once he came up, smirking. He grabbed his engorged cock and rubbed it on the tip of my clit. I ached for him...I wanted him in me. I wanted his weight on top of me. I wanted to squeeze him in further and further. I moaned excitingly at the sight of his gaze and his knowledgeable hands.

I had a good shot of his face. I didn't want to miss a moment of his reaction. God, I could barely contain myself. So, I stopped him again. Then, I pushed him down to the bed, flat on his back. I wanted to sit on *it*.

From there, I jumped on top and showed no mercy. I held him and put him in. He felt deeper and deeper in me. I'll never forget it. I was in charge and we both liked it. I held his hands down. He pretended he was trying to break free. I let my tits touch his face with every lunge. I could tell by the way his mouth was open and with his timed breathing, he was in paradise.

He then sat up a bit and wrapped his arms around my body. Sure enough, he hauled me over onto my back. We never lost connection.

The way he threw me down made it even more exciting. His grip had a manhandling way to it, yet without the brute force. The move was firm and quick, riddled with it was his eagerness.

It was then I felt that thick, swollen cock go deep inside me again. I could barely catch my breath. I dug my nails deep into his back, he had me going at laser speed.

"You like that?" he whispered. His voice was a coaxing rumble. I arched my back in response, letting him know he was moving in the right direction. I then wrapped my legs around his waist, panting more by the second.

I loved it. It felt like there was no end to the new things he was doing. He did a thrust, I copied him. I did something. He did it back. We were in perfect rhythm with each other.

Every time he pounded, a yelp of pleasure escaped my throat. I was so fucking close. I wanted us to go at the same time…I wanted it all over me.

So close! Two more moves, I'd be there. It was then a wave of hot and calm washed over me. My head was spinning. My body was shaking. I closed my eyes and simply escaped into euphoria. The flood of sensation was spectacular. It was like going down the tallest part of a rollercoaster. Every ounce of energy was sucked from my body…from my fingertips down to my toes. I shuddered against him. My vagina was pulsating. He looked into my eyes, smirking, knowing what he felt he did to me.

My hair was tumbled. My face was glowing. I smiled back at him, laying there as I felt him accelerate inside of me.

He began kissing me on the lips, hastening faster. He was taking my breath away even though he was doing all the work. I felt another one coming.

Could we time it? Could we both explode together? I felt his hands grab my thighs and I told him with what little voice I had left, "Fuck me, Jack….fuck me harder, HARDER!!"

And it's coming closer
And it's coming closer

My breathing grew irregular again. I can't focus on anything. I lost myself. My whole body stopped moving. I clenched up, enjoying the explosion that's erupting throughout my entire body...and all over my stomach. It was overwhelming yet so awesome.

He sat up, breathing heavily as his finish appeared to be just intense as mine. Drenched in sweat, his hot rugged body, and the smell of sex in the room...I was in another world. I was beat. "You're simply amazing," I uttered. He didn't reply. He smiled, coming to kiss me on the forehead. As much as I wanted more of him, I was exhausted. It had been a long day...with a *phenomenal* ending.

We had a little pillow talk, but eventually, we both fell asleep. The sounds of the ocean were soothing me into my sweet slumber.

I woke up in the middle of the night to the sounds of vibrations next to our bed. Half asleep, I looked over and noticed a phone was going off on the nightstand. Thinking it was mine at first, I grabbed it to look at the screen. I then realized it was Jack's phone. Nosey me...I read the texts anyway.

One of the messages that came through was from Caz...ugh! It read, "I need to see you tomorrow night. Call me from an outside line." Fuck that scumbag, I always trusted him the least – *delete message*! The other one, however, read from Dr. Dan at SICH. His news was a bit more daunting.

"Hi, John – I wanted to let you know that Desmond Carter's son, Nathan, passed away tonight." Immediately, I woke Jack up from his rest.

CHAPTER TWENTY-FIVE

The wide shades cast from the evening dissolved into the gathering darkness of the nighttime. The summer air cooled over while car horns and police sirens sang an all-too-familiar street melody in the background of the city.

Returning to the bleak Badlands of North Philly, Desmond and Jerome sat side-to-side and inhaled the urban ether on one of the long-standing stoops in their old block. They watched the cars drive by on the overpass in silence for a few minutes while they collected their thoughts.

"I still miss my brother, man...I know Nathan is up there with him now, watching his back," said Jerome, smirking before shifting his head towards his friend. He then glared at the concrete below him.

Desmond remained quiet. Instead of responding right away, he stared up into the dark sky, studying the smoggy clouds that typically curtained the stars.

In the far distance, he could see a mere glow in-between them. It wasn't the scape of the buildings piercing through like a jagged mountain ridge. This was a warm radiance.

Above the millions of lights glittering from the dense mass of skyscrapers was one solemn star amid the atramentous blanket. It wasn't just bright...it burned as it shined. He knew right then and there...his son was smiling from above.

Desmond looked back down, smiling to himself. He shed a tear, thinking about all that he'd give to have Nathan back. There wasn't much he could've done at that moment. Yet, he nodded his head knowing his son was watching over him.

"We gotta act, man!" exclaimed Jerome, interrupting the bliss. "I ain't fuckin' doin' it, homie," replied Desmond, standing up from the stoop. He turned his back and looked towards his home, merely a block from where he and Jerome were. A few kids on bikes rode by, lurking the streets. The moonlight was their only glowing guidance at this hour.

As Desmond began walking away, Jerome stopped him, grabbing his arm before he got far. It was then he explained to him how important it was to retaliate. There was no other option.

"Our names are mud on the streets if we don't blast back, man! I'm talkin' anybody related to this…they gotta go!! Anyone who knows anyone who conspired against our neighborhood. Justice needs to be delivered."

Desmond's silence spoke for itself. It was the kind of quietness that fell right before you get knifed in the back. The kind that would send a shiver down your spine and make your blood chill in the veins. However, it didn't faze Jerome. He persisted.

"My brother is dead. Your son is now dead, D," he told him, looking directly into his eyes. "Avenge his honor!"

All of a sudden, Desmond's cell phone went off ringing. It was the perfect kind of noise to break his muteness.

The buzzer went off like an annoyed rattlesnake and the ringer sounded like a firetruck barging through the city.

"Hello?" he answered.

"Desmond…it's Jack McCool," the other line spoke. "I simply do not know where to begin," continued the Irishman

"What the fuck you want, McCool?" asked Desmond, looking over to Jerome who was still sitting on the stoop. It was then, he rose up to his feet.

"I am sorry to hear about Nathan…I can't even imagine this kind of loss," said Jack, scratching his beard up and down methodically.

With another look, Desmond nodded his head towards Jerome, finishing up his conversation on the phone as quickly as he could.

He began with saying, "Man…all I gotta tell you…" before pausing to add a bit of suspense to what he was about to end the chat with.

Jerome reached for his Glock nine at the side of his hope, showing it to King Carter to remind him it was there for whatever he needed it to do.

"Watch your fuckin' back, nigga!" concluded Desmond, raising his tone a bit with such powerful words in his message. He then hung up the phone.

CHAPTER TWENTY-SIX

After an unnerving call with the renowned *King*, I put the phone down on the kitchen table and thought of what to do next. His closing statement was anything but settling to me. I had to respond in a timely fashion due to the unique situation at hand. I just wasn't sure how to yet. Either way, I knew this conflict starting between us was far from over.

I pondered as I sauntered slowly through my kitchen, pondering on my way back to continue watching the Phillies' game with my little buddy, Andrew.

I had just finished making us each a plate of macaroni and cheese to eat to enjoy while staying glued to the bottom of the seventh inning.

"You scoring this thing or what, buddy? How many hits do the Phils have without looking at the television?" I asked him, standing in front of the screen to put him to the test. He was very intent with the scoring sheet I gave him, watching every move of the players. He penciled in the rows with data methodically. It was as if he didn't want to make one single mistake and let me down.

"Six hits, two runs, zero errors," he responded, without fail. Man, I was impressed! Both with him and myself. The smile on my face showed that. To see my teachings come alive was great. Andrew was a smart kid.

I looked at the table next to my television. There sat one of my proudest, most prized possessions next to my photo with Ron Jaworski.

It was something significantly important to me. I hadn't touched it in many years…an autographed baseball signed by the great number 38, Curt Schilling. He was one of the most legendary pitchers to ever put on a Phillies' jersey. I grabbed it from its stand, holding in the palm of my hand. It felt just as sacred as it did the day he signed it for me during the 1993 World Series.

I then looked over to Andrew. "This is for you." Underhandedly, I tossed him the ball. He caught it quickly, holding it in front of his face. He was looking at it from every angle. He simply couldn't believe it. His eyes lit up as if I handed him a small bag of gold.

He got out of his seat, ran over to me standing next to the TV, hugging me tightly. I could see his smile growing wider the tighter he squeezed me. His head only came up to my waist. However, I know he felt twenty feet tall with such a prized piece of sports history.

I crouched down to the floor to look at him, eye level. "Maybe it will bring us luck when we go to the game next week!" I said. That was when I revealed my second surprise from my pants pocket…a pair of tickets to the Phillies-Mets game for that following Thursday night. His mouth dropped to the floor. His eyes lit up the room. He hugged me again, firmly around my neck. He kept telling me that he loved me and how thankful he was. For this very moment, I was just as grateful to see him so happy.

In walked Nina, quiet and quick. She was listening to us intently from the other room. Her body language told me all I needed to know about her current mood...something wasn't making her happy. I was sure I'd find out within the moment. "He can't go to the game with you, Jack."

"Why?" both Andrew and I said at the same time, looking at her like she had ten heads. Nina picked a few clothes up off the den floor and stormed out back into the kitchen and towards the laundry room.

"Sweetheart, what's the matter?" I asked softly, chasing her, trying to match her fast and furious walking pace.

"Andrew has his first week of school coming, Jack. I need his sleep pattern to be routine. He can't be up late like this with you," she replied, whipping around to look at me at laser speed.

I put my index finger up in front of her. "It's one night, Nina...I don't think it's going to be the worst thing. It will be so fun."

Looking from the corner of my eye, I could see Andrew sitting back down on the couch in the den, head down and glued to inspecting the ball. Another letdown...he was used to it in his life. Yet, now I was starting to see one of the main reasons behind it.

Nina then stopped in her tracks to tell me, "Listen, I love how you're getting close to him...but he isn't going to the game with you. That's that."

She grabbed the laundry basket and began fiddling with the clothes, one by one.

I grabbed the basket form her and put it down on the ground. I then took my hands, placed them on top of hers. I began leading her in into the direction of the main living room, away from the laundry and far from Andrew for a moment.

Descending slowly, I then sat her down on my loveseat by the front window and looked at her directly in the eyes.

My stare spoke for itself. However, I could tell she was trying to get me to voice where I was going with this kind of gesture.

"I guess I am just confused, Nina. You were in a good mood minutes ago. Did I say or do something?" I questioned.

She gave me the old "look." A slow batting eyes, pursed lips and a glance in the opposite direction.

"No."

The silence was poisonous, cruelly underscoring how vapid our conversation had become.

It was a part of her routine: pushing me away. I didn't know what the spark that ignited in her each time. It was odd. Was it the way I kept getting closer to Andrew? Was it how I tried to make a better life for her? I couldn't figure it out.

Each time, I'd do my best in trying to make her happy again. "How was your day?" I asked, doing my best to soothe her. I held her hand as she turned away from me once more, responding in a passive-aggressive tone.

"Fine, I guess…how was yours?"

Suddenly, there was a hasty fire next to us. Within the first second, I didn't even hear anything…I merely felt the window glass shatter and spray above my shoulder. Blasting gunshots cracked into the air as loud as thunder with the raw power of a summer storm.

Frak!!! Frakkkkk!!! Frrrrrrrrrrrraakkk!!!

I grabbed Nina by the arm, pulling her down to the ground with me. Luckily, we were right under the piercing booms as they began pouring in. "ANDREW, DON'T MOVE!!!" I yelled at the top of my lungs towards the den.

The firing shots of multiple machine guns continued spraying above us. The window, the curtains, the top of the sofa…obliterated! It was the scariest moment of my life. After it was done, all I could hear was a ringing noise in my ears.

CHAPTER TWENTY-SEVEN

Agent Davey was on a mission. He hadn't heard from Martinez nearly all day. Not a phone call, not a warning he'd be out on PTO…nothing! He felt excluded. He knew something was missing, more than just his partner's presence.

He was walking down the long, narrow hallway at Headquarters, turning the corner and peering into each office on the way to the men's room. He needed answers. He needed them quick.

Rock's office was the only one that looked busy. He was fussing with papers and fiddling with the laptop on his desk. Occasionally, he'd peek over to the laser printer in the corner of the room. "Where is Martinez?" It was far from a subtle welcome, but Davey couldn't help it.

"Down in AC!" replied Rock, trying to talk over his hands typing vigorously.

"What brings him there?"

Rock laughed to himself, keeping quiet. Of course, Davey acting like a statue with the perfect scowl at the entrance of his door demanded he needed to spill the beans.

"Well, it looks like McCool is higher up in this gambling thing than the Italian Mafia is. He has the connections down there at the Jersey shore. Martinez is there, talking to the locals."

"How do you know that? How do you even know about the *gambling thing*? That was confidential information we received recently."

Davey looked at Rock as if he were from Mars. Not only that, he walked closer to his desk, wondering what made the young agent so knowledgeable in the ongoing case practically overnight.

"We just do," replied Rock, pausing to look at Davey. In no time, he was back to the keyboard, pounding away.

"WE? What is this, I'm not a part of the *Operation Cardshark* now? They put you on it?" yelled Davey. Now, he was staring at Rock like an upset parent.

The brawn, bald presence of Rock stopped what he was doing and stood up as if the seat had water on it. "Davey, I'm not saying that. You know how badly Martinez wants to take down McCool," he told him, extending his hand out.

It was too late. Something wasn't adding up here. He felt like he was being pushed onto the case and Rock was being pushed towards it. He needed to speak with Martinez at once!

Meanwhile, outside of Skinny's Lounge, a restless McCool was on the hunt. There was no stopping him. The dark look in his eyes slid over to the sign at the entrance door: *closed*. He banged hard on the glass, demanding for entry.

Four guys in blue jumpsuits all rushed to the front. One of them opened the door nearly an inch wide, begging the question, "Can I help you?" Without saying any words, McCool gave his answer. He grabbed the door, pulling it open forcefully, inviting himself in.

"Where is Caz?" he yelled, looking on either side of where he was standing.

"He is by the bar," said one of the blue jumpsuits, pointing towards the back. All four remained standing in front of McCool, staring at him as if he were the schoolyard bully.

He forced himself through the pack, on his way to the bar. "Relax, relax…we are just the clean-up crew. We don't want any trouble!" One of the guys even showed Jack a bottle of Pine-Sol Lemon Fresh in their one hand while another held a mop in both. They slowly inched away from him in perfect unison. All had their hands up in the air, assuring they were not going to stand in his way.

He proceeded along, looking around the club before he approached its owner. Caz sat, hunched over in his stool, chain-smoking cigarettes until the bar around him looked like foggy London. It appeared he had more on his mind than McCool did.

"Where the fuck have you been?" asked Jack, walking swiftly over to Caz who was attached to his stool. Immobile. Jack was in no mood to be discreet with anybody. His intense stare told it all. He didn't recognize himself when he looked in the mirror behind the bar, where liquor bottles sat on the shelf below.

"I messaged you the other night…you never got back to me," replied Caz, taking another drag of his umpteenth cigarette. He looked away from McCool quickly, glancing over at the same mirror in front of him. He wasn't able to look at himself in it long either.

"No you didn't," noted Jack.

"Yes, I did."

Instead of continuing to go back and forth, Black got right to it. He didn't have much time to waste, and he was in desperate need of a counterstrike strategy before it was too late.

"Listen, Caz…I need your help here."

Putting out his short into the ashtray on the bar, the skinny one blew out a final cloud of smoke above. He then looked directly over into Jack's eyes, solidifying the fact he was ready to hear whatever he had to say next.

The Irishman went on. "My house was shot down last night. My front window that the couch is in front of, bullets came pouring through like a hailstorm. Nina and I were sitting right there," he filled him in.

Caz did not respond right away. Both elbows were planted on the bar. He grabbed his pack of Marlboro reds and took out the last one. Immediately, he lit up once more while Jack continued.

"Luckily, her son was in the other room. Nobody was hurt. Still…this ain't good, Caz. I'm fuckin' livid."

"I know," replied Caz, closing his eyes, scratching the side of his face vigorously. *Puff, puff, puff.* He couldn't stop.

Jack looked to Caz, demanding, "Whoever did this, I want them gone...smoked!" Finally, he sat down on the stool beside him. He stared straight ahead, folding his hands and continuing to play 'guess the shooter' in his head. Desmond Carter was the only one he could think of. He was convinced.

All of a sudden, he heard a sniffle to his right...then a long exhale. There was a long, somber series of panting that followed. He looked over his shoulder and couldn't believe what he was seeing.

Profusely, Caz was crying. The tears burst forth like water from a dam, spilling down his face. Confused at first, Jack turned towards him and put his hand on his back.

"Caz, what the fuck is wrong with you?" he asked, trying to figure out what was happening with his friend. He was bewildered as one could be.

Caz looked over and stared back at Jack while his eyes remained pouring. He shook his head sideways. Jack removed his hand from Caz's back. It was then he knew who planned the attack. He couldn't believe it.

"You miserable son of a bitch," he said to him. He was in total shock. He didn't know what to do or say next. He felt the life being sucked out of him.

"Fuckin' Vinny...he gave the order. I just brokered it. I tried to stop it at the last minute...but the wheels were already in motion. That's why I messaged you to call me from an outside line, I wanted to tell you to not be in your house that night!"

It was a text Jack never received. He looked down, shaking his head. This was absurd. While he was trying to figure out why he'd be betrayed by Caz, the answers were already pouring from the skinny one's mouth. "I have to tell you something else," he said to him, shaking while he said it.

With his fists clenched tight, Black remained silent. He sat still in his seat, eager to hear what was ahead.

"Vinny never planned on keeping you around long. He knew from the beginning, the first time we went to see him at the jail. He knew we'd all join in on the initial hit on Paulie and The Connor Brothers. He only disagreed with you to distance himself."

Jack was revolted. His insides curled up. He kept his gaze off him. He couldn't bear to look his way. If they had made eye contact, he thought he might vomit.

"He was getting in your head that day! He was using you, kid. He wanted to use you for your manpower to bring down those guys…then get you close to Lou only for you to bring him down too. That's why I was so miserable the night we met," Caz went on. "After that, Vinny was going to have you killed. It was his plan all along."

Jack took a deep breath and brought his head up for a moment. He didn't know whether to shut Caz up or to hear him continue. The sickness inside was spreading as the skinny one's story went on.

"From there, me and the boys were to run the show." Caz put out his last cigarette, his hand trembling while doing so. He wasn't sure if it would be the final one for the night...or for good.

"It went too far though, Jackie. The Caribbean Connection...Carmine dead, Tony in jail. Vinny's plan went to shit!"

Caz took a gulp in-between his confession. After a few breaths, he went on. "Plus, I got too close to you. I got to know you. From there, I knew I couldn't whack ya out myself."

Having felt like he heard enough, Jack stood up from his seat. Leaning in, he got closer to coming face to face with Caz. "No...you just had others do your dirty work for you, you miserable fuck!"

"They weren't my people, Black. After Vinny learned there was no chance of you taking Lou out on your own, he simply gave me the names and numbers to call. It was as if he did it himself."

"Bullshit!"

"I didn't want this to happen!"

Caz then felt his throat close in like a vice by the hand of the raging McCool. The fire in his eyes was burning. Quickly, he let him go once Caz stopped gasping for air.

BAM! Jack gave him a punch in the nose. "You cocksucker!" he yelled. BOOM! BOOM! Right hook, left swing.

"Those sons of bitches came after not only me...but my girlfriend...and her son! Are you fucking crazy?" yelled Jack. Caz was on the floor, continuing to cry and beg Jack to understand.

"YOU FUCK!"

"Jack, please!!! I'm sorry. I was a coward. I should've never made the call initially. I'm a fuckin' idiot!"

Jack kicked him in the stomach, hoping to knock some sense into the guy. "Vinny wants me dead? Fine! Kill me on the streets…kill me at Lou's…kill me here! But to go after my family? At my home? A fuckin' disgrace you are…you and that rotten fuck!"

Jack grabbed him by the shirt and held his back against the bar. He then pulled out his Springfield XD, shoving it right into his mouth like he was feeding it to him. Enough was enough!

"How many were there shooting at my house? How many, Caz?" he yelled, shoving the gun deeper into his mouth.

A voice from the opposite wall of the club then echoed, answering for him, "Four!" Before Jack could even think of a response, the yell was followed by gunshots, spraying in the direction of McCool.

The rapid-fire continued coming at him. PING! POW! BOOM! The bullets were breaking apart the mirror behind the bar and the bottles below it. Releasing Caz, Jack ducked down as soon as he heard the shots. He then got on all fours and began crawling over to behind the bar as quickly as he could.

The four blue jumpsuits from the entrance continued blasting away as McCool took cover. He scuttled behind the bar. He waited until the shots stopped firing, making sure the Springfield was loaded and ready to respond.

He listened for just the right moment of silence. Walking on his knees, Jack came out from his shelter. When it was time, he stood up. He began blazing gunfire back in their direction. He locked in on each one of the blue jumpsuits, shooting them each before they even saw it coming. One, two, three, four.

"Clean *that* mess up with your Pine-Sol, cocksuckers!!" he yelled, doing a double-take just to make sure none of them were breathing.

McCool made it look easy. Although, there was nobody to see it. The four lifeless jumpsuits were the only bodies in the room.

Holding his gun in front of him, he looked around the entire club for Caz. Every corner, every booth. He was nowhere to be found.

CHAPTER TWENTY-EIGHT

A landmark building. A world-renowned collection on its walls. A place that welcomed everyone. Known for its elegant events that hosted only the most formal citizens, the Philadelphia Museum of Art was in the midst of holding its most notable function yet.

The annual "Spirit of Philly: Hospital, Non-Profit and Charity Award Banquet" was off to a good start. The city's most celebrated medical workers, volunteers, and philanthropists were all being recognized on this night for their hard work and contributions the past year in their respective areas.

Groups arrived by the dozen. They all sported expensive tuxedos and ball gowns. Greetings were offered out along a rolled-out carpet stretching the length of the historical museum steps. From afar, the surplus of colors made it look like a Kaleidoscope.

Various photographers fought through the crowds, trying their best to capture the most graceful moments of the evening to be the first to give all a glimpse into the night's magic.

Many knew they belonged at this event. Then again, there were those who knew they didn't. For starters…Jerome, Desmond's top guy, parked a block away. If anyone was out of place within a hundred yards of the vicinity, it was him.

A sweet melody of small talk and business conversations drifted through the busy atmosphere, carrying its way inside. Starting through the double doors, moving past check-in and towards the coat room. Finally, making it to the main ballroom.

Jack McCool, one of the night's premier award winners, examined his watch every thirty seconds. He stood in the foyer by the blue ballroom entrance just as dinner was being served inside. Knowing the great turncoat, Caz still lurked the streets out there somewhere made him antsier than ever. Additionally, one of his two guests for the evening had not arrived yet. He was getting the feeling he was being stood up.

It was the same waiting feeling he had the night of their very first date at the steakhouse. The uncertainty…the anticipation…the hands on the clock moving faster than ever. His heart started to keep in rhythm. It was all too familiar.

However, Jack reminded himself good things come to those who wait. So, he remained patient. He paced back and forth while the champagne waiters cautiously passed by cackling women. They were all apparently on glass number three, positioning themselves at critical angles in their group walks.

In another corner, exchanges of gifts were made between one aristocrat and another - bottles of Rose in return for crystal dishware…both of which would be lost to the hawk-eyed scroungers of the party.

A collection of violinists, harp players and pianists were placed at the far end of the hall. All of a sudden, Jack could identify the smells of lavender soaring through the air. It wasn't just the incense placed at various intervals around the museum earlier that day, it was the smell of his second guest finally making her arrival...the love of his life.

Yards away, Nina stood, idle, for a few seconds, checking in with the ceremony staff. As the music came to a brief pause, she was approached by the mile-wide smile of the Irishman who invited her.

Given it was many weeks after the shooting at his house, Jack was looking to make Nina feel safe again in any way possible. He hadn't seen her since the night it happened.

"Hi," he said, taking a deep breath before he did so. Smiling back, she muddled the same, "hi," with a quick glance at the commotion behind him. She then tucked her hair behind her ear, looking away. Her gestures suggested she felt forced to be there. She wasn't comfortable in her surroundings.

The way these two were acting as if they were a boy and girl at a fifth-grade dance. Neither one of them knew what to say next. "Thank you for coming. You look gorgeous," commented Jack. She smiled again in reply.

Jack was in a black tuxedo while Nina was in a long, sparkling silver dress. Her hair was curled to perfection, soft around her face.

"Is everything okay? You haven't been answering my calls, babe," he then inquired.

Suddenly, the smile vanished from her face. "Are you kidding me?" she snapped. Several folks in the hallway looked towards the two. She lowered her voice a bit. "Why don't you start by telling me what the *fuck* is going on with you?"

"I have *tried* explaining, Nina, but you won't answer me when I reach out to you."

"Here I am…tonight, just for you. Or wait, am I in the line of fire at this place too? Are we going to get shot?" she asked, sarcastically. Jack pleaded with her to keep it down. She huffed and puffed, beginning to walk towards the ballroom entrance.

"Nina, hold on!" he yelled, grabbing her arm before she got too far away. "Now, I know you don't feel safe with me. But, if you come over tonight after this…I can explain everything."

"Are you kidding? I'm not going over to your place! I wasn't even going to come here tonight. I came to support you winning this award and to get some answers. So, give me the decency right now and tell me what is going on with you. Are you still in danger?" she demanded, her green eyes widened and as severe as ever.

McCool looked around where he was standing. How could he tell her everything about his life that led up to the shooting in five minutes? In the midst of these people around him? Seconds away from being called to stage? To spill the beans to her all at once…reveal his darkest secrets? Here went nothing.

Jack took a deep breath, closed his eyes and grabbed both of her hands, holding her tightly. "I can tell you this," he began. His sentence was finished for him. From behind his back, he felt a hand on his shoulder. "I can tell you, young lady, that you have not yet met Lou Gorgeous," said the voice. There he was, the second guest on McCool's list...the enigmatic don, out of the shadows and into the light.

The gorgeous one smiled while Nina remained still. She was speechless. These two had never been in the same room together...until now.

She wore a fake smile to hide how she really felt about Lou. His grin was making her even more uncomfortable. "It's a pleasure, dear," smoothly commented the charming Sicilian. He came closer to Nina, took her hand and kissed it on the top.

"My pleasure as well," she replied, tilting her head and still smiling yet wanting to vomit all over his thousand dollar suit. Perhaps it was his smooth voice that didn't make her feel safe...or the way he raised his one eyebrow in a snake-like fashion. She just didn't trust him.

"What was your full name again, my darling?" he asked her, coming a bit closer.

She paused, looking at Jack before replying. "Nina Constancia,"

"Ah. Nina Constancia, Beautiful name," he responded, breathing in and out, loud and winded as if he was inhaling her.

Closing his eyes, he walked over and put his arm around Jack. When he opened his eyes, he continued to stare at Nina. He wasn't sure what to make of her either. He couldn't tell if he was intimidated...or infatuated.

"Forgive me, Nina...I don't make many public appearances. This is a rarity for me," continued Lou. She gave a brief laugh out of courtesy but didn't say anything back. "What do you drink, love?" he asked.

"Mojito," she replied.

Lou then requested, "Listen, we are all sitting at the same table, Nina. Why don't you go have a seat, they'll get you a Mojito. Let me speak with Jackie Boy here a second?" as he pointed to the entrance.

Jack nodded his head, assuring he'd be right over. She then scurried away towards the ballroom. She did not want to be around any more than he wanted her there.

Jack and Lou then walked away, heading over to a deep, dark corner of the museum foyer. They wanted to be far from anyone nosy enough to listen to them. Cheers and applauds continued to erupt inside the ballroom.

"You alright?" asked Lou. Jack replied, "I guess. She still doesn't seem to feel safe around me after the shooting."

"She's a woman, Jackie…they're excitable."

"I guess."

Lou chuckled, continuing to keep his arm around Jack, telling him, "Good ass though, I'll give her that." He chuckled, patting him on the back. He took Jack's silent smiling as agreeance.

"Nothing from Caz?" asked Lou.

"No. And you?"

"Nothing. Listen…more importantly, I looked at the bags of cash this week from the Caribbean. Not good. Want to explain?"

Jack didn't quite know what to say at first. It was a shift of conversation he wasn't expecting, especially on what was supposed to be his special night. Touchy topic too. "Business is light. Trust me, I'm worried as well, Lou."

"I feel it's more than that," responded the gorgeous one, raising his eyebrow again.

"What do you want me to tell you?"

"What I need to hear, not what I want to hear."

That was when Jack heard his name be announced in the midst of the audience's applause. He was receiving the honor of the *Citizen's Award for Outstanding Volunteer in a Private Philadelphia Hospital.*

"We will continue this later. You better get on stage, Hollywood," Lou told him, winking one eye and walking away and towards the tables. Jack adjusted his bow tie, shot out his cuffs from his shirt and hustled over to the stage to receive his award.

Outside, Jerome was sitting still in his car a block away, waiting for the right moment to charge inside the museum as a "last minute guest." He called Desmond on his cell as he waited. "Hello?"

"Yo. Are they there, Jerome?"

"Yup. McCool, Muchetta…both in the flesh."

"I see 'em! Watching on TV. Go to work, J!"

While Desmond sat at home, watching the ceremony on television, others were doing the same. Agent Martinez was also keeping an eye on the evening's events from the comfort of his couch.

Back at the museum, Black was reveling in glory. "You ain't seen nothing yet, Tim Bryce…we are going to save this hospital for generations to come!" Jack said to the hospital CFO, sitting a table he passed on his way to the stage.

"I was wrong about you, kid. You're on the path to greatness here," replied Tim Bryce, coming up to hug Jack and to tell him how proud he was.

Once he made it to the stage, Jack arranged the microphone on the podium a few times until it looked right to make his speech. After that, he sent many thanks to those who supported him, first and foremost. He looked around the room at all who gathered. He watched Nina and Lou at the same table...on opposite ends.

"I grew up in this city. My parents passed away when I was very young. I didn't have anything...not a home, not a family, not a vision. It wasn't til' I was adopted and taken under strong supervision of Saint Isaac's Children Hospital at the age of five. They brought me in. They gave me guidance...direction. They didn't treat me like a patient without insurance. They treated me like family!"

Applause erupted for the first time during Jack's speech. Jerome remained in his car, shining his Glock, getting ready to make a grand entrance.

"There were and are still many hospitals in the city and the areas surrounding...some of the best. As a matter of fact, the finest in the world."

Lou kept looking at Nina as Jack continued speaking. She could almost feel the hole he was burning into her head. He was observing her every move; the way she fixed her hair, the way she'd eat.

"However, when you and your family come to SICH, you experience a different feel. The staff has

class, charm, and a sense of warmth. These are things you don't find anywhere else."

Dr. Dan and Bryce were never more fulfilled. They looked around the room, grateful to know a man like Jack McCool.

"With the way this country is and the state we are in with the Medicare crisis, the insurance companies robbing away...it's nice to know that whoever you are and wherever you're from, you always have a room at SICH! No outsiders!"

It was almost that time. Jerome put the bullets into the gun, ready to come in heavy. Meanwhile, Agent Martinez texted Rock to begin the process of looking into auditing SICH's donation receipts with the team in the morning...and to expedite it.

"And that is why the planning board, the finance committee and the nonstop generosity of the volunteers share my vision in giving the care that this city needs and deserves!!!"

Waiters scurried around the floor, collecting plates of the uneaten cookies and lemon bar desserts. Guests at the tables were oblivious.

"We will keep SICH open!! This is only the beginning. I thank you all...this was absolutely a team effort!! Let's continue to drive forward!!!! It's up to us to be the change!!"

While Desmond watched McCool from his television, his anger was hotter than ever...like water boiling over a stove. He couldn't take it anymore.

"That being said, we are creating a new scholarship going into the New Year! It is going to be for inner-city kids the hospital supports looking to

go to college. Not only are we going to keep this place open...but we're going to give back as well."

Jerome stepped out of his car. He took a deep breath and started to walk towards the museum.

"The scholarship will be in the name of a recently passed young man involved in a horrific tragedy. His memory lives on as the spirit of the hospital. Not only was this kid a giver of fine words in his short life...but he gave from the heart as well. He had a magical way to him, expressed by his family and by his peers!"

At this moment, Agent Martinez practically stopped watching the ceremony while Desmond was on the edge of his seat, unable to take his eyes off it.

"The Nathan Carter Scholarship Award will be implanted this coming spring!"

Desmond closed his eyes. He couldn't believe it. Was he really throwing his son's name out there like that? Unreal. Putzing around to take his mind off the TV program, he took another look at the unopened mail on his coffee table in front of him.

"God bless you all!!!" concluded McCool.

The celebration went on into the night. By the end, everyone was dancing as if they'd forgotten how to stand still. Many faces burst with excitement.

"Things will only get better from here on out," Jack said to Nina after making a ton of introductions to her after his speech. Still, she acted aloof. Her head down, simply nodding...no words spoken.

Outside, Jerome was walking up the museum steps. Continuing to check his side to make sure the piece was still there, ready to unleash is wrath on who had it coming. The chill in the air was a reminder that he needed to bring the heat inside.

All of a sudden, his phone went off. It was Desmond again. "What up, D? I'm about to do this, baby…you good?"

"Call it off, man…call it the fuck off."

"Why? What the hell you talkin' about, man?"

"Turn around and get the fuck out of there. We aren't doin' this tonight, J. Not like this!"

"C'mon, man…you can't be serious."

That was when Jerome turned around, looking back at his car in distraught. Did he really make it halfway up the steps only to turn around and forget the mission at hand?

"Nah, Desmond, I ain't turnin' back now. I gotta settle this! For your son and for my brother!"

Just as he took the phone from his ear, he searched the screen for the red button to end the call. At the same time, he pulled out his piece.

He climbed a few more steps before he came face to face with another gun, similar to his…Umberto's. "Where you think you're going?" asked Lou's top guy, cocked back and ready to squeeze. Jerome's jaw practically dropped to the step in front of him.

Desmond hung up the phone just as he heard the voice on the other line in front of Jerome. He proceeded to prepare in departing his residence. He wasn't taken any chances. He grabbed the one letter he was glad he opened from the mail pile on his way out…the notice that all Nathan's medical bills were fully paid off. Signed, with love, *Jack McCool*.

CHAPTER TWENTY-NINE

Tony Boy was anything but comfortable in a Federal penitentiary. To him, it was all too familiar…the cold bars of the cell, the screaming sounds into the night, the taste of the lousy food they served. He had just been there less than a year prior.

There was nothing to hear in his prison chambers but the sound of his own breathing, escaping his lungs. At times, he'd flick the iron bars with his fingernail, just to hear something different, to make a tune. He would look forward to the rare occasions when all prisoners could join in the courtyard. It was there, many were able to convene in various conversations.

Tony would have this thing he'd do, not talking to any of the others. Usually, he wouldn't say anything, not even make a sound. He'd just stand in a far corner in silence, occasionally turn his head to see if it was time to go back inside. He'd lean himself and his orange jumpsuit against the chain-linked fence, his hands behind his back. Sometimes, a frown tugged at his face. He preferred it this way, it is how he got by. But one afternoon, he couldn't help himself. He had a guest.

It was the first time he had seen Vinny during his stint. The beat-down, weathered senior walked his way, limping as if he needed a cane. "Vincenzo! It's about time I come face-to-face with you in here!" greeted Tony as the little one staggered closer. He pushed himself off the fence to welcome him.

"You know how it goes in the can. We can all get lost in the midst of losing ourselves!" Vinny replied, coming close enough to Tony to whisper.

"Well, I'm just glad to find you here in the courtyard, Vinny."

"After what I did in Fairton, boy…they had to make sure I wasn't clinically insane. They held me up most the year, but they're acclimating me back to normalcy now. It's good to see you, Tone," said a coughing, gasping Vinny, trying to catch his breath. Tony replied, "You too," with a bit of concern as he studied Vinny's decline by the minute.

It was then, at the same time, these two both noticed Pretty Paulie from afar, fraternizing with other prisoners by the dumbbell weights. Contrary to Vinny's weakened state, the pretty one was active.

"That fuckin' piece of shit," commented Vinny.

"I'm with ya. Every time I pass him in the hallways or out here in the courtyard, I think of stabbing him with whatever object is close by," replied a furious Tony Boy, crossing his arms.

Vinny laughed, telling him, "Hah! At this point, they'd give me the chair if I pulled a stunt like that." After that, he let out a violent wheeze before he continued, with his hand over his mouth. "But, I don't give a fuck anymore. What's right is right!"

Tony looked at him, grasping the old man's shoulder. "I gotta say…I'm looking forward to getting out of here soon."

"I know. That's why I wanted to see ya, kid."

"What's on your mind?"

"You already know!"

Tony chuckled, replying, "Let me guess…the pretty one, the gorgeous one, who else?" Vinny was silent for a few seconds. He then cleared his throat of a large flood of mucus which he spit loudly to the grass. "That two-timing cocksuckin' bastard of an Irishman," he finally uttered.

"McCool? I thought he was being handled?"

"Don't you keep up with the times since you got in? He actually went into business with Lou instead of wiping him out like I asked."

Tony shook his head sideways. He then said, "That little fuck. What's Caz doin' about it?"

"Nothing! I thought he had it under control. But, he let me down. The little Black Irish prick is still breathing!" *Cough, cough, HACK!* "He's no good, Tone…this McCool." Again, he spit.

"You know I never liked him. He disrespected ya, Vin. Not that we were ever going to let him live anyway, but still."

"It doesn't matter…it's all fucked up over there now," detailed Tony, huffing and puffing, kicking the ground.

Vinny was quick with his response. "The fuckin' kid still has to go….I want you on it!" Tony hesitated. It took him a few tries, but he finally got it out of his mouth. "Vin, I don't know." He chewed the inside of his cheek, mulling it over.

"What don't ya know? Him and that snaky fuckin Lou. They're both a disgrace," Vinny went on, continuing to keep his eyes on Paulie from afar. He was still a social butterfly.

Tony's silence thickened while the little one continued. "And I'll handle this asshole in front of us at some point!" Vinny's eyes widened, his face was scarlet red. He was no longer coughing and hacking his lungs up. He simply stood restive like a hungry bear, ready to attack anything that displeased him.

"I'll always be loyal to you as my don, Vin...you know that. But, I got out of here the first time with the intent of starting over...ya know, retirement?" hinted Tony, admitting he wanted no parts of killing anyone once released.

As his skin turned more vermillion, Vinny yelled to Tony, "There's no retiring from this, Tony, you took an oath. Duty always calls! This needs to be done. It should've been done right the first time. He's caused multiple problems! He's the fuckin' reason you're back in here."

It was then Vinny made his strongest point yet.

"Most importantly, Tony...he's not one of us. He's not Italian. In the end...how can you trust a guy who doesn't bleed the same as you? Do it for Carmine...for Primo...for Chrissy!!!"

Without warning, Vinny fell to the ground, panting before Tony Boy could respond. He held his hands on his chest the whole way down. Screaming for help, Tony called for all prisoners and guards around the helpless old man. All the while, Pretty Paulie never flinched, watching from a distance, grinning wide as his eyes were glowing. All he kept thinking was, "Vinny's end was near."

CHAPTER THIRTY

It had been a long few days. I never shook so many hands and kissed that many babies in such a short time. Yet, I was proud of my recognition for receiving the volunteering accolade. So were plenty others. Needless to say, I had been exhausted since the night of the award ceremony. So, when Lou called me in to meet him at his auto garage at the end of the week, I was anything but enthusiastic about it. Though on the phone, he said it would be a subtle visit.

However, as soon as I came flying down the flight of stairs leading to the basement, Lou's office was far from subtle. There was an abundance of Brooklyn muscle he called in from the Commission. Wiseguys I had never seen before. They stood like robots in assembly lines around seven-by-three-foot long wooden tables. They were counting mountains of cash on top of the tables, vigorously placing dollar bills into small stacks.

At his desk, Lou was opening up empty duffel bags, handing them off to Umberto to distribute among the groups. I had never seen Lou like this. He looked disturbed as if he were preparing for the rapture. "Did ya have a good time the other night?" I asked, scratching my chin at the counting process, trying my best to initiate conversation.

"Yes," he replied quickly and in a monotone pitch. He swiftly handed me the key to my house I lent him. "My guy went in, Jackie. Your window is fixed, everything is bulletproof and secure. Quit staying at the Holiday Inn already, would ya?"

That was a relief. It was nice to know he had the connections to turn my place into Fort Knox…just in case another shooting incident would arise. "And don't worry, I made a duplicate for myself. You'll have painters come in this coming week to touch up some of the work the contractors didn't make pretty and nice-like." Before I had the chance to thank him for all that he did, he proceeded to hand me two duffel bags, heavy as a ton of bricks.

"Here…I need you take these and store them somewhere," Lou instructed. He went back to fluffing up bags on his desk, refusing to tell me what was happening.

I then followed him, walking around. Unable to determine where to start, I opened my mouth to let out a constant, "umm." Just as I collected my thoughts, he gave the answer to the question I was about to ask.

"Word from my Federal connect on the inside is that the bulls are looking into your bookies down the shore, they're trying to see what they will tell them about a *certain* operation."

"You're shittin' me," I gasped, eyes wide open.

I couldn't believe it. The Caribbean Connection had a leak in it? How could such a thing happen when I was so meticulous about my process?

"You think I'd fuck with you on this, boy?" asked Lou. I was speechless. "Though it explains why we're seeing less money lately," he continued.

I stared at the two bags of cash in my hands, trying to think of the best place to keep them. Right as I was going to inquire about the future of the operation, Lou beat me to the punch.

"I don't know how or when they are making their move yet. So, we're pulling out of the entire thing as of this morning to be safe...collecting whatever is left and allocating to the right places. Now, get out of here and keep this money safe. When I need it, I'll call you. This is in case shit goes down...it's for both of us."

I didn't like the feel of this situation. It was all so sudden. I began to speak my peace. "Lou...I don't think that's...," before he interrupted me.

"Also, about Caz...," he began. I was all ears, keen on what he had to say next. "Nothing. Nobody can find him," he continued. "But you can be certain that when we do, he will pay the ultimate price."

I nodded my head as I started to walk away slowly. Umberto was trotting back and forth between Lou's desk and the long tables, slightly bumping into me each time he'd pass.

Meanwhile, Lou went on. "Caz may not be our only concern. Let's just say Umberto had to do some damage control the other night outside the museum."

"What? How so?" I inquired, looking at both Lou and Umberto. I had no idea what or who he was referring to. The whole thing was puzzling.

"Never mind that for now…get those bags somewhere safe, Jackie. Your house, your basement…wherever."

I responded with a slight bit of topic change. "Well, Nina was delighted to meet you, Lou," I told him, obviously lying.

He grinned in a spine-chilling way, crooked and mischievous. "I bet she was. Nina *Constancia*, right? Did I say that right?" He was pushing it. I didn't like his uncanny tone when it came to her.

How many times did he need to hear her name? It was getting annoying…and creepy. I simply nodded my head in return, trying to walk away once more. Instead, Lou stopped what he was doing and walked up to me to get in close range.

"Do yourself a favor with that piece of cooz, eh…fuck her a few more times, then dump her. Trust me." Again, I was speechless. It didn't stop him.

"From there…you're better off cumming into a tissue than trying to keep a relationship."

I shook my head sideways, reminding him he was wrong. What Nina and I had was something special, more than he could have ever understood. He didn't appreciate the same views I did; family, future. He yelled as I turned towards the staircase, "I've told ya. C'mon. Love makes what we do financially unfeasible. It's a drain to our fortune."

"Lou…she *is* my fortune," I replied on my way out. The last thing I could see as I made the turn was Lou quickly pulling Umberto aside in a fishy manner. It was as if he was putting him on another critical task. It was very odd.

I didn't care. Once I got to the parking lot, I made it safely into my car after tossing the duffel bags into the trunk. Looking around before I did so, I took a glimpse of the only thing on my mind that mattered above all...the sparkling three-carat diamond ring I had just purchased for a special someone. It had been in my possession for weeks. It was ready to come out and shine brightly!

It took some begging and pleading, but I was finally able to secure a night with Nina and Andrew that weekend. She wasn't too keen on coming to my place just yet, which I understood....neither was I, even with the restoration. Upon her request, I came over to hang out at her parents' house back in the old neighborhood. It felt like the beginning when we first met, very nostalgic.

I spent some quality time with the two of them. The later it got, we all began to wind down. Andrew fell asleep on top of both of us on the couch in her living room. Nina was fading into the wee hours after telling me how eerie she felt Lou was. As exhausting as he was to discuss, I was wide awake!

"Want to watch a movie?" she asked, following an extended yawn. I figured the Bruce Springsteen album I had playing on my phone had been on repeat for too long. *Ohh, ohhhhhh, ohhh...I'm on fire.*

"Nah, I'll probably just call it tonight," I said, staring straight ahead. My thoughts were racing a mile a minute.

"What?" she asked, taken back for a second.

"I'm just tired, ya know?" *But, I really wasn't.*

"You're never tired, McCool." *She was right.*

"Tonight, I am." I kept it brief. I had a lot on my mind. It wasn't my intention to be so distant. Yet, she could sense something was wrong.

With Caz on the loose and the Caribbean Connection coming to an end, I didn't know where to turn. Plus, I had the ultimate question to ask her. I needed to make it all come together somehow.

"Oh...now look who is being stand-offish!" she commented, calling me out on my own words to her, many times. I certainly couldn't spill it all out to her. In fact, not even a smidgen. I remained silent.

"Come on, tell me a story," she pleaded.

"About what, Nina? The summer I was a male stripper?" I admitted. True story.

All of a sudden, she perked up. Her mouth flew wide open. She almost woke Andrew up, lying across us, quiet as a church mouse. "Get out of here!" she gasped, love-smacking me on the arm.

"Well, half a summer," I noted.

"You're messing with me."

"I needed the extra cash, ya know? It was after I came home overseas before I got into working AC and the card game in the northeast with Fitz."

She rolled her eyes. "Jack...c'mon. Tell me something else...tell me about these overseas days." Now, she was digging. That was a no-fly-zone for me. She knew I never liked talking about my military experience.

"Don't go there!" I demanded.

"You never tell me anything, McCool. Why are you being like this?"

"There's a limit here, Nina."

"Fine, tell me about work then."

"Hah! I'd rather talk about the War."

"Alright…tell me what really happened."

I gave in. I figured it was time. If I was going to ask her to marry me, she might as well know the truth about my past. I took a deep breath. The story about those nights haunted me for long enough. This, at least, I could try to get off my chest.

"The shit I saw over there in that fuckin' desert, Nina…no person should ever see. I remember it like it was yesterday. Every grueling moment. Everyone I witnessed die in front of me, it made me sick, especially innocent women and children. We tried so hard to save them. I couldn't stomach it. I felt like I was lookin' for a way out the minute I got there."

She readjusted her position on the sofa, doing her best not to wake Andrew. I continued my saga. I took my time, making sure she experienced the full account with every bit of detail.

"There was this prick lieutenant we reported to, a real yuppie…ya know, your typical West Point kind of kid. 'Baxter' or something was his name. He was always on my ass about something. The abuse he delivered to me, and the many who I served with…it was more than what we deserved. Anyway, he knew my roots back home. Although he didn't know me personally, he did know where I grew up and who I was associated with. He never liked my kind…he thought I was a thug. I mean, I was…but I never did anything bad to him! There was this one time, he made us sleep outside the fort., shoulder to shoulder during a potential sandstorm. There were recent attacks too. It was all dangerous as shit. We could've gotten wiped out...but, he didn't give a fuck!! That's the kind of guy he was...like the first half of Full Metal Jacket, except worse. So, I couldn't take it anymore! I had to get out of there! I was on patrol one night at a checkpoint with another one of my fellow troops. It was dark, windy...real ugly out. I'll never forget the sky of the wilderness either...arid, dry. There were these jingle trucks that pulled up, really colorful. They were decorated with these elaborate floral patterns and calligraphy on the sides. We pulled them over for inspection. Anyway, it turned out that they were two truckloads full of heroin, black...in its rawest form. I'm left to guard the trucks with some Afghan troops en route to Kabul. On the way, one truck breaks away, and the troops let it *disappear*...if you know what I mean?"

"Was it you?" she asked.

"Yes. I saw an opportunity present itself. The kid I was with, we made a deal with the Afghans. We made an excuse as to why we let them go later on. At first, it was just too easy."

"So, then what happened?"

"The shit bag lieutenant found out. He was on me right away once he got the news. He got to the kid who was with me, he spilled all the beans under pressure. Lieutenant threatened to court-martial me."

"Then what?"

"So while I was pending the court-martial, I kept up with my duties at the base. One night, our unit gets ambushed...full-on. It was some the goriest shit I'd ever seen. I'll spare details! Lieutenant turns tail and runs...I was the only who saw him do so."

"Where did he go?"

"I found him hiding in a mud hut, the next day. Fuckin' guy shit and pissed his pants, sitting in the fetal position like he was waiting for his mommy."

"Oh my God, Jack. That's terrible."

"So, I turn, and I walk away. Later on, though, I find out some of the troops I'm with took video with their phones showing the shit-ridden, coward lieutenant. The boys fought for me before my trial and told the lieutenant, 'you drop this bullshit, and we don't tell the world you shit your pants. You keep your perfect little West Point golden boy image.' So, he did. Lieutenant decided he had his facts wrong. I was given an honorable, early discharge due to 'PTSD related' issues. I came home, and that was that. Next thing I knew, I was in with Fitzy, started counting cards in AC before I got in on the exec game...then jail...rest is history."

"Wow. Did you ever second-guess any of it?"

"I mean, I felt bad about what I did...but at the time, I was just looking out for me, ya know."

It was as if I just got over a cold. I never told anyone that story. Once I did, something came out of me. It was a feeling of relief, opening up. Yet now, I gave Nina a full glimpse into my criminal background...moments before I was about to pop the question. I wasn't sure how she'd take it all.

"You've seen so much," she commented, appearing aghast. "Nothing like seeing you, dear," I replied, leaning in to kiss her softly. It was the first time we did so in many weeks. Though, something wasn't right. She didn't have the same warmth in her return. *Did my stories really get to her?*

"Tell me more about the card counting and exec games with Fitzy," she pried. I shook my head sideways. "C'mon. Tell me about Lou. Tell me what you got goin' on now," she continued, aggressively.

"How about I just show ya something?" I asked her, kissing her again. Still, nothing...no spark. It was as if she was over me. It was like kissing a fish.

She yawned as I stood up from the couch, doing my best not to wake Andrew as I rose. It was now or never. I had to make a move and make this right.

I ran upstairs quickly, silently as I could. In my gym bag in the bedroom, there it was. It was right next to the blue sea glass Nina found for me on the beach last summer. It's most precious...the diamond engagement ring. It was now or never. I had to ask her...she was the one! I could not lose her...even if it meant changing my ways! A fresh start!

When I rushed down the flight of stairs, I came to the bottom and looked at the sofa. Nina was passed out! Cold! Immobile. It just wouldn't have felt right to wake her. I let out an exhale of defeat.

"Another time," I told myself, second-guessing, I even pulled the ring out once more from my pocket to look at it on my way back up the steps, thinking of when would be a better time to do this.

CHAPTER THIRTY-ONE

The boardroom in SICH was cool, calm and collective the beginning of that following week. Jack, on the other hand, was hot as a pistol and ready to shoot his financial guns anywhere they would blaze fire. The planning committee gave him a statement he was not happy to hear.

Tim Bryce, CFO, was the bearer of the sad news that morning, removing his glasses and fumbling with a stack of balance sheets at the head of the conference table. "Jack, we are still short going into the end of the year. I'm sorry...it's not looking good for Q1. We did our best. You, my friend...you did amazing this entire time."

It was a shot to the heart for all. Everyone remained silent...including Jack, sitting directly next to Bryce at the long, mahogany table. The query for many was what to do next once the hospital would close. However, for Mr. McCool, he had a different question. He wasn't ready to throw in the towel.

The Chief of Finance continued on, giving the Irishman proper tribute for his efforts. "I was wrong about you in the beginning. For that, I am sorry," commented Bryce. It took a lot for him to apologize. It was quite the gesture coming from him.

"It was a hell of a run," he continued, extending his hand out to shake. Instead, the only thing Jack shook was his head sideways.

"I'm not done yet, Bryce! I appreciate it. I respect you too…but I think we can keep going!" The whole room gasped. They couldn't believe the tenacity of this kid.

"Jack, nearly three million extra on top of what's expected this month is due. It's just not attainable, I don't care *who* you are."

Then again, perhaps Bryce didn't know everything like he claimed to have. Immediately, Jack thought of the duffel bags Lou gave him down in his cellar. He tried to guess how much was in the bags by the weight in which he carried it. Either way, he figured it would be enough.

Sure, they were meant to be for a rainy day. However, these were different kinds of weather patterns he was dealing with in the boardroom.

"I can find the money," admitted Black.

Bryce looked around the room. He then whispered to him that it was more than just that. "Jack, we have another problem," he admitted.

"What is it?" asked Jack, leaning over, whispering at the same volume. Bryce then asked the room to clear out so he could speak with McCool alone. What he had to say next was for his ears only.

After it was just the two of them, Bryce kept at it. "The FBI contacted us this week. They wanted to see statements."

"Did you show them?" asked Jack.

"I didn't have a choice. They came in here like they owned the place."

Jack stood up in distress. It was if his world was cracking. He was in fear that it was soon to be crumbling. Staring into the abyss, he didn't know how to pull away from it. "What the fuck?" he asked, both to Bryce and to himself. Jack grabbed fistfuls of his own hair in frustration.

"It has me scared a bit," admitted the CFO.

"So, what happened? What did they do?"

"Nothing. They didn't see what they were looking for."

"Fuck em' then, Bryce…I'm getting that money for you," said McCool, pointing at Bryce, standing up from his chair.

"Jack, please."

"Give me until the end of the week to figure it out! We're not giving up…not yet!"

Jack then stormed out of the conference room. He didn't say goodbye to anybody on his way out. He was on a mission!

Sitting in his office, Agent Martinez kept staring at his watch, eager to get home. It was long past seven o'clock on a Monday evening. Not that he minded staying late, but he knew the person he was waiting on was intentionally keeping him there, out of spite. Frustrated, he began impatiently tapping his fingers on his desk.

Just as Jay was looking outside his office, Agent Rock passed by on his way to clock out for the day. "Can I get anything else done for you before I leave, sir?" he asked, peeking in through the open doorway, doing his best to kiss up to his boss.

Martinez smiled in return, shaking his head sideways and sliding back in his swivel chair. He then put both hands behind his head. "Just keep an eye on that fuckin' Agent Davey, Rock...would ya? He seems a little high strung with me these days." He then winked at him.

Chuckling, Rock knocked twice on the wall next to him, assuring to Jay he knew what he was implying and that he was on the mission. Coincidentally, Davey was walking by in the hallway just after the comment was said. With that, Rock was out. The scowl Davey wore towards Rock made it clear he wasn't happy. Although, Rock wasn't sure if it was because he was in a bad mood or because he had just heard what Martinez said. Perhaps it was both. Either way, he went in the direction of where Davey had just come from.

Davey didn't even look into Jay's office when he passed his doorway. He kept it moving, quickly. He had things to do as well. It was checkout time, and his agenda entailed other things on it besides touching base with his 'so-called' partner, who barely seemed like a co-worker these days.

During his exit, a beautiful young lady came walking towards him in the hallway. Although he recognized her, Davey evidently did not make it known. He looked down to the ground as she walked past him.

There were plenty of women who worked for the Bureau...but none like this girl. The way she walked, wearing glasses and a business suit was the perfect combination of sexy and sophisticated.

Everyone loved it when she made it to HQ, which was rare.

She found herself in Martinez's office, appearing to look even more upset with him than Davey was. Yet, differently…for various reasons.

Once her presence was known, he was far from delighted himself. Before his opening line, he pointed to his watch, looking directly at her. "Where the fuck have you been?" he questioned. She kept silent. Hesitant, she sat down in the chair, facing his desk.

The puzzling expression on this girl's face was one he had never seen before. She stared at him as if they met once and she forgot his name. Although, it was quite the opposite. These two were extremely familiar with one another.

Trying to snap her out of her mystified look, "Michelle?" Jay asked, with inflection. He was tired of this *Nina Constancia* alias she was living by. It was time for him to get a return on her undercover investment.

"I don't want to talk about it," replied Nina…or rather, *Michelle*. Instead, her watery eyes fogged up the glasses she had on. Instantly, she removed them to wipe the tears that came falling down her face.

"Agent Lesandi…I am tired of you going MIA and resurfacing like this out of nowhere. You work for the Federal Bureau and for *me*. You are currently destroying this case."

"I don't care anymore, Jay!" she exclaimed. Anyone who was on the same floor with them would have heard her outburst. Realizing she needed to stay professional, she did her best to keep her composure. So, she took a deep breath and lowered her volume.

"This isn't for me anymore," sighed Michelle.

Perturbed, Jay stood up in a rage, flinging whatever was in front of him on his desk; pens, papers, folders. He was tired of her attitude the past twelve-plus months. She was neglecting her duties as an agent lately.

"So, the entire undercover mission means nothing now? You're just going to throw your career away? More than a year's worth of work hangin' in bars and getting close to McCool to ultimately penetrate what's left of the Philadelphia organized crime element?" he interrogated, making his way closer to her. "For what, McCool...FOR LOVE?!?!?" he continued, now screaming in her face. You could tell Jay was taking it personally. Yet, it was almost too harsh for Michelle to hear.

"Don't act surprised. I have told you numerous times before today...I can't stomach it. I need to come clean to him," she admitted, still crying in-between every sentence.

"Yes, you do. And you need to make the arrest personally!" instructed Jay.

Michelle's eyes widened. It was as if he told her there was a ghost in the room. "What? That wasn't a part of the deal!" she stammered.

Jay was adamant about wrapping this up. He didn't care about any deal with an agent who reported directly to him. "It's time. We need to get him in and link him to Lou Muchetta to the online gambling racket and put Operation Cardshark to bed! You need to make it happen! You have dinner with him this week, right? First time at the house since the shooting?" he asked.

"There isn't even enough evidence to make an arrest."

Scurrying over to his desk drawer, Jay grabbed a manila folder inside it. He then tossed it onto Michelle's lap. He told her, "We have the recorded lines hooked up to his cell phone."

"Nothing of use was said," she replied, tossing it back to him like a hot potato.

"Enough was said to use in court, Lesandi. With the testimony from the bookies and your word on being there on the forefront in Atlantic City, we can get him convicted and begin a RICO trial."

Michelle then stood up, fixing her business suit, admitting, "I won't say shit." Jay cackled back. "That's okay, the money coming into the hospital says enough," he responded.

"That was all volunteer donated, every penny. I got the memo on the audit we did this morning…I guess you didn't."

He was stunned. Historically, this was a girl who took no crap and knocked every case she ever worked, out of the park. She was one of the greatest undercover agents in the history of the office. This was a first for Jay to see…her so smitten for this Irish gangster and so far gone from the initial reason they assigned her to the project.

"What happened to you, Lesandi? You were so gung-ho about this in the beginning."

Michelle then turned her head to the side, replying softly, "I just...," before interrupted by Agent Martinez.

"You fell in love. That's what just happened!" he bolted in, finishing her sentence for her. She did not finish. They both knew he was right. Silently, Jay walked back to his desk, taking off his watch and throwing it on the bookshelf behind him.

Michelle's eyes continued to drip with tears. She sat back down in her seat. Her inner walls that held her resilient for so long continued to collapse. Moment by moment, they fell.

Finally, Jay changed his tone. He rubbed his eyes with his hands, telling her what was going on behind the scenes, "The director is breathing down my neck. I have to make this stick in order to...,"

This time, she interrupted. "In order to what? Get your promotion to DC?" Jay didn't know what to say back. They both knew that was true too. Finding her strength, Nina went on. "This is the same shit you've been talkin' about for years, Jay. This is more than that now, and you know it! You saw I fell for McCool and...," she preached, raising her voice every other word.

Jay cut her off. He rose from his chair, rolling it back to hit the wall on his way up. He pointed his finger at her. "That's enough!!! You have twenty-four hours, Lesandi! Lure him in at that dinner you have at his place. We will be close by!" he assured, with both hands on his desk, leaning towards Michelle.

Although, she still was not hearing him out. "This is ridiculous. I will leave the department then. I want no parts of this takedown!"

"Oh yeah?"

"I'll even tell him everything. We will flee this city together!"

Jay then began laughing so hard, he fell back into his chair. He maliciously responded to her little threat. "That's fine, Lesandi. You will be fired for insubordination. Then, when we find you…you'll be taken into custody with him for being an accomplice to his criminal activities."

It didn't seem to faze Michelle. Back on her feet, she headed towards the door. Just when she thought she'd cut away from the department and call it a career, Jay said the one thing that made her stop. "And your kid will go into foster care!"

She turned back around. Now, he was playing dirty. "If you think I can't make that happen, just fuckin' try me!" Jay told her, raising the pot.

It was an ultimatum she had no other choice in deciding on. She'd do anything for her son. There was no denying that.

"So…you need to decide. It's him or your kid, Lesandi."

Suddenly, Jay tried to play Mr. Nice Guy. He walked up to her and put his arm around her back. "You get too emotional, Michelle…too involved. It's clear to me now why it didn't work out between us years ago!"

She then whipped her head around, ripped his arm off her back and responded, "Fuck you! It didn't work out because you were a prick, Jay! You'll do anything to get ahead!"

"I was great to you and Andrew. It was the first time he had a father figure!"

"Please! You're a workaholic! And a fucking asshole!"

It had been years since they spoke like this. Even when they dated, it never escalated this seriously. The breakup was somewhat civil. Although now, the stakes were higher than ever. Old wounds were opening up with more pain than before.

"He calls himself a man?" he whispered. "What kind of a man puts you in danger where you can't even feel safe on his couch because you might get shot at?"

Michelle scolded him then turned away. Jay reassured the mission at hand before she left. "Rein McCool in…either way, we will have squads there at 8:00 PM tomorrow coming into his house to take him ourselves if we have to!"

She put her head down and began walking out of Martinez's office. Before she was all the way out, Jay had one more important detail to throw in. "Oh, and Lesandi…just so you don't give him any ideas…I want you wired up til' it's done!"

CHAPTER THIRTY-TWO

Arriving on time for once was Michelle...or rather, *Nina,* in the eyes of Jack. She had the weight of the world on her shoulders when she walked through the front door of McCool's home. The load wasn't getting any lighter after his welcoming. Jack's smile lit up the room following her entrance.

How could she possibly tell him this awful secret she'd been hiding from him their whole relationship? The reason she was who she was with her behavior – aloof, reserved, protective. It was the mere explanation of her entire demeanor.

Not only that, how was she supposed to utter the four hardest words she'd ever say to the one she loved? "You are under arrest." It was making her sick to her stomach simply thinking about it.

It was quarter after seven. Jack was tremendously busy in the kitchen, rapidly bouncing from one side of it to the other. He had a big, white chef hat on along with a tacky checkered apron around his waist that read with big letters, "kiss the chef" in the center of it. If she couldn't tell, he was excited to put this occasion together.

Staring at the diamond ring he was hiding for later and preparing the ultimate feast had consumed the majority of Jack's day. This was a dinner he did not want his special lady to ever forget.

"There she is! How are you, dear?" welcomed Jack, hugging Nina tightly and giving her a swift peck on the lips before beginning taking her hand, racing back to the stove.

Nina followed his direction, gently replying, "Doing well, and you?" The sick feeling in the pit of her engulfed most of her senses. She looked at the clock by his staircase, knowing the next forty-five minutes would feel like five.

"Great!" he yelled. He was deliriously giddy. After clarifying with Nina that her parents were okay watching Andrew until late in the evening, he led her through his hallway, into his kitchen and over to the table to walk her through the delectable menu.

He took his position by the oven before explaining. "Okay…there are three courses tonight. My special garden salad. Mixed to accompany it, my homemade vinaigrette dressing. Although, I know you don't like that…so, I got you regular Italian dressing. Then, chicken parm for the main…just the way you like it with a side of rigatoni pasta."

She forced a smile. In a typical setting, her mouth would be watering, waiting to inhale each piece of fantastic food he put together…but this was far from the typical situation. Jack, however, was oblivious. "And then, for the *piece de la resistance*, Tiramisu dessert…*that*, I didn't cook."

"Sounds wonderful," she told him. Gradually, Nina sat down in her seat at the table. Glancing at the setup Jack arranged in front of her, she became more enamored with him, finding it even harder to continue on with the night.

A vase of roses next to a lemon bowl centerpiece, two lit candles, and the most elegant crystal ware and China…she did not feel worthy.

"Start you off with a Mojito?" asked Jack, getting the rum, limes, and mint together by the cutting board.

"Yes, please." She needed to take the edge off. She rested her elbows on the table, folding her hands and placing her chin on top of them. Finally, Jack could sense something was wrong. Nina was far from being talkative. He could barely get her to smirk. "What's the matter?" he asked.

"Nothing. Just a long day at the office."

Noticing the top to his fresh Bacardi Silver bottle came off a bit too *easy*, Jack knew he had to make Nina's Mojito *hard*. She looked like she had a day that put her through the hell. He wanted her to unwind and give her a little piece of heaven.

"Well, tell me about it. I want to know every detail," he continued before making his way over to the fridge to grab a few ice cubes.

Instead, she grabbed her napkin in front of her and unfolded it to place on top of her lap. "Let's just eat, Jack. Come on…tell me about your day. How's the hospital?"

"No, no…I want to know why you're wearing that puss on your face. I know you too well, honey."

She looked down, twiddling her thumbs. When that didn't take enough of the pressure off, she began peeling the paint off her fingernails. "It's not that easy to explain," whispered Nina. She couldn't look him in the eye.

"The numbers were wrong in the accounts payable department? People didn't get paid? What was it?" joked Jack. He put the finishing touches into her drink and walked it to her, removing his chef hat.

"Nina?" he asked. She accepted the glass from him, took a small sip and then placed it on the table. Still, she was remaining silent.

Fussing with her blue button-down shirt, the wire she had taped to her stomach was anything but comfortable between clothing and skin. Not just for her...but those listening. Every time she fidgeted with it, static erupted on the headphones of the several agents tuning in. *Frikkkk, frakkk!*

"I'll be right back, I have to go to the restroom," she said to Jack.

He couldn't figure it out. He was losing her...in more ways than he even realized. Jack looked into his pocket and pulled out the ring. "Real nice," he said to himself, both about the diamond and sarcastically about the way Nina was acting. He knew the answer to her enigma was close by...he was just unsure of where to start searching. The way Lou Gorgeous was calling his cell phone back-to-back, he knew he wasn't going to find it with him.

During Nina's breakdown, Agent Rock set himself up on watch duty across the street from the front of the McCool household. Listening to her every peep along with Martinez and a few others nearby, he could hear the awkwardness cultivate by the second.

"Rock, you have a good view of the house?" radioed in Martinez, not far from the scene. It was approximately 7:32 PM.

"Both cars in sight. The two of them are still inside," replied Rock, grabbing his handheld portable. "Over and out," he ended it.

That was when the agents heard sobbing cries on the radio. Nina was in Jack's bathroom, unable to look at herself in the mirror. She simply sat on the toilet, fully clothed. She couldn't get her mind right. She knew she wouldn't be able to go through with the plan.

Was she really going to wait until 8:00 when Jay and his crew would suit up and come in for a raid? Even then, what was next? Jail for the both of them? Jack never trusting her again? What did it mean for Andrew? Could she really believe Jay? Would her kid go into custody? Her brain was racing…so much, it was starting to spin out of control.

After the last set of tears fell down, Nina fixed her mascara, looking in the mirror, taking a deep breath. With a long exhale, she almost threw up in Jack's sink. Her nerves were creeping up and twisting around inside like a pretzel. All of a sudden, she had another plan…one that involved *true stealth*.

She unbuttoned her shirt. Like ripping off a Band-Aid, she yanked the wire off her stomach, tossing it into the bathroom toilet and began flushing away!

SHHHHKKKKK!! SHHHKKKK! The signal shorted out. "What's going on there, Rock?" asked

Jay on the radio. They went from hearing Michelle's sadness…to nothing. White noise.

"I don't know. The batteries are dead, or she canned the wire. Either way, still no movement," stated Rock.

"Okay, hang tight…hang tight," he said. Jay then looked to his crew that surrounded him. He began signaling them to gear up. He told the boys to get their equipment ready. By the sounds of things, they were going to have to move the plan up.

Nina came rushing out of the bathroom just as Jack started placing food on the table. He greeted her return with a smile while she responded with panicked eyes. The clock was ticking.

"We need to get out of here!" she yelled, running over to her Mojito, chugging it to gather some liquid strength. She slammed the glass down hard, exclaiming her announcement.

"What the fuck's going on?" asked Jack, plate in hand. The drink was catching up to her. Unaware of how strong it was, Nina's face curled, gulping down the last bit of rum. She looked like she had been sucking on a piece of Warheads candy.

"Anywhere, Jack…please. Let's just go! I'll tell you on the way! Let's go out the back though."

Jack looked at his front door then back to his girl. "Nina…sit down, please. You're scaring me." He stopped her before she ran over to the foyer to get her purse. He sat her back down.

"I…I….I. We can't go out the front, that's all," said Nina, antsy to leave that very second.

"Calm down. Just talk to me…what is it?"

"I need to tell you something, Jack."

Eagerly listening, Jack reminded her that she was able to tell him anything. He continued gathering food to put on the table.

She opened her mouth. Then, couldn't close it. It was the strangest thing. She stood there, soundless…motionless. It was as if she lost her breath. Jack kept looking at her, anticipating some kind of response in any way. He was getting nothing. She appeared to be choking.

"Rock, do you see anything?"

"No, Jay…I don't know what's going on."

"Fuck it. The crew and I are coming early.

"Want me to go in?"

"Not until we get there, Rock."

Nina's mouth remained frozen, wide open. Her eyes were begging for help in any way. The feeble silence was the scariest part of witnessing. Whatever the blockage was in her throat became so airtight that she couldn't cough, shout or even splutter.

She wrapped her hands around her own neck, unsure of what was going on. McCool dropped the food he was holding, shattering the plate to pieces on the floor as he rushed over to help Nina. He began smacking her back vigorously. *Whack! Whack! Whack!*

Nothing was helping. Not a single thing. He was starting to panic, looking around the room for an answer. "Nina, oh my God...Nina!!!!!" he yelled, continuing to slap her back. Still nothing!

It was then she tumbled out of her chair and onto the floor. A frantic Jack got on top of her and attempted his best version of the Heimlich, the way he learned it when he was in the Army. Yet, it only seemed like he was making matters worse.

As Nina slowly turned her head up towards McCool, he noticed her face change to a deep shade of rosy red. Her eyes were bulging and watery.

Jack was now frantic. He had never felt so desperate. He tried again to help her breathe...and again, it seemed impossible. He grabbed fistfuls of his hair out of frustration, trying to keep his composure and think of what to do next.

Nina's arms and legs started moving in a frenetic, almost involuntary way one had never seen before. Blood began pouring out from her nose as if a faucet inside had just been turned on. It wouldn't stop. Her eyes were now bloodshot in every direction.

McCool then remained frozen himself. He was frightened. He was thinking of everything and nothing all at the same time. His eyes grew even wider in shock. This was a situation so grueling and sudden, he wished it wasn't real.

Without wasting any more time to try and mitigate the situation himself, Jack rushed to his cell phone resting on the counter to dial 9-1-1. *Ring, ring, call failed. Ring, ring, call failed.* This kept repeating. Over and over. The dials he was making weren't going through. He looked at his phone in disarray. "This makes no sense," he said to himself. Not only that, McCool was getting constant, incoming calls from Lou at the same time. If only the gorgeous one knew what the kid was dealing with.

End call. He went back, jumbling through his screen and tried 9-1-1....again, again and again. Nothing! It was as if the phone was manipulated with prior.

Just as he was about to rush out the front door and yell for whatever neighbor would be outside to help, he finally heard Nina utter a loud wheeze. She was heaving, spitting up all over herself. It looked like watery oatmeal coming out from her mouth. He darted over to her aid and answered the next incoming call from Lou. He figured he'd ask him to call an ambulance...right away!!

"Lou?" asked Jack, picking up the phone, panicking as his voice began cracking with his cries. He looked down at Nina. Her face was now a dark purple, much like a plum.

"Jackie, you alright?" asked Lou, sounding worried.

"Lou...I don't know what is going on...I need your help, please!!" replied McCool, supporting Nina on the floor. With each word he spoke, he wiped a new drop of sweat off his forehead. "I'm trying to dial 9-1-1," he continued.

Although Lou sounded calm, it was no help in soothing Jack. "Take it easy. Talk to me, buddy. Slow down. What's wrong?"

He took a few deep breaths. "It's Nina…she's on the floor. She's choking right now…I don't know what to do. My phone isn't working right. Can you get an ambulance over here?"

"Are you serious? That's terrible," Lou replied, controlling the situation.

"Lou, help me…I got nobody. Please!! Call 9-1-1 for me!!!!" Jack then yelled frantically.

He paused for a moment as he looked over to Nina. He didn't hear anything from her again.

"What's the matter, she have too strong a Mojito?" questioned the gorgeous one, finally raising his voice from the other line.

"Huh?" Jack was confused. He stopped walking and looked at his phone.

"Is she having spasms yet?" asked Lou.

Jack then glanced back over to Nina. To Lou's narration, she *was* having spasms. It looked like a scene from *The Exorcist*. She began to vomit, except it wasn't pea-soup green…it was scarlet red. She was throwing up her own blood, buckets of it.

"Yeah…but…what? Lou? How the fuck do you know this?" asked Jack, looking around the house as if Lou was watching from one of the corners.

"Yeah, she's done. I told you she was no good, kid. To hell with her!" said Lou.

Gasping her final breath, Nina locked eyes with Jack once more, picking her head up off the ground with the last bit of strength she had left. Seconds after that, her head fell back to the ground quickly. She was dead.

"You...what? What the fuck is happening?????
YOU DID THIS!!!! YOU FUCKIN' SCUMBAG!!!!
YOU'RE FUCKING DONE!!!! WHERE ARE
YOU??" screamed Jack, putting his free hand on his
face. He could not watch a second longer.

"The only scumbag is the one lying dead on
your living room floor."

It made no sense at all to Jack. Not only was his
world crashing down, but it had also practically
ended right there on his floor. McCool began
hyperventilating, trying to control his breathing so he
could hear all Lou's answers.

"She was a Federal agent, Jack. I don't know
how you didn't fuckin' see it before."

"What?" he asked. He looked back at Nina.
This was way too much to handle. His body was
now involuntarily shaking. Unable to figure out what
to do with the tornado of emotions he was feeling,
Jack merely walked around his first floor in circles
while Lou continued talking on the other line.

"Yet, that's what happens when the penis takes
over the mind...the pussy clouds our judgment. It
makes ya blind."

"Lou...no!! Why? WHY??" McCool cried out,
bursting into tears. He fell to his knees, barely
keeping the phone to his ear.

"She was going to arrest you tonight. Whatever
they have on us over there, they're running with it."

"No...no...it can't be."

"Her real name is not *Nina Constancia*, you
stupid fuck...it's Michelle Lesandi, Special Agent,
FBI."

McCool nearly dropped the phone, he was so shocked. It was as if he never knew the girl at all. Then again, Lou was one heck of a manipulator. Was it really true? Jack proceeded to ask how he would know such classified information.

"I told you that I had people on the inside, Jackie. I conducted multiple layers of research on your girl. My instincts kicked in after meeting her at the ceremony and hearing the way you talked about her the other day when I handed you the duffel bags...I felt it had to be done. None of it made sense, she looked too familiar. Low and behold, I'm glad I did what I did."

"I can't fuckin' believe any of this," responded Jack. His trembling overwhelmed his breathing.

"When I fully investigated her, I got the whole scoop on her life beyond those pretty little legs of hers. I just wish I caught it earlier, I mean she *was* in the picture of the Terry Green body discovery in the river...I'm mad at myself too. However, I would've fuckin' killed ya both long before they'd have a chance to do what they're doing now!"

"You piece of shit. I'll find you and fucking kill you!!!" screamed Jack. Not only was he furious, he wished he paid more attention to the photos Lou showed him back when they were revealed.

"Not once you hear what I have to say, you won't."

In that very moment, Jack broke down to his knees, mourning Nina. He was motionless, wanting to simply die with her.

"I would've gone to prison for her, Lou. I would've done anything for her! This didn't need to happen!"

"I know you would've. You're young, dumb...I figured this. But, I would've gone down with you as well for the Caribbean Connection. And I'm not letting that happen."

"FUCK YOU, LOU!!"

"Plus, I wouldn't have gotten what I wanted first."

"You ain't gettin' shit from me, you two-face fuck! I'm callin' the Feds right now myself to get to the bottom of this." Jack ran towards his front door. He noticed a strange black Chrysler, unmarked sitting across his street.

"That, you also cannot do," Lou told him. Jack came to a screeching halt, curious to hear why not. "I've set up your phone to where this is the last fuckin' call you'll get. You can't make any outgoing dials, not even to 9-1-1 as you've already realized. Nobody can hear us. There are devices I've planted in your house, blocking anyone from listening. Unless, of course, your girlie corpse is wearing a wire. Even if so, I imagine she hadn't kept it on, or your place would be swarming with Feds by now."

"How the fuck?"

"Good question. I had your phone tampered with earlier while you were sleeping. Additionally, I poisoned your Tequila...I knew she would be thirsty. I did it to the Italian dressing I know she liked as well...just in case that didn't do the trick. Thanks for lending me the key. You just made it too easy, sweetheart."

"Cocksucker!!" Rage boiled deep in Jack's system, as hot as lava. It churned within, hungry for destruction.

"The clock is ticking. They're suiting up for a raid with or without her making the arrest to you. Your house will be bombarded soon with the entire department, I am sure of it. From what I've learned, they're watching you now!" instructed Lou, smiling as sinister as he could. It was as if he was taking pleasure in this entire madness.

Indeed, Martinez and his fleet were on their way. Agent Rock continued to sit in his car, ready and willing to come into the house and take down McCool if he had to. Whatever it took to impress his boss.

"Rock, what's happening?" radioed Martinez.

"Nothing still, Jay. Can't hear anything either."

"I'm coming with the team, we're loading up! When you see our trucks pull in…come out and be ready to fire! Unless he comes out, take him down yourself…her too if ya gotta."

"Copy that!!"

"You're not getting away with this, Lou!" screamed McCool.

"Actually, I am."

"I'm going down, Lou, I'm taking the heat…for everything, I don't care. And bringing you with me when I do!!!"

"I figured you'd say all that. You go through with that, your dead cunt of a girlfriend's precious little Andrew next to me...I'll rip his fuckin' throat out and shove it up his ass, you shit bag!"

Next to Lou, the tied-up nine-year-old, gasping for air spoke up above the tears that covered his face. "Jack, help me...please!!" he sobbed.

Jack's world turned into a blur, and so did all the sounds. The touch. The smell. His balance. Everything was gone. Everything darkened into nothingness. He was dealing with real evil. Now, he was locked in. He had to play Lou's game.

The gorgeous one went on with his details. "If only Little Miss Agent's parents put up a better fight. Don't worry, they're still breathing. They complied, alive and well. But, they are searching for their grandson....they don't want to find him fucking DEAD!! Nor do you. Nor do the Feds. I'll make sure the blood is on your hands along with the death of his mother's."

"You're a psycho!"

"You bring that two million in cash to me to the Delaware River docks tomorrow at 7 PM...or you and your little buddy here will be sleeping on the bottom of the river next to it. I know it ain't at your house because I searched high and low. Had you kept it there I suggested, this could've been avoided."

Jack shook his head sideways. He couldn't believe the mess he was in. Not only him but Andrew as well.

"How am I supposed to leave here if they're watching my house?"

"You better go out your back door. Do it and do it now. It's a quarter to eight, but I guarantee the Feds are already on their way. They ain't waiting too long for ya."

"You miserable bastard...how could you do this?"

"Have my money at the docks, and I'll have your kid. Or Jackie...the things I'll do to precious little Andrew, man, it'll make what I did to Carmine...what I did to Frankie...and what I did to his cunt rat of a mother look like a walk in the park!"

It's like someone took a knife, edgy and dull and cut a six-inch valley through the middle of his skull.

Jack threw his phone at the wall. The feeling was an unstoppable knot in the pit of his stomach. He couldn't concentrate. As his heart continued to pound faster and faster, sweat started to pour all over his body. He began pacing around irrationally. He flipped the kitchen table upside down. Glasses, plates and whatever else shattered in its tumble. He threw a few random things in the room at the wall before punching a few holes into it.

He had to think, and he had to do it quickly. A little boy's life was on the line. The stakes have literally never been higher for him. He was all in on a hand he was unsure of.

In his car, Rock began to panic after hearing the mess McCool was making. "I heard something, Jay!

Sounds like things being thrown in the house. Lots of glass-breaking noises. Still nothing out front though."

"Rock, go check the back of the house. We're minutes away, trying to get through traffic!"

Getting out of the car, Rock packed his heat. His bulletproof vest that said FBI on the back wasn't slowing him down. He trotted down the yard. When he got to the rear of the McCool house, he saw the door was open. He let Jay know on the radio.

"Rock, go inside. Go now!" instructed the boss.

Rock made it up and into the house, gun in front of him. He saw nobody. All he saw was wreckage. There were food and liquid stains splattered next to punched holes in the wall. Smashed glass, scattered lemons, fallen roses, and other types of jagged debris covered the ground. What was left of a broken phone laid on the edge of the floor. However, the most horrific sight of all was the lack of consideration for Michelle's bloody, swollen, dead body.

Agent Rock stood in awe. His eyes widened. His knees, violently shaking, buckled as he hovered over the loss. As he reached for his radio, his hands trembled. He raised his voice to let his boss know he was in the midst of true devastation. "Code blue, Jay...CODE BLUE!! McCool killed her. He killed Agent Lesandi!"

Part Four

White Noise

CHAPTER THIRTY-THREE

Excruciating. I didn't think my heart could continue to ache worse as the minutes went on. This was a pain I was not familiar with at all…a kind of pain I never knew existed.

Although I was aware I'd never return to my house, there would always be a part of me left there after my escape. It was the part that refused to let Nina go, the piece of me that needed our bond to extend past a mortal life together. I still didn't want to believe Lou's accusations could have been true.

I didn't sleep a wink. I remained stationary in the kneeler of the last pew in my church that next morning. It was the only place I felt safe during a time like this. Looking down at my folded hands, I began reciting what could have been my final prayer. I looked up to the statue of our Lord on the cross at the front of the church. I felt myself dying slowly much like The Almighty did when he was crucified.

Tears continued to fall down my face. I wanted to curl up and rot away. I did not want to witness life go on. How could it when my world had already crumbled, and my life was already over?

Yet, I had no choice. I had to keep going…for Andrew. I had to save him. I stood up, knelt at the end of the aisle while I blessed myself on my stride towards the altar. I could not waste another minute. Time was not on my side. This madness had to end.

I jumped over the pulpit step and trotted to the tabernacle along the center of the wall. Carefully, I opened the small door that led me to the wine chalice and Eucharist tray. Behind the two sacred items, a key...that of which unlocked the cabinet beneath. Voilà! There they were...the duffel bags of money I was hiding for Lou.

Time to go!

Without thinking, I grabbed the bags and made my way back down the aisle as quickly as I could. I was racing to get out of the church and to never look back once I did. However, it was when I made it halfway, I could hear a recognizable voice behind me, telling me to halt.

It was His Holiness...the Chaplain...Monsignor O'Brien, prepared to lecture me. He walked at the only pace he knew, slow and steady. Yet he still wore the big smile he was known best for.

Although I could've used some of his wise advice, I simply had no time. Nor did I want to listen. Out of respect, I stopped to hear him out. The old man came and stood next to me like a father would to their son.

He reached out for my cheeks and spoke. "Find your faith...find it for whatever you are looking to do, my son." I was speechless.

With my mouth wide open, I had intentions to lend him my voice. Instead, I was filled with evil. Too many terrible things happening around me were barricading me from having the chance to feel fulfilled...let alone, have any faith. "Look within yourself to find God," he continued.

But there was no God in me at that moment. There was only a lost, broken soul...the place that harbored the secrets that never left my lips.

Again, I stared straight ahead at the cross for a few seconds before turning back to O'Brien. I patted him on the shoulder, thanking him for letting me take refuge under his roof, in times of distress like these. I attempted to walk away, remaining speechless in beginning my departure.

"Whatever you are looking to do...don't do it alone!" he yelled to me.

I stopped dead in my tracks. Turning around with ease, I was curious to see what Monsignor meant by his statement. Before I had the chance to ask him to elaborate, something behind him caught my attention even more...and it wasn't the stained glass on the wall.

Swiftly, I dropped the duffel bags to the ground. My sadness turned into fury. My face was fiery red, and my blood was hot at boiling temperatures. The person coming down the aisle behind O'Brien was one I hated just as much as Lou Gorgeous.

"Caz? You got some fuckin' balls coming here, you piece of shit!" I screamed, pacing towards the no-good bastard. My eyes were bulging and my fists were clenched, ready to connect with his face. Monsignor put himself in my path, holding me back. He began telling me not to curse within the church walls.

"Monsignor, why is this traitor here?" I interrogated.

"John, please!"

"Get him out of here! I want him gone!"

"Just hear him out, John…come on! Give him a chance!"

All I kept listening to were the voices in my head, giving me different ideas on how to kill him. He should've stayed in hiding like a coward. Whatever made him think he was safe talking to me in my church had me believing he was more brainless than I thought.

Monsignor kept holding me back. I knew I could push him away quickly. However, I was trying to be respectful. I put my hand on his shoulder once more and kindly asked him to move. "O'Brien, I'll kill him. I swear to the cross I'll put a bullet in him right in your church here!"

"JOHN!!! LISTEN TO ME!!!!" he screamed powerfully, slapping me in the face hard enough to send me looking the other way.

The old man still had some muscle to him. I felt it! I held my cheek in shock. I didn't quite know where to go from there.

"I've told him your situation, John. Listen to the man," he instructed, pointing his finger in my face. Allowing Caz to come up to me, I figured I would give him half a minute.

The closer he got, the angrier I felt. For this was a man who squealed away the very second I had a gun to his head.

"The prodigal shithead! What makes you come back to me now? What changed, asshole?" I inquired.

It didn't take much to sense how ashamed he was to be in my presence. He had guilt and embarrassment dripping out of his pores.

"I was sorry to hear about the girl," he began.

I remained silent. The things he was sorry about meant very little to me. I had more important things on my mind.

"Whatever she was...Fed, not a Fed, it doesn't matter," he continued. "It's a disgrace. To kill a woman. It's not what *this thing of ours* represents at all. Lou Muchetta goes against every principle we stand for. The man has no limits."

"Neither do you," I replied.

"Jack, I don't want to argue with you. I've crossed multiple lines. For that, I am deeply sorry even though I know you could never forgive me."

"So then...what is it you want, Caz? What will make you happy enough to leave me alone?"

"Let me join you this one last time to take this guy down with you. We need to bring justice! He's out of control."

I shook my head sideways. I certainly wasn't buying it. "What is it, Caz? Did that scumbag in prison get a hold of you and tell you what to do again? Did he tell you to come here today...to see me?" I scoffed.

"I'm here on my own, Jack...not on Vinny's accord. He won't even speak to me anymore. The man is about to die anyway. Believe in me...Tony Boy and I are in your corner now, kid. I've spoken with him. He's getting out this week. We agree...nothing else matters anymore."

Hah! I didn't believe him one bit...especially the part about Tony Boy, being released within the next few days from the same prison building that Vinny was in. How could I trust such terms?

Nonetheless, Caz kept talking. "We ain't doin' this for Vinny now. This is for me...and for you." Again, I tried to turn around and leave.

"For the kid," he went on. I spun my head around and looked at him, admitting, "The kid's life is all that matters to me now. That's why I'm doin' it Lou's way. I'm not doin' what you're implying here, Caz."

"It's the only way now, Jack. There's no way he can be trusted, especially with your little boy's life. You know that. Come on!"

Caz kept coming closer to me. His hands were folded in front of him. Hat in hand, he continued apologizing to me.

"Let me make things right with you."

Again, I turned to O'Brien. He always told that pride came before the fall. For so many years, I heard him but never listened.

"Let's wipe this dirtbag off the God damn planet...together! And get the kid back, safe and sound!" Caz concluded.

I kept contemplating. Yet, I was in-between a rock and a hard place. Considering this was the ultimate time I needed whatever assistance came my way, I gave in. I had no other options. I decided to put the past behind me and let bygones be bygones.

"Marine terminal Port by the Walt at Dusk…7 PM. He's expecting me! Come blazing…because I'll be frisked clean, for sure," I instructed.

The skinny smiled one ear to ear, telling me, "I'll make a stop…then I'll see you there."

He opened his arms, looking for a hug. However, I didn't even want to shake his hand. Not just yet! I didn't know what I was getting into bringing Caz back in my corner. All I could do now was hope I wasn't going to regret it.

Mistakes happen, awful things might occur in one's life. This is for certain. Yet, I tried something new for this venture that was ahead. I tried looking at the brighter sides of things. At least I had somebody with me for it.

I looked back to Caz and said loud enough for O'Brien to hear me, "We take this cocksucker tonight!" Grabbing both duffel bags tightly on my way, the church bells rang, just striking noon. This told me I only had so long. Seven o'clock would be here before we knew it. I said one last prayer before I went out the door.

CHAPTER THIRTY-FOUR

It was late and rainy that afternoon. Caz was going to pull out all the stops in preparation for the night. This was a matter he wasn't taking casually in the least bit. Neither was McCool. Lou went too far this time, and they both knew it. The record had to be made even, once and for all. It was now or never.

That being the case, he wasn't going to arrive at the marina without coming there ready to shoot it down. In his basement, he had every firearm known to man to choose from. He called it his "finishing closet." It was used only to get the biggest of jobs done.

One key opened it. Very few knew about it. Rarely was it ever unfastened. Black steel cages encased some of his most valuable possessions.

Assortments of different types of pistols, revolvers, submachine guns, rifles, carbines, shotguns, and hand grenades held high and mighty on a massive armory rack that stretched far across one of his basement walls. It almost covered the entire thing. Extra clips and magazines for each weapon were lined up like soldiers.

If there was ever a significant battle to prepare for, Caz was the guy you wanted to go into the trenches with. You couldn't go wrong with his deadly selection.

Looking around, he picked up each one of the armaments carefully. He was very meticulous with what his choices would be. Thinking about the night and all possible outcomes, he wanted to make sure he showed up with the appropriate arms. Mistakes were not an option at this point.

He came out of his house with more metal on him than a Green Beret. Two Colt Python revolvers resided on each side of his belt. He placed a Smith and Wesson Model 686 behind his waistband and a 38 in his ankle holster.

Lastly, for the main act, a Norinco Type 84S assault rifle was placed carefully in the trunk of his Cadillac. This was one of his prized pieces. Smuggled in from his connects over in China, it was the last gun he purchased before he went away to prison in the 90's. That being said, it was only used once…for target practice. Tonight would be the first time its blazing hot barrage would meet flesh.

Caz shut the trunk door and looked around once more, just to be sure he didn't spot anyone in the neighborhood staring at him strut around like the walking pack of ammunition he was, ready to fire at a moment's notice.

Just as he was about to open up his car door, he paused for a moment and stared down the block. He pulled the black hood on his coat over his head. Something wasn't right.

Pellets of rainwater were bombarding up from the puddles in the street. They were firing in all different directions like lightning.

The breath of the rapid winds aerated a little stronger. Chills were running down his spine with what he was now staring at.

Two very familiar black limousines coming down the road were catching his attention. The water they were spraying from the ground was high enough to powerwash the row homes on either side. They were heading in his direction at top speed.

Fumbling through his keys, Caz was trying to find the remote to unlock the driver's side door. He was panicking to escape. The limos were moving too quickly for his liking. He had to get out of there before it got ugly.

SPLASH! Down went his keys as he dropped them into the rain puddle below his car. "FUCK!" he yelled. He plunged to his knees, scrambling, trying to pick up the set and dry off the remote.

He hopped back to his bases. However, it wasn't quick enough. The limos were getting closer. He clinched the remote tightly. As much as he continued pressing the unlock button, nothing was happening. The water must have gotten to the battery. Now, it was a fight to get the actual key to open the car.

It was too late. The limos were passing by him, and some eerie heads were poking out. They weren't friendly looking...neither were the black and shiny Glocks they were holding in their hands.

The set of Cadillac keys fell to the ground once more. This was no time to try and drive away. As Caz bolted from the scene on foot, he was avoiding a different rain than what was falling from the sky...the rain of bullets shooting rapidly in his direction.

Turning the corner of his street, he made his path to the alleyway behind his row home. He kept looking back to see if they caught up to him.

Down he fell over a few metal trash cans, landing face first onto the asphalt. BANG, BANG! More bullets were coming. Two of the shooters made it out of the limos and were speeding up to Caz.

There was no time for him to hold the blood pouring from his face. He had to get up and keep running. The rain was now coming down harder. It was falling as if it were attempting to wash away all in its path.

There was no greater equalizer than Mother Nature. Even from the lowest slung cloud, she exploded with pent-up fury. Gusts whipped the frigid drops, sending them hurtling in every direction but still straight down.

By one of the homes, Caz found a white shed to hide behind, finally gaining his composure. From both sides of his belt, he flung out his Colts and started twirling them in each hand like a cowboy. He was ready.

"COME ON AND GET ME, YOU FUCKIN' COCKSUCKERS!"

He peeked down the alleyway in the direction he just came from, trying to see what was moving in-between the raindrops. Besides trash tumbling and dust grazing the air, nothing was in plain sight.

All of a sudden, two shots came at him, missing him by a few inches. One bullet hit the shed, and the other flew above the hood on his jacket.

Caz got up to his feet and started firing both revolvers away. One after the other. With each shot, he yelled for the guys to come to the forefront. He strolled stealthily around the dumpster. Not being able to see what was down the alleyway made him wary.

"COME ON, YOU SON OF A BITCHES! FACE ME LIKE A MAN!"

He made it to the other side of the dumpster where he rested under the canopy of a window to keep him dry. The sounds of the tip-toeing made way in his direction.

"STANDOFF IN A QUICK DRAW!!! LET'S GO, YOU PUSSIES!!!"

Catching his breath, he listened to the steps come closer and closer. He waited for the last bit of rain to beat off his face. Caz then looked at the two barrels he was holding, closed his eyes and jumped out from his hiding to showdown with whoever was near him.

POW, POW, POW, POW! Down went the one guy of the duo. He crashed like a ton of bricks into the puddle beside him. Another splash!

His partner sprinted away from the scene, quicker than the bullets that were flying. Caz caught him before he made the turn back into the street. One to the head! Down he went, as well!

Yet, Caz knew he was far from done. As he started his journey back over to where his car was, he could see from a distance that the limousines were gone.

Putting his hands in the air, he began laughing uncontrollably. "WHERE THE FUCK YOU ALL GOING? I'M JUST GETTING STARTED!!!" he yelled throughout the neighborhood. He even fired a shot straight into the sky, feeling lucky. He dropped both of his revolvers and pulled out his 686 from the back of his waist.

"I'LL TAKE YOU ALL DOWN!"

He stood still for a moment under the gloomy clouds. Blood was dripping down his face. The water coming down from the sky was getting colder and fiercer. Caz stood with his gaze fixed on the horizon, looking in every direction for whoever else was hiding, waiting to catch him off guard.

As the clouds continued crying, he turned and walked away. He came closer to the two bodies he shot down by the dumpster.

Noticing the first guy he connected with was still breathing, Caz laughed. The guy crawled his way out of the puddle and down the alleyway. Caz looked down at him, pointing his shooter directly at his head.

BANG! The man's head exploded like a melon. Pieces went flying everywhere. The skinny one stood and stared, laughing a little louder this time. He looked to his left again, just to be sure that his partner in the distance was undoubtedly dead. He got him in the head the first time…but one could never be too sure.

Caz laughed once more, extremely loud this time. Anyone around would be able to hear him. He was very pleased with himself.

"Hey, you!" a voice softly whispered into his right ear, behind his back. He turned around and aimed his gun in the direction the sound came from. As it turned out, they were the last words he ever heard.

All he saw next was a semi-automatic Desert Eagle firing round after round at him until he, himself was on the ground next to the guy he just put down.

Ten bullets took him flat to his back. Caz looked up at the man holding the gun, trying to respond. There was no use. One in the head put his lights out.

Lou's top guy, Umberto, stood above him with the handgun, smiling that the job was done while Caz's blood poured from his dead body into the alleyway puddles.

CHAPTER THIRTY-FIVE

Massive vessels awaited to be stocked and unloaded with cargo from the harbor. Gulls filled the foggy air with their beating wings and cries. It was the salty breeze blowing in my face that reminded me how chilling this experience had been. I didn't see it warming up anytime soon.

Genuinely, I thought about many things, standing by the intermodal containers on the white, freshly painted dock, awaiting my fate. How it all came down to these moments blew my mind. Yet, I was determined to make something right in the midst of all the wrong this journey had led me to.

The Walt Whitman Bridge in the distance was a marvel of steel and cables. It spanned the river six lanes wide. It suspended seamlessly between two states for almost sixty years.

The view of the river and New Jersey across from it brought a moving place to rest the eye. It was serene in comparing it to the hustle and bustle of the city behind me. It was where the clouds soared freely above – this view unhindered by the rising of the buildings' skyline.

But above all, it is where I would have this ultimate meeting, the pinnacle of all meetings I ever had before. A meeting in which I had no idea how it would begin or end...but my focus would remain on Andrew.

Anxious, I was hoping to see Caz by this point. I arrived a half an hour early just to be extra prepared. The rapid-firing rain had just turned into a light drizzle. Standing there alone at the dock with the duffel bags in my hand, I was ready for anything!

All of a sudden, the sound of tires hitting gravel whispered from afar. Three all-too-familiar black limousines finally began sauntering down the tarmac of the shipyard, slowly and with caution. It was then I realized, I certainly wasn't alone anymore.

Sternly, I stood…by myself. I had nothing but my gray jacket, flat cap and torn jeans on. The exterior was hiding the sadness within me like a blanket over a dead body. The animosity in me was spreading like a virus, more by the minute.

I remained confident notwithstanding my duty….a blinding blackness; a promising future I once had now vanished into nothing. My only hope was to keep this kid alive long enough to get him to safety…long enough before these animals had their way with me.

For a moment, I thought I heard Andrew's cries from one of the limos as all three pulled up and parked in sequence. It was the same gang of Brooklyn wiseguys I recognized from the basement. Two men apiece came out of each limousine. The last pair…Lou and Umberto, standing tall.

Donning his signature overcoat and fedora, Lou ambled over in my direction as if it were routine. Umberto, right next to him, in his Member's Only leather jacket confirmed his seriousness to me, cracking his knuckles. Immediately, he came and frisked me head to toe.

"He's clean, Lou," confirmed Umberto.

I didn't want to waste any more time. "Where is the kid?" I asked, still holding the bags tightly. I was in no mood for games. I wanted this to all end, right then and there.

He wasn't answering me. "Lou?" I yelled, frustrated with the way he was nonchalant. He stood sternly with his signature empty grin, shifting his eyes over to Umberto and back to his army of men rallying around him like a pack of wolves, ready to attack me at any minute.

"Where is my money?" he then spoke. He put out both arms as if he wanted me to come and over and simply place the bag handles over his palms.

"Right here, in my hands." I extended both arms with the bags to show him I clearly came prepared.

Lou looked over his shoulder at his top guy, snapping his fingers twice in a row. "Umberto...go count it up. Make sure it's the full three million." With a pistol in his hand, arm resting at his side, Umberto came back towards me with a long grimace. As he did, Lou continued bantering in the background. "Any extra, you can take and buy yourself a new coat."

Snatching the bags from my possession, Umberto hurried to unzip both and scuffle through them, checking to make sure it was worth its weight in paper. He was looking for a decoy...a fake...something!

"It's all clean, boss." He then brought the bags over to the malevolent don, standing in the wind, holding my fate.

"Impressive," he remarked. I was getting fed up. Now that he had what he wanted, I was waiting for a little reciprocity.

"Lou, come on. Where is the boy?" I shouted.

The gorgeous one smiled as he and his goons began marching closer to me. It was like a horde of zombies coming to attack the living.

Only one of the guys stood by the limousines. "There has been a change of plans, McCool," announced Lou, looking around at the docks surrounding us in his walk.

"What the fuck do you mean?"

"Your buddy, Caz…he is dead."

"What?" I questioned. I didn't know what to say next. How was I to respond? My jaw dropped to the ground. Before I had the chance to question why he did what he did, Lou explained in detail.

"Based on the stack of weapons he had with him at the time, it leads me to believe he was planning an attack."

The gusty winds intensified. The rain was coming down harder once again. My mind was racing. I shook my head sideways. How could this have happened?

"Any ideas?" Lou inquired.

"So, you killed him? Just like that?" I spoke up.

"The stupid fuck showed up at his house. We were still hunting for him since he came after you. This was initially your call, kid." Go figure!

He kept coming closer to me…and closer. I could then tell by the way Umberto was staring at me, they didn't plan on making this exchange a pleasant one. My fate was long decided before the clock struck seven.

"Yet, based on your reaction…I can see you two joined forces recently. Didn't ya?" interrogated Lou, raising his voice.

I closed my eyes for a second. I tried to envision my next move. Everything I did from here on out had to be calculated. It was time to be extra meticulous.

How was I going to overcome this psychopath and his squad all alone? No weapons, no backup…no way out.

"Lou, just tell me…where is the kid?"

"You were going to try and take me out…weren't you, Jackie boy?" he continued, not letting this matter go.

So much for being smooth. Something came out of me. I forgot how to keep it cool and merely lost my mind. "Lou, what the fuck? Answer MY question!"

"You've already got the answer! You try and cross me, cocksucka…it's the last thing you'll ever do!!!"

BAM! I fell down to the ground before I even realized what was happening. Umberto's fist connected with my nose. I didn't even have the chance to think. Two guys behind him came over to join the fun, beginning to kick me in the stomach…in my back, my ribs, my arms…anywhere their boots would connect.

"You should have known better, McCool!!!!" yelled Lou, turning his back to me while his goons persisted tearing me apart.

"Now you die…and so does the kid."

The sole henchman by the limousine finally opened the door. He reached inside to pull out and show me the only important matter to me in these critical moments…the nine-year-old boy whose life was in the hands of insanity.

Andrew was pale as a ghost. His messy hair and dark circles under his eyes indicated to me that he was taking constant abuse, far from what any child should. They tied him up as if they were trying to make a mummy out of him. The cloth around his mouth muffled any screams or cries he was attempting to deliver once he saw my face. He was helpless. So was I. The wind being knocked out of me at that moment was preventing me from doing the same.

I then looked to Lou, getting back into the limousine. "You fuckin' scumbag!" I kept thinking. I wanted to say it, I wanted to scream it. But, I had no voice.

"Get him the fuck out of here!" screamed the gorgeous one. Before I knew it, two more punches connected to my jaw, followed by a bag that went over my head. I couldn't see. It was all a blur…a white nothingness.

CHAPTER THIRTY-SIX

Arising from my heavy slumber, there was a chill that ran through my veins once I started to move. It must have been the cold air drifting through that woke me up.

The ground beneath me was lumpy as if I were on a bed of rocks. My clothes felt as damp as grass in the dew of the dawn. I stood up slowly, studying my surroundings. As familiar as it all appeared, I still couldn't put my finger on my exact location.

There was no sense of time. My breathing was steady, but my heartbeat was racing. My mind wandered all over the place. I kept prompting myself, "If there is a way out of these quarters, it is just a matter of searching thoroughly until I find it."

The dark basement felt like a bunker, all concrete and no personality. The walls and ceilings had a yellow-tar sheen on them. The once-whitened floor was dark grey and gritty with grime.

The stagnant aroma made it dungeonesque. The unsoftened echo of my shoes sliding on the ground brought an eerie feeling of confinement.

I was starting to feel claustrophobic. The dimly lit ceiling lamp in the center of the room shined upon my face, but it wasn't shedding the kind of light that I needed. I looked around the room for some sort of clue in its darkest corners.

The only signs of hope were the multiple sheets of layered plastic on the far side of the room from where I was standing. The industrial-sized sheets were nail-gunned into the ceiling, draping down. They were covering something, I just wasn't sure what. The more I stared at them, the more I noticed a light peeking through. I then asked myself the question…where was this radiance coming from?

Slowly, I made my way to the other side of the basement. I cracked my neck and stretched my aching back out on the way, trying to readjust myself after an awkward sleep. The fresh bruises and scrapes all over my body were an indicator that I surely didn't make it to this destination willingly. Although, I was still kind of foggy on the details.

As I got closer the plastic, I noticed a rusty crowbar leaning up innocuously on the wall in the very same corner of the room. I went to pick it up, knowing it could come in handy for multiple uses.

Immediately, I used it to chop through the plastic dangling down. Pulling from one way and tearing apart in the other, I was able to remove the mess and see the light brighter with a few clean sweeps from the crowbar. The musky smell had dwindled. Scents of oil and tire rubber began swirling their ways down the steps.

Low and behold, a breakthrough…a staircase. It was old and wooden. Up at the top, an all-too-familiar white door. Everything started to become more evident…true déjà vu. I quickly realized I was in Lou's basement beneath his auto shop…only empty. What once held a desk, a rare wine collection, and operations led by the most sadistic Mafia don's was now nothing…a silhouette, a vast emptiness.

I had no idea what I'd walk into on the other side of the door, up the steps. However, I knew I wasn't going to survive long in the empty crypt that I was standing in without quickly making a move.

I held the crowbar in front of me for protection. It was my only hope of keeping me safe. Step by step, the deep creeks reminded me that this was only the first part of a journey that would be uphill the entire way.

Finally, at the top of the steps, I stood hesitant, facing the door. This was the gateway to something terrible. It was just too easy to get up here, there had to have been more in store for me. I fiddled with the doorknob, quickly realizing it was locked from the other side. Accepting the challenge, I decided it was time to put this crowbar to use and bust the door down.

With the crowbar wedged in-between the door and the wall, I applied all of my force down, pushing it away from me. With a little wiggle and a bit of tussle, I broke the lock and opened the door. *CRACK!*

Too easy. This has to be a set-up!

There was nobody around in the garage I stood in. The only things in sight were boxes of tools…claw hammers, wrenches, and work gloves. Old paint cans and ladders rested near the car lifts. I made my way into the main lobby.

All of a sudden, a grizzly bear of a man moseyed out from the break room by the front counter as if he just woke up from a nap. He was six-foot-six with a long beard and a belly that burst at the seams. Looking preoccupied and unprepared, this was all telling me that my entrance was unexpected.

We locked eyes at the same time as if we were drawn by magnets. I lunged in his direction. As I did, he ran over to the counter, hastily reaching across it. Before he had the chance to use what I knew he was grabbing, I connected my crowbar to his knee with a swift, stable whack.

POW! He and the M1911 pistol he obtained during his reach-around went tumbling to the floor. The thud he made was so hard, everything in the auto shop shook and vibrated as if a sonic boom came passing through.

"Where the fuck is Lou?" I screamed, holding the crowbar in front of his face, assuring him I'd deliver more blows to his body if I had to. He remained sitting on the floor, grasping his knee in excruciating pain. I noticed on his chest, the left part of his boiler suit, the name "Earl" was embroidered on it.

"Who? What?" asked Earl, looking towards the pistol that went flying across the floor as if he really thought he had a chance of getting it back.

"You know who, Earl! Your fucking boss!! Lou Muchetta…where did that piece of shit go with my kid?"

"I don't know what you're talking about, man!"

Clenching the crowbar tightly in my hand, I savagely thrashed it across Earl's other knee. He turned to lay on his stomach, protecting his head with his hands. I beat him over the back with my weapon three times. BAM! BAM! BAM! His cries of agony didn't stop me any.

"Agghhh!!! Noooo!! Please!!!" yelled Earl.

Once he came up for air, I gave him a shot to his left wrist. He curled himself into the fetal position, crying for me to stop.

"GIVE ME SOMETHING, COCKSUCKER!! I'M NOT FUCKING AROUND HERE!!!!"

"I don't know...I DON'T KNOW!!!!"

I continued to hammer him down with the crowbar until I was able to connect with each and every limb. The force of my wallops were like a cars crashing on an interstate highway. With each fresh strike I delivered, he yelped a new scream. The tears from his eyes were pouring out just as quickly as the blood was all over his body. His vessels were bursting. His arms and legs were trembling. He begged for mercy as I maliciously stood above him, continuing to put the poor man into more agony.

For the grand finale, I whacked the bar across his face, sending a few teeth flying across the floor and landing next to where the gun sat. This sent him to his face.

I stared down at him at a point when I thought I knocked him out cold. I didn't feel bad one bit. I wanted answers. Nothing was going to stand in my way at this point.

After catching my breath, I dropped the crowbar to the tiled floor, letting its painfully ringing sound pierce Earl's eardrums in its fall. This alerted him. He slowly sat back up.

Still sore from my own beating I had just taken, I needed to rest my arms. I went over and picked up the gun that rested a few feet away from him. I kicked away his loose teeth next to it.

Gradually, I made my way closer to Earl, hovered back over him once again. "Don't make me do it!" I screamed, cocking the piece back and pointing it at him. "Last chance!" I confirmed.

He looked at me while his body kept quivering. "What do you want me to say?" he asked, now with a lisp from losing teeth. I had it! BANG! One shot to his foot.

"AHHHHHHH!!! AHHHH!!!!" He let out cries like a little baby. He even rocked back and forth again in the fetal position, holding his foot as if it was falling off. Still, I showed no mercy. I cocked back the gun again and aimed it now at his face.

"Tell me something, you piece of shit...or this next one goes off into your motherfucking head!!!!!"

Earl put his hands over his face and shouted, "Alright, alright...I will talk!" while continuing to cry. At last! I finally put the gun down and let him speak. But, I wasn't going to give him all day to do so. Time was limited.

"Lou's coordinates are on the back of that invoice on the counter!" he said, pointing to a stack of papers resting evidently on the counter. I made my way over to them, smiling.

"He leaves tonight!" included Earl.

"Was that so hard? Why did you make me beat you to a bloody mess for that?"

The poor guy continued laying on the floor, holding onto his foot for dear life. I saw a few towels resting on the counter. I tossed them his way. "Clean ya self up, would ya?" I instructed to the messy mechanic.

Scooping up the invoice Earl instructed me to see, I turned it over to glance at the coordinates in which he swore held Lou's location.

40°18'46"N 75°07'44"W

"You got a loaner?" I asked Earl, tucking the invoice into my pocket.

"Take the Malibu out front, keys are already in the ignition." He was barely able to get the words out of his mouth. It looked like he was about to pass out. The amount of blood he was losing was exponential.

There was a portable landline phone sitting upright on the counter. I picked it up off the receiver and tossed it to him, next to the towels. "Wait twenty minutes after I leave to call an ambulance! Remember…I was never here, Earl!!!"

I was just about to scurry out the door and make my way to this location Earl gave me when something held me back. Something I stared at on the counter was telling me there was more to where I was going.

Beneath the invoice, I noticed a piece of paper with a phone number on it. The closer I stared at it, the sicker I became.

I was looking at Federal Agent Jay Martinez's personal cell…hand-written!!!

Just as I was about to question why he'd have such a number, the answer was right below it. This was even more nauseating. It was Federal paperwork filled out by Lou, confirming him a cooperating informant. It was dated the same day with his signatures all over the documents. I also checked the calendar on the wall to be satisfied. This meant I was only in the basement overnight and whatever he was doing, he had just put the wheels in motion.

What in the world?

This gave me even more reason to hate the man. I knew he was a malicious nutcase…but a cheese eating rat? This had gone on far too long. I had to get out of there. I had to let Lou know his awful basement wasn't going to keep me hostage. I was ready to take him down…and whoever else he had with him.

Popping open the register in front of me, I grabbed as many quarters in the tray as I could. The only payphone I knew of nearby. I had to make a call or two.

I ventured outside, hopped into the loaner and wasted no time in my escape. Knowing I was still a wanted man by the Feds, I crept out as stealthy as I could. It was going to be another long night.

CHAPTER THIRTY-SEVEN

It was just the way I expected it. The trees gave way to an empty, barren road nearly twenty minutes into my ride. The path that started as civilized quickly became a no-mans land.

I knew my voyage was finally coming to its destination when the abandoned warehouse in front of me matched the coordinates from Earl's invoice. I was roughly thirty-five miles outside of the city.

Old machinery lined the road covered in dirt and scavenged into skeletons of whatever they were at one point.

The big, old abandoned shack had a curved roof like an aircraft hangar. The walls were made of corrugated tin. The broken tarmac around it was empty except for an old yellow forklift – I figured that it must have been in use again, just like it was many years ago.

A chain-linked fence surrounded it along with an assembly line of Lou's Brooklyn muscle, standing in perfect accord, prepared for war. They looked lean, mean and ready to spray gunfire. I didn't care though. No amount of bullets in the world would keep me from trying anything.

I kept thinking, "It would be just a matter of time before I am within the warehouse walls...even if I have to shoot them all on the way."

On my ride over, I purchased an old GO FLIP mobile from a corner convenience store. Standing tall, I opened it up, punched a few numbers on its surface, let it ring a few times and then hung up. I then proceeded to put it back into my pocket, next to my wallet. I was hoping what I just did would come in handy later on.

I parked the 2000 Chevy Malibu loaner on top of dirt and leaves just outside of the fence. Not long after, I came out of the car and fixed my jacket before looking at each of the thugs as coldly as they were staring at me.

I smirked, strolling to the gated entrance as two brawn bruisers, double my height, came to meet me on the other side. They had perfectly trimmed mustaches, big black aviators, and slicked-back brown hair.

Just as I was opening my mouth to tell them who I was there to see, they beat me to the punch. "Lou is expecting you," the one said with a deep, reverberating voice. All of a sudden, the gate opened up, ready for me to cross it. I couldn't believe what was happening. This was all just too easy. I remained convinced…something was awry.

My puzzled expression said it all. There had to have been more to this cryptic quest I was venturing on. Among the many questions I had, I was hoping the answers were within the warehouse walls.

The row of thugs continued to stare at me as I walked towards the entrance. I took one last breath before I made my way in.

My footsteps echoed on the concrete floor as I shut the door behind me. The stillness of the room sent shivers down my spine.

There was water dripping from the roof, rhythmically, generating a melancholic melody. The door hinges were all rusted, and the glass windows were shattered like my broken dreams. Plastic sheets did their best to cover them.

None of that mattered more than what sat in the middle of the giant space. It was young Andrew, tied tightly to a wooden chair, motionless…soundless. He was disheveled. His clothes were torn, his body was beaten down, and his eyes were tired, squinting and ready to close at a moment's notice.

His skin was white as chalk. His mouth was frozen, wide open in an expression of stunned surprise. Although he was staring straight at me, it appeared he wasn't able to notice me at all. The sick fuck that did this to a nine-year-old needed to pay…big time!

"Andrew…Buddy!!" I yelled, smiling for the first time in days. Yet, I knew I couldn't sigh with relief. Something somewhere was lurking and watching…I just didn't know what or where.

First, I looked around the room, keeping my 1911 pistol in front of me. Then I made my way over to where Andrew was sitting. He remained silent, too traumatized to utter a single word.

I knelt down and looked at him, aghast at what they did to him. I pushed his hair out of his face and kept telling him how much I loved him. As soon as I grabbed the thick rope to being untying him, I heard the cocking back of various guns in the distance. I kept attempting to unfasten him from the chair.

All of a sudden, five men appeared from the back of the warehouse, behind the shelves and crates. They were pointing their weapons directly at me…one of them was Lou.

"Just in time, McCool," he announced. The weight of his words carried across the warehouse. Its sound ricocheted from one wall to the other.

I stood up and spoke my peace. "You cocksucker! What are you…a Federal informant now, huh? You rat fuck?" I asked, holding my pistol up and pointing it at him.

His penny loafers made a loud clicking sound on the concrete as he and his squad continued walking towards myself and Andrew. He danced around my question, merely replying, "As the old adage goes…the pen is mightier than the sword!"

"I am tired of fuckin' playing games here, Lou," I stated, losing my patience. I even started to sweat a bit.

"Well, that's a damn shame, sweetheart…I've only just begun," he replied, pulling out a gun of his own from the side of his overcoat, pointing it at Andrew.

"Step away from the kid for a minute!" he demanded.

"Fuck no, Lou…tell me what's going on first!"

POW! He shot a bullet to the back leg of Andrew's chair, breaking it off its balance and sending him to the floor. The kid let out a terrifying scream, followed by continuous cries.

"Do it…or the next slug goes into his skull!!!" commanded Lou.

I backed away…but I kept my arm steady. My gun was still pointed at this bastard's head. It took all my power and my will to not squeeze the trigger and watch his brains splatter everywhere. I tried to keep my composure.

Once Lou made it over to Andrew on the floor, still strapped to the broken chair, he began finishing untying him. After that, he scooped him up with his free arm, practically choking him. He then put the gun to his head, staring straight at me.

"Let the kid go, Lou!" I yelled. "This is between me and you…he's seen enough." We were about ten yards from one another. The four hoodlums behind Lou stood still as statues, inching their way closer in my direction.

"If only it were that easy, McCool," Lou told me, applying pressure to Andrew's neck by squeezing his arm around him. The poor kid was about to pass out.

"What the fuck are you talking about?" I countered.

"I led you here on purpose, my little Irish friend," continued Lou, raising his one eyebrow. He held the gun harder into Andrew's head, keeping his free arm around his neck. I could tell it was painful by Andrew's jerking reaction in his face. "I kept you alive in my cellar so you'd get out and find the coordinates from my guy easily!"

"I figured that, Lou. Now, I need answers. What was this with the Federal informant paperwork I saw in your shop? What else is it that you want from me?" I screamed. In return, Lou merely laughed. It was a dangerous type of chuckle, one you'd expect from the devil himself.

"It's not about what I want. It's what others want," he replied. I couldn't determine where he was going with the point he was trying to make. My silence suggested he would need to elaborate.

"The Caribbean Connection, the murder of a Federal agent, the kidnapping of your boy here...," explained Lou before I interrupted him.

"What the fuck are you saying?" I asked, furious as ever. I knew what he was implying...I simply didn't want to believe it. This fuckin' guy!!

"Just as I was about to kill you after the docks, I realized somebody needs to take the rap for all of this shit. It sure ain't gonna be me, sweetheart. So, I made the call to Martinez myself and put it all on you. In the next twenty minutes or so, this place will be swarming with Federal agents...more than any of us have ever seen."

I couldn't believe it. I shook my head sideways, closing my eyes briefly. He disgusted me. The man had no code. Just like that, he was trying to throw my life away, piece by piece...whatever was left of it. Meanwhile, Umberto stood in the distance, eyeing me up along with the rest of Lou's guys. The look on my face grew more frustrated as the gorgeous one continued to speak.

I questioned him once more, "What makes you think you're so fuckin' innocent, Lou? The blood is on your hands, not mine!"

He wasted no time to reply to me. "I have no past record, you do. Your dialogue with the Costa Rican speaks for itself, I never spoke to him once. Your bottle of Tequila, poisoning your girlfriend...I was never there, not one time as far as they know. And your car parked outside shows you came here voluntary...with a weapon in hand. And the kid, well...his grandparents wouldn't know you from me or my men from The Temptations. Now, it all points to you, McCool."

"You fuckin' piece of shit. We are even in this!! You are just as guilty as me!!!"

Laughing, Lou went on. He began enlightening me on his plans for the aftermath, "In payment for the light I shed to Martinez, I'm given a pardon. Instead of fleeing and hiding for years...I'll have peace of mind while you sit and rot."

I kept my gun steady at him. I screamed, "I will make sure you go down! You ain't puttin' me away, motherfucker! NOT TODAY!"

"It's all over, McCool. Twenty more minutes...just hang in there. That...or you die along with the boy. I'm sorry it had to end this way...but there is no other way."

"There's no way I'm going away just for you, Lou! I'll tell them everything! I don't give a fuck!"

"What can you prove? The only time we were in public was at dinner and for your benefit. Even then, there was no business discussed."

"Nina knew about you. She had to have mentioned your name to them."

"Ah yes, Agent Lesandi. Say McCool…it must have been something else to watch that little bitch die. The way she choked on her own spit, the way her face turned as purple as an eggplant. Hah! The way she fell…only to spew blood all over the floor before you ran out like a pussy."

This guy was pushing it. The more he talked, the more my stomach turned.

"If it were me and I stood there watching the little cunt die…I would have at least put my cock in her one more time!"

"FUCK YOU, YOU MOTHERFUCKER!!!" I screamed. I was losing my mind, letting him get to me. Meanwhile, I was running out of time the more I kept wasting it. I had to stop giving him the upper hand here.

Lou went on, "Luckily, for me, she's fuckin' dead. I'm sure she spoke about me. However, any suspicion of my involvement would have gone in the grave with her…there's nothing to back it up. If so, I'd be behind bars already."

I had to think of something quickly. I couldn't let him win. However, gathering my thoughts became more difficult with him, continuing to ramble.

"All of this is detailed in my official pardon which was arranged this morning with my lawyer and the Federal government."

I had to rely on fate. Thinking back to the card game days at the casino, an old lesson came back to me. If you're down and out and about to lose it all, go big…bluff!

"What if I recorded everything? Every conversation we ever had?" In truth, I didn't. However, I pulled out the GO FLIP from my pocket, waving it in the air as if I were doing it that very moment. "Yeah, that's right! Everything you told me today!" I told him.

He was quiet, looking down. Did I have him? Was I able to take the pot just like that? I was praying to come out of this game a winner.

"Does a name Marc Baxter ring a bell to you?" he asked me. My heart sank. That's when he threw out the royal flush on the table.

"Why?" I asked.

"Oh, McCool...you know I love my research. I didn't stop at Lesandi, I continued to look into you once I started. As it turns out, your honorable discharge from the Army wasn't entirely honorable if you know what I mean."

Unbelievable. The last thing I imagined being an issue was now in his favor.

"Your boy Mr. Shit-and-Piss Baxter didn't forget the incident in the desert. He's got unfinished business with you, boy!!!"

This was bad...real bad. Once I heard this, I knew it was over. There was no more doubting it. He was undoubtedly going home with the gold.

"How do you know this?"

"He works for the Federal government now."

Of course, he did. Why in the world wouldn't he? This only made things a catastrophe. I couldn't talk my way out of it anymore.

"As soon as I turned you in, he came forth. He's having the Army look further into your mess. And when they do...hah...let's just say you won't have a jingle truck to get away in."

I felt defeated.

"So, you can record me. You can scream and yell...do whatever you like. But everything I said along with the shadows of your past coming back to haunt you...I'm not the one going to prison today. I assured that you wouldn't beat me, boy!"

I was finished. There was no turning back now. All I could do now was my best to fight off these goons alone while keeping the kid alive. Was it time? To sink or swim? To rise or fall? To break the chains that held me or to stay imprisoned?

"Clock is tickin', McCool. Any last words to the boy, you tell him now."

Just as I was about to give Andrew my final 'I love you,' salvation hit my ears. The sweet sounds of new engines growling in the distance reminded me that there was still hope for Andrew and I at this very moment.

"Lucky for me, asshole...I didn't come here alone either," I said, smiling back as full as Lou was prior.

It was then I saw him look behind me and outside the smashed front windows. He was staring precisely at what I wanted him to see. Five camouflage green Jeep Wranglers arriving at the scene. They crept in gradually. Yet, once they parked...those who came out of the vehicles were anything but slow.

It actually worked! The call I made before I crossed the chain-link fence. Inwardly, I prayed and thanked Duffy in heaven for the old carpet cleaner business card he gave me that night outside McCluskey's.

I continued to Lou. "You lay a finger on me or the kid...you, and all your men die. These men I have here are trained to kill in warfare. They are armed with military-grade weapons and explosives. They know just who to kill and just who to keep alive...don't ever underestimate the Irish."

All I heard outside was yelling. My guys were must have been standing off with Lou's henchmen. I didn't look back. There was no time.

Lou looked around the warehouse, now the one feeling defeated. His men seemed a bit clueless as well. For the first time during this visit, he had nothing else to say. His mouth remained wide-open as if it were searching for the words through thin air.

"Until the Feds get here...we stand. You tell them the truth, Lou...we both go away and the kid remains safe."

Still speechless, I noticed the gorgeous one bring his weapon down a little bit. His breaths were getting heavier. His mind was racing at the speed of light, I could see it through his troubled eyes.

"Or I'll make sure we both get buried in the ground tonight."

Finally, he replied after clearing his throat. "Good form." He said it softly as if he was already beginning to lose his voice. His tug on Andrew was easing up a bit as well. He looked at him, questioning what to do next.

"We're both taking the heat for this, Lou. If I'm going down, you're going down with me! One way or another."

He nodded his head.

"But the kid lives!" I yelled, firmly holding my gun stable.

Various men dressed in fatigue coats, cargo pants, and steel-toe boots came out, armed to the teeth began poking through the window.

On their heads, balaclavas covered their faces. Their hands were equipped with either an AR or an AK, cocked back and ready to do some damage. When it came to the IRA, they never underdressed or underprepared for any type of occasion.

I looked directly at Lou while his head remained on a swivel, eyeing the new guests to our "party" here. The rest of his body paralyzed itself. The hurt spread through like hot, liquid metal.

I clenched my fists as I hesitantly took a few steps closer towards him. I then noticed his feet tremble. His legs twitched, fighting the impulse to whirl around and sprint to the outside and run towards nowhere.

My throat became dry. "They are here all night if necessary," I told him. My jaw was getting tighter. *Was I finally going to end this thing and win the battle once and for all?*

I kept my gun steady, waiting for an answer from the gorgeous one. *I could just take him out…right here and now. He is becoming vulnerable.*

He finally spoke. "I don't need all night!" Lou then fired his pistol at me before he turned around with the kid still in his arms. I fell to the floor. In that very moment, I could hear the explosions between my guys and his outside. A bloody battle was brewing.

CHAPTER THIRTY-EIGHT

Guns were blazing hot. Bullets jingled on the metal warehouse walls, bouncing around like we were at a ping pong tournament.

Pt'choo! Ding!

My left arm felt as if flames were bursting through my veins, burning me to a crisp. Yet, I wasn't going to let the shot lodged in-between my bicep and deltoid take me out of the game yet. Not for a second. The reason being...I didn't *have* a second to spare. The Feds were on their way over. More importantly, a little boy's life was at stake.

Lou jetted towards the wide-opened garage door in the back of the warehouse. He was carrying Andrew over his shoulder like he was a sack of potatoes. It was hard to keep up. He was moving quicker than I had ever seen him go, even with the added weight. Every other step, he'd turn around and wave his pistol at me. He fired a few more back each time I'd catch up. Luckily, his aim was worse than his moral decency.

However, I wasn't going to rely on him not getting lucky and hit a moving target. This had to end! I couldn't let his ultimate plan come to fruition and have the Feds come and take me away.

I didn't trust any of what he had in store. I kept thinking, "I'd rather die on my feet than to live on my knees!"

There were a few of Lou's henchmen I had to faceoff within my path, ducking and diving behind different shelves and crates towards the exit. They would stop at nothing to be the one to kill me.

In the very moment I thought I was outnumbered, Duffy's IRA guys stormed into the warehouse to back me up. I could hear their AR-18's and AK-47's going off like fireworks, tearing apart anyone and anything that stood in front of its madness. I avoided their direction as well.

Nobody had a chance going head to head with the Irish Republican Army. They were too militant of a force.

One of Lou's men had automatic gunfire unleashed on him so severely, he was unrecognizable. He went from human to looking like a pound of raw meat, beat down to a bloody mush by steel rain.

The guys who tried to blend in on top of the old wooden containers for safety were the ones in deepest trouble. Once they were spotted by the guerillas, it was like a wildcat rushing to its victim and climbing up a tree to attack.

Instead of fangs, they delivered piercing blows with Ka-Bar knives to their stomachs. They were the same kind of blades used after World War II.

Those who fell victim were sliced apart so viscously and deeply that when they fell to the ground, their bodies exploded. It was as if a tomato dropped and splattered. You could see the freedom-fighters smiling, even though the black ski masks were covering their faces.

Bodies from both sides of the skirmish laid everywhere like dolls on the floor. Limbs were at awkward angles and heads held in such a way you knew they weren't merely sleeping.

There were two more rows of steel shelves I had to pass before I came in arm's length of the garage exit. More of Lou's men appeared. He seemed to have an endless amount of muscle, multiplying by the minute. They were now gaining an advantage, moving in on the IRA guys. Surreptitiously, I slithered around them like a snake.

Nonetheless, there was one more face I had to encounter before I'd be on my way out towards Lou. It was his top guy, Umberto. He had his beautifully polished Desert Eagle pistol aimed right at my skull once I got close. Five yards away...I didn't have a chance as it shined right into my eye.

I could see and hear it all coming to an end right there. I simply closed my eyes that very second and prayed he would just finish me quickly. This was my time. Not how I wanted it to go...but I made it further than I thought.

Umberto was a sure shot, unlike his boss. While he grinned at me, he cocked back the hammer as his other finger on the trigger moved slowly.

All of a sudden, the next thing I saw was a bayonet on the end of an AK-47. Umberto's eyes were wide open as if he saw a ghost. His Desert Eagle fell to the floor.

A long steel blade jammed deep into Umberto's throat and wedged far into his neck. The IRA man kept digging his weapon through him until the tip reached the other side of his head.

I didn't stay to watch the blood spray. Instead, I sprinted out of the garage exit as if the place were on fire. Finally, I could continue my great pursuit of the gorgeous one. The evenly-matched war inside between both forces remained behind me.

The maze of the woodlands in back of the warehouse was an endless puzzle of fog and sounds of the night. The view that was once so calming in my mind was now giving me chills. It was not out of freight, but out of unrest.

Even on such a warm wintry eve, I was shaking. The trees sheltered so many secrecies in front of me with their spreading canopies of green perplexity.

The little bit of light unfettering from the moon brightened up the dark scene. Yet, it was not enough to truly see where I was going. Every tree I bumped into could have been a disaster nearby.

I kept walking with my 1911 pistol in front of me. My hands were on it, holding it with my arms straight out. The bullet wound was still piercing my left bicep, but I did my best to act as if it weren't.

Creeping around like a slinking panther, I tried to listen for footsteps on the brown leaves that covered the ground. All I heard were frogs, crickets and full branches weaving in the wind.

I found a yellow birch to briefly lean up against. Something had to give. *He's out here somewhere.* However, Lou was making himself harder to find the more I continued to sneak around.

I bent down tie my shoe. POW! A bullet smashed into the grand tree. Thankfully, I moved. Had I stayed where I was a second longer, I would've felt the wrath.

Out of the blue, I caught Lou running in-between two trees, fifteen yards away. BOOM! I fired off, only to send a round into the mist. I had to be careful…he still had the kid in his arms.

I was down to my last clip. I had to make it count. The line separating life and death for me consisted of fifteen nine-millimeter pieces of ammunition, ready to be released.

It was quiet again. Tip-toe, tip-toe I went.

I planned to slip around the corner I saw him dart to, stuff the magazine into my burner then put one right in the back of his head before he could even turn around.

Yet, once I got to that particular tree, Lou had already disappeared. I stood there, scanning the landscape once more. I was hoping for another noise, a sign…even the slightest murmur would help me.

BANG! Another shot fired. This time, my right forearm took the sting. This one burned worse than my left bicep. It felt like a bone shattered.

My knees plunged to the ground. I dropped my pistol beneath me to hold the wound. Blood was gushing all the way down to my hand. The agony wasn't enough to stop me, but I needed to regroup.

I picked up my head. Taking a deep breath, I closed my eyes. Once I opened them, the unsettling mist that surrounded me was swirling like a whirlwind and turning into a thick fog.

It was then, out from the vapors appeared Lou Gorgeous, walking with his arm around a weak, weeping Andrew's neck. At this point, he was practically dragging him by his shirt. It made me sick.

Cuts and bruises on the kid hurt more to look at than the two bullets painfully piercing each of my arms.

Yet, I was still on the ground. Just as I was about to get off my knees, Lou's Jericho stared at me in the face. Its deep, dark barrel was telling me this was all over. The game had to end, and I was going to lose. This was my curtain call.

Praying one of the IRA guys came to save me, I closed my eyes once more. Although I could hear screaming voices, they were probably too far away.

"Five more minutes...I should let you rot in a cell. Instead, I may just kill you both because I'm tired of lookin' at yas!" said Lou, pulling the hammer back on his gun. One last time, I inhaled the smell of cedar profoundly and held it in.

PT-CHOO! The bullet went flying into the trees, missing my head completely. All I kept thinking before my sight came back was, "His aim is getting worse as the night goes on."

That was until I saw him with his hands on his privates, holding them like they were about to fall off his body. By the grace of God, Andrew was given the strength...at least in his elbow. Just as Lou was about to pull the trigger, the kid threw one back to his old jewels, saving my life at that very moment.

A shot of adrenaline poured through me. I was up quicker than Lou's balls exploded into his stomach. To add insult to his injury, I headbutted the slimy son of a bitch right in his forehead, sending him and his gun to the ground. Payback was a bitch…and I had plenty to cash in on!!

Right when I went to pick up his Jericho and put an end to this miserable night, he rose to his feet and speared his shoulder into my stomach. He was tackling me like a linebacker in a football game. We both fell into the leaves and twigs, pillowing our plunge. The gun fell out of my hands and back into the rubble.

Poor Andrew stood there, continuing to sob as he watched what no child should see at nine-years-old, let alone anybody in a lifetime. If I didn't have any sympathy or care for him, I'd yell for him to grab the gun and shoot Lou himself in the middle of our scuffle. But, I couldn't do it. I wouldn't let him live with that. This was my battle…not his!

During our wrestle on the ground, Lou and I grunted as we took handfuls of each other's clothing in an attempt for one of us to escape the scramble first.

I was tired of this gridlock. I started jabbing him in the ribs with my left fist. It wasn't my best punch, but from my right forearm and down, it still felt like needles were slicing it apart. It was the best I could do with the resources I had.

Lou grabbed my hair, bringing my face down sharply onto his bent knee. Blood flowed from my now-broken nose as he staggered back up to his feet.

I looked up. Right as he lifted his leg to give me a stomp, I moved out of the way. I rolled, planted my stems to the ground, and put my fists in the air!

We came eye to eye. Blood was running down our faces onto our dirt-stained clothing. Even in those moments, he still smiled like the sicko he was.

Andrew's eyes were swollen, and his chin was trembling. He stood, watching in fear as this animal and I duked it out. He wanted to scream, "Stop," but I don't think he had much of a voice left or the courage to do so.

Lou swung at me with a haymaker. Luckily for me, he missed. He tried again...big miss! The third time, not even close! My face was hardened, and my knuckles opened and closed rhythmically. In those few seconds, the silence was absolute, nobody even breathed. I took my right hand, the bad one...and delivered a punch square-on to his nose.

As he turned around, I grabbed the back of his shirt and swung him to the ground like a bag of bricks, releasing him as he tumbled.

From there, I didn't stop. I pounced on him like a lion to a wildebeest. He wrapped his hands around my neck, firming his grip like a vice closing in on my throat.

Quickly, I escaped his choke and returned the favor, strangling him back! Then, another head-butt. This time, I slammed into his teeth.

Right hook, left hook...I kept going.

POW! SLAM! BOOM! I was screaming in anger, excitement, sadness, and regret. All of these emotions were forging together and exploding. Gushes of blood shot out from his face.

I didn't want to stop punching him. I tried to keep going until his brains fell out of his ears. Yet, my hands wouldn't allow it. They were numb as if they had been in a freezer for thirty minutes.

I stood up to catch my breath. Lou was immobile, lying down flat, gazing up at the murky sky. He looked done to me! It was time for me make sure of it.

Glancing over at Andrew, I smiled. "It's all over, buddy. I'm gonna get us out of here." As he looked back to me, I could tell he was still frightened from his eyes all the way down to his feet. Yet, it was understandable. He just witnessed a massacre.

That was when I heard sirens for the first time in the night. The "boys" must have gotten to the warehouse, which was now far in the distance away from where we were standing.

I kept telling myself it was time to make a move. Lou wasn't going to stay down much longer before he'd rise up and come back at me for more. "Look away, buddy," I told Andrew. Immediately, he turned around.

I limped over to grab my 1911 that rested in the dirt where I dropped it. Checking once more to make sure the clip was packed tight, I picked it up with my left hand and swayed over to Lou, still trying to catch my breath and keep my balance.

I could see his stomach moving up and down which told me he was still alive. "Not anymore," I told myself. "Not after I put one through his face."

I smiled and firmly told him, "Say goodnight, you fuckin' scumbag!"

I pulled back the hammer again and moved my finger on the trigger. BANG! BANG! BANG! Three shots went off...but not from my gun! Two hit my stomach, and one hit my chest.

"NOOOO!!! JACK! NOOOO!!" screamed Andrew, hysterically crying once again. He fell to his knees where he stood, yelling for help.

The scream was primal. It had a raw intensity to it that conveyed urgency, a desperate need. He was terrified.

We both descended. I collapsed to the ground like one of the dead trees nearby would slam down in its final minutes. I couldn't breathe. I could barely move. Yet, my sight wasn't affected.

Out from the mist, there I saw...the only...Tony Boy Tomasello. Who else? Just another loose end I didn't tie up. I should have known better than to call him from the payphone for help. However, when he didn't initially show up...I figured he was done with me. Well, he was...he just had a different way of showing it now.

Slowly he walked, proudly holding his Kahr K9 gun as if he were a hunter who just captured the buck of the season.

"Vinny Veccuto sends his regards, cocksucker! You stepped on the wrong motherfuckin' rattlesnake!"

Panicking, I tried to lift the piece I still had in my hand, but my arms were becoming less useful. Tony stood above me, about to give me the ultimate "goodnight kiss" as he aimed the gun right at my eyes. Just when I thought this would certainly be my final moment, once and for all, I watched his head crack open like a watermelon.

Did Andrew pick up a gun and save my life?

No, he didn't...thank God. I still didn't want any blood on his hands. He probably wouldn't even know how to work the thing, even though his mother was a Federal agent.

Tony Boy met his demise, dropping to the ground before my legs. Just as I noticed Lou aching, crawling to get back on his feet, I saw another surprise guest of the evening...Desmond "The Motherfucking King" Carter, holding the gun that executed Tony. Well, there was one of the two calls I was glad I made.

I was speechless...both because I had nothing to say and the fact that I was choking on the blood pouring from my mouth.

Perfect timing. It was right when I needed an ally. Yet, now I needed one more favor...the most important one of the night.

I backed up, scooting towards a tree to lay back on it to keep my poise. "Finish him," I whispered over to Desmond, holding my throat. Right when Andrew was about to run towards me, a still-alive Lou Gorgeous scooped him up with his hands like the last slice of pie.

"Get your fuckin' paws off the kid! You ain't doin' to him what you did to mine!" yelled Desmond, aiming his Glock at Lou. "Let him go!"

Out came the signature "L" blade from Lou's pocket. He flipped it open then pressed it into Andrew's cheek so hard, the kid started to shed blood. He then moved the blade towards his throat.

"I'll fuckin' shove this knife right through him if you don't put the gun away!" screamed Lou with a menacing stare. His eyes were of a vermillion hue while the drops of red continued to pour down his head, falling down his face.

"You think I give a fuck, you black bastard? If you shoot me, this stupid kid's neck gets sliced apart and explodes open like a tomato! TRY ME!!! COME ON!!!!!"

Desmond pulled the hammer back on his gun and kept it steady. "Settle this man to man, Lou...you and me. You leave the kid out of it!" he told him.

All the while, Lou let out a sinister laugh with his eyes wide open. "HAHAHAHAHAHA!!!" He was pressing the knife harder against Andrew's throat while the tears continued pouring out of the kid's eyes like a waterfall. "COME ON, YOU NIGGER MOTHERFUCKER!!!!!!!!!!!!!!" he yelled, echoing throughout the entire woods.

"COME ON!!!!!!!!!!!!!!!!!!"

CRACK! Enough was enough. With the last bit of strength I had left, I leaned up and released a round into Lou's eye to finish him off. Finally!! Thank God my aim was good because my sight was now becoming terrible. I was losing consciousness.

Andrew ran off and out of the man's dying grasp, over to where I was laying. Just to be sure he was dead, Desmond came over and shot Lou three more times in the face. "Piece of shit! That's for my son, my boy Jerome, and his brother!" he yelled. "Who's the nigger now??"

With his arms around my neck, once he scooted onto my lap, Andrew was telling me how much he loved me, repeatedly asking if I was okay. He had such a good heart.

He sobbed into my chest unceasingly as his hands clutched at my head. I held him in silence, rocking him slowly. His tears soaked my shirt more than my blood.

A tiny lapse let him pull away, blinking his lashes heavy with more tears before he collapsed again. His howls of misery were worsening.

I could see the blood from my gunshots spreading all over him. Taking a deep breath, I whispered, "It's going to be alright, buddy!" while I pulled him off for a second, trying to wipe it all away off his face.

Desmond ran over to me, extending his clenched hand in front of my face. I looked at it for a second...then up at him staring down. I gave him a fist pound, thanking him for making an appearance.

"Thank you for the money...and the scholarship named to my boy," he said. "I was wrong about you, man. I'm sorry."

I sat in silence, persisting in looking up at him, nodding my head. There weren't many more opportunities for me to utter much else. This was the beginning of the end.

"I'm forever grateful to you, Jack. Thank you," he continued, looking on to the lights and sounds by the warehouse coming closer in our direction.

Meanwhile, Little Andrew's eyes shifted to me once again. They became glazed with a glassy layer of tears. As he blinked, they dripped from his eyelids and slid down his cheeks. Continuously, my heart began to sink. I was not ready to tell him this would be as far as we'd go together.

His lower lip shuddered as words slowly made their way out of his mouth. "I…" he began, yet what followed was engulfed in the tremors.

I couldn't bear it much longer. His hair was pulled and frizzed, looking like he had volts of electricity shot to it. His face was battered and bruised, cuts in every direction and of all sizes. His blue shirt was torn with blood stains all the way down it. His brown khakis and sneakers, filled with so much dirt and debris, you'd think he was homeless.

"We gotta go. Let's get you two to a hospital before the police find us," demanded Desmond, lending his hand out to us both. For the first time that day, I smiled wide…and genuinely. "I ain't goin' nowhere…you take the kid, and you get far away from the shit storm that will be here soon!" I replied.

"No…Jack…no!!! I can't leave you here. I just can't, please!!" sobbed Andrew, continuing to cry.

"I wish it could be different, buddy…but this is the only way."

Coming in closer, Desmond asked me again to join him. He stared at me, deep into my eyes as if I didn't have a choice but to listen.

"I ain't goin' back!" I yelled.

"Back where?"

"Back to jail."

That's exactly what they would have done had the hospital repaired me. They would have called the local police, the Staties, and the FBI; all in that order. They all wanted my head on a platter.

I had nobody left to help me get out of the jam I was in. To them, I would undoubtedly be guilty as charged.

"I ain't NEVER goin' back. Leave me here so I can die in peace, Desmond. Take the kid and go while you still can."

In those final moments of being face to face, he told me he did not want to leave me alone, not again. "I'll always be near. Every time you watch the Phillies, I'll be scoring the game with you," I gently reminded him. Tears continued to fall...for the both of us.

The burning suffering that was spreading had quickly turned into an icy numbness throughout my entire body.

"Take care of the kid, Desmond. Promise me!!"

My blurry vision blackened along the edges. The only thing I could hear was my heartbeat. My breaths grew shorter. They then turned into gasps.

From a distance, the blue and red lights were growing brighter. It was time. Desmond picked up a restless Andrew and carried him out of the wreckage. They were headed far and away from this war zone and distant from the Federal ambush that was about to come my way.

The kid's horrifying screams reverberated as Desmond carried him in his arms onward. "NO, PLEASE...NO!!!" I wished there was more I could have done. He would be out of my life forever now...just like his mother would be out of his.

Seconds passed, feeling like hours once Desmond and Andrew vanished. The dead bodies of Lou and Tony Boy were the only things keeping me company. It didn't matter though, I would probably be joining their rat asses soon to meet the almighty. I didn't care. I took comfort in knowing I'd be able to leave the pain behind.

Fighting to keep my eyes open, I looked around at the mayhem. Even though it was blurrier than a distant memory, I was fully aware of the course I had chosen. After that, all I began seeing and hearing was white noise.

In the midst of everything, there was plenty to be upset about, plenty to be saddened by...yet I smirked once more, satisfied knowing Andrew made it out alive at the very least. I cried again, knowing my light was dwindling. *Was this really the end?*

I then felt something in my pocket, poking at the only nerve I had left. It was telling me something different. However, I was having a hard time trying to figure out what it was.

CHAPTER THIRTY-NINE

This was all too familiar to Desmond. The smell of iodoform circulating the halls and into the bedrooms. The sounds of nurses rushing, doctors dropping their clipboards, and electrocardiograms chiming in perfect rhythm with their beeps. The haunting memories lingering on. Ingrained in his mind was the image of his late son, Nathan laying in the same type of bed as Andrew. Same building. Similar look.

However, he made a promise. For whatever the relationship was between him and Black McCool, Desmond told himself he would always fulfill the wishes of a dying man whom he respected. It was in those moments he missed Jack more than ever. He only wished he had given him a chance to know him a little bit better.

It had been two weeks since the night of the carnage. Desmond slept very little. He sat in Andrew's room at SICH each night. He vowed to be there and to make sure that the kid received the treatment he deserved. All its employees rallied around the renowned king and the kid's recovery.

Andrew's problems merely started when everything ended. In addition to the bumps and bruises he endured during his abuse, the trauma led to several panic attacks during his stay. He would pass out at the drop of a hat.

His blood pressure was out of the roof, behavior was up and down by the hour, and his sleep schedule was all over the place. The doctors believed he developed PTSD given what he had to witness.

Yet, he was making progress, thankfully. The hospital was discussing releasing him to his grandparents' custody within the next day or two.

Sitting there, staring at the young boy sleeping, Desmond pondered. He looked back at his entire life, harking on what he could have done differently.

The heartache was like cancer eating at his insides, tearing its way to his trembling core. It threatened to devour him, feed on him entirely and leave nothing but scraps behind.

Yet, deep down…he knew he was stronger than that. He refused to be the scraps left from this vicious life. He would rebuild himself and fight off the demons, but right now he didn't know how. So he did his best to ignore it.

He had no choice but to overlook this feeling once two special guests with special badges came to visit him in Andrew's room. "Desmond Carter, Special Agents Jay Martinez and Davey Leodore."

His entire mood changed, quicker than the bullets flew through the air two weeks before. Immediately, Desmond rose up from his seat.

"I'd like to speak to you outside, Mr. Carter," said Jay as he stood at the front entrance, tall and militant as always. Davey remained behind his partner.

"You can speak to me in here. I ain't leavin' this kid until I decide I am going out for coffee," replied Desmond.

Silently, Jay met his demands. He slowly walked towards Desmond, tucking his badge into the pocket of his suit jacket. Davey stood by the door while he did so.

"It's commendable what you did, Mr. Carter. This kid is the son of a Federal agent. We'd like to reward you for bringing him to safety," explained Martinez, folding his hands in front of him.

Standing stern, wearing the greatest scowl he'd worn in days, Desmond replied, "I don't know nothin' about that. I was just helping a friend in need. Everything else that happened was unexpected. You don't need to reward me." Clearly, he was no fan of the Federal Government.

Jay smiled, shaking his head sideways as he began pacing back and forth from one end of the room to the other.

"I know who you are, Mr. Carter," he admitted.

"I don't really give a shit...do I know you?" asked Desmond in a sarcastic tone.

The pacing then stopped. Martinez came closer to Desmond, looking him in the eyes as if he was ready to start a staring contest with him.

"You were a badass in your day. And the mess you were in two weeks back. Some high profile people were there. Cosa Nostra, K&E Crew, IRA...I can go on," explained Martinez, raising his voice. Davey stood by the door, rolling his eyes at Jay.

Shushing him immediately in fear of him waking the boy, Desmond put Martinez in his place as quickly as he could.

"I am fuckin' retired, man. None of those things mean anything to me. Those groups, those people. That ain't me. I'm done with that shit. I have been since…,"

"Since your boy died?" asked Jay, half-smiling at Desmond.

The anger was steaming. The old proclaimed king wanted to wipe the smirk off the agent's face so badly, it would tear his face away with it.

"Get the fuck out of here, you piece of shit. I got nothin' to say," concluded Desmond, turning his back towards the agent and facing the door.

"I know you know where he is!" yelled Martinez. At first, Desmond did not know who he was talking about. It was then, the agent continued. "Your boy, Black McCool…where the fuck is he, Carter?"

Laughing and looking around like he was talking to a crazy man, Desmond countered. "You some kind of sick fuck? He's dead, man. He was at the wasteland y'all showed up at…right next to everyone else. Maybe you didn't search well enough!"

"He wasn't there!" chimed in Davey.

Just as Desmond was about to turn around again, he halted his steps. Puzzled, he looked once more to the two agents in the hospital room.

"What the fuck you mean he wasn't there?"

Jay cracked his knuckles, quickly looked to Davey and explained more in detail to Desmond. "We found a lot of the departed. Lou Muchetta, Tony Tomasello, some of Lou's guys, some of the IRA guys…but no McCool."

"What?"

It was strange to hear. Desmond watched him give up his fight in the middle of the woods and fade away. "How could this be?" he thought.

"Your buddy ran a multi-million dollar national gambling racket that led to murder, extortion, and chaos. Now, in my heart, I don't believe he killed a Federal agent and kidnapped her kid…but he still needs to speak to the money he stole and the murders he actually did commit! He also has a pending case with U.S. Army Court Martial coming up. And I won't stop until I find him, Carter…I got every department in the country looking for this fuck!!"

"That's all bullshit."

Jay came closer to Desmond. He didn't want to speak too loudly. "Make sense of it, Carter. You brought the kid back, that's the only reason I'm happy with you right now. Other than that, you're no better than him if you stay silent in all this."

It appeared the agent was done. He was about ready to leave. Desmond spoke his peace once more while he had the chance.

"I did not bring the kid in for you guys…I did it for McCool."

Martinez took a long, deep breath and looked around the room. He reached into his coat and pulled out his business card, handing it to Desmond.

"Here's my number if you ever smarten up. Until then, watch your back."

Desmond looked at the card, crumbling it up and throwing it in a nearby trash can. He then walked away from Martinez, exiting the room and the hospital for fresh air. The impatient agent shook his head sideways. Once outside the room, he and Davey went the opposite direction as Carter.

On his way out of the hospital, Jay pulled his partner aside. "Davey, get to the office…look into recent intel on Desmond Carter. I want a full case opened on what he has going on and his involvement at the warehouse massacre," he instructed, putting his aviators on before walking out the door.

Scoffing, Davey shook his head sideways. "Oh, you're actually gonna include me on this one? Is that what you're saying?" asked Davey, sarcastic as ever. Jay then stopped in his tracks. "Huh?" he asked.

"Do the guy a favor, Jay…back the fuck off!! And don't go and get your boy Rock on it, that one-case-pony." He had enough. He was tired of getting pushed aside recently. It was all coming out.

Martinez didn't know what to say next. He took his shades off. While he kept trying to figure out why Davey was acting this way, his partner was beating him to the punch.

"Just leave him alone. His kid just died last year. Haven't you ruined enough lives?"

"Ruined lives? Davey, what do you mean?"

"Hah! C'mon, Jay…you knew what you were doing with Agent Lesandi. You put her in harm's way that day at McCool's with those animals. You knew every step of the way what the stakes were."

"Davey...did I do something to you?"

"If only you knew." The fed-up Davey shook his head sideways to the arrogant agent before he continued. "Now, Jay...you listen to me for once. I'll help you in finding McCool...but Carter is left alone. And I'll make sure that goes to DC!"

Immediately, Davey walked away. He was tired of being thrown under the bus. It was time to start standing up for what he felt was right.

"Wow. You gotta be kiddin' me. When did *I* become the *bad guy* here?" Jay sneered, asking himself. He put his shades back on.

The sunny skies above him set the stage for good things to come. It was a sign. Desmond was prepared to leave the darkness behind him. There was plenty to be thankful for. It was a new day.

In his walk towards his car to drive off and grab a coffee, he could see from a distance that there was something on his windshield. It looked important. He sped up hastily to see what it was.

"Shit, they better not be giving me a parking ticket here!" he said out loud to himself. Yet, as he continued running and came closer...he realized the message was far from one being sent by the law.

The long beige envelope rested beneath the wiper. It was innocuous enough not to draw suspicion. However, the big letter D illustrated on the front with black permanent marker was loud enough for Desmond to grow apprehensive. He curiously picked it up to peeling back the metal on the Columbian clasp slowly.

Inside, there were three items shoved in. A long hand-written letter and two smaller beige envelopes big enough to hold keys or jewelry of such. Once he began reading, he couldn't believe it. Did this letter come from a ghost?

King Carter,

I am writing to you from a safe place. I cannot tell you exactly where...but do know it is flourished with green fields, a blue ocean, and a clear sky! Maybe a shamrock or two nearby...

It has been a long few weeks. First, I want to thank you for everything you did for me that night by the warehouse. Without you, I'd be dead, and a little kid would have been in the hands of darkness.

I told you I wasn't going back to prison. I knew you were too good a guy to let me sit there and rot. But, the hospitals would've never let me see the light of day after they'd get the Feds involved! It was a situation in which I already knew the end.

With this letter, I leave you two small envelopes. In the one with the phone number written on it contains one of my proudest possessions. Open it up!

In the middle of reading the letter, Desmond undid the seal on the smaller beige envelope as instructed. For what was inside was grand. This was the essence of McCool's journey.

It was something very precious. It shined brilliantly as he held it to the sun above. He even tried fitting it on his finger, but it didn't quite slide on as smoothly as it did with Jack or Fitzy at one point. It was the rare Claddagh ring. He kept reading.

It is worth more than just its weight in gold. Call the number, it's my lawyer. He will put you in touch with a dealer. Take what the dealer gives you...it will be a lot. Please then bring it to Timothy Bryce and the committee at SICH hospital as soon as possible. You don't have to say who it is from. I don't know if it will be enough to keep the place open or not...but it's all I have left to give.

Next, open the envelope with the shamrock.

Desmond did just that. The second envelope had a shamrock drawn on the front by black permanent marker. He couldn't quite decipher the item inside. It was like nothing he'd ever seen.

It is blue sea glass. Give this to Andrew when he is awake and feeling better. His mother gave it to me as a sign of love, a symbol of friendship. The color of blue represents peace, tranquility. Lodged in my pocket, it was the only thing that kept me alive in those woods.

Remind him how much I love him. I will always be thinking about him. Better yet...with this sea glass, his mother and I will always be with him.

Most importantly, keep an eye on him for me, D. Teach him the right way. Teach him how to live and how to lead...how to bring good to the world. Not the fucked up courses we chose in our paths.

I'm on the run, D. There is no telling if I will ever be back. The Feds won't quit until they find me and put me away, you know that. I'm sure I will be on their most wanted soon. Plus, I killed the boss of an Italian Mafia family...every fuckin' wiseguy looking to make a name is after my head too!

Fear not, my friend. I will be okay where I am.

This life is short...take a chance. Those who go furthest are the ones willing to do and dare. Get out and make a difference, D...in a positive way! Be creative. If not for yourself...do it for Nathan.

Choking up, Desmond nodded his head as he cleared his throat. He told himself he would fulfill these wishes, no matter what. This was a good man, deep down. Reading on, he finished the rest of the letter, taking a deep breath while doing so.

Forever in your debt and always in your heart,

"Black" Jack McCool

P.S. – Don't worry, I am staying busy. I still have one more fish to fry – if you know what I mean!! ☺

CHAPTER FORTY

It was a long morning at Allenwood Maximum Security Prison. Between two fights in the cafeteria, one inmate attempting to escape, and the guards being short-staffed, it was quite the scramble between the walls of the old cells. By the end of the day though, it would be the least of the overall concerns considering what was shortly ahead.

Being that it was the first nice day in awhile, many prisoners were outside in the courtyard, trying to take advantage of the fresh air. Whether it was lifting weights, playing basketball, or reading a book, extracurricular activities were of the plenty. For Pretty Paul Muchetta, however, he was taking part in another type of exercise.

Two bald men approached him as he was sitting down on a metal bench in the far corner of the court. He was gazing into the sunlight, wondering where all the brilliance went in his life. As his fire burned out a bit more each day, he was starting to become grateful for every moment he had left. He was living to appreciate the finer things for the first time in his nearly seventy-seven years.

One of the bald guys sat down, handing him a white letter envelope. Inside, a stack of one-hundred dollar bills, fresh and crisp rested richly with the smell of new money. Paulie took a peek at the cash, bringing it into his hand to sniff.

"Don't pull that out so quickly...not here with so many people around," said the second guy, looking around at the many eyes in the courtyard gawking. Afterward, he handed him another envelope. This one was a bit lighter in weight. "That one, you can open."

The old man grinned, looking at both baldies as he chuckled. He didn't say a word. He simply peeked inside the envelope, pulling out the big prize. A piece of wood.

"Not just your regular popsicle stick," the second guy chimed in, seating himself down as well. Paul looked at it, edge to edge. The end of it was sculpted to its sharpest point like a pencil. "This ought to do it," commented the pretty one, still inspecting every little part of the hand-crafted shank.

All of a sudden, the first bald guy snatched the envelope of cash from Paulie's hand. He sat there, clueless as his eyes remained on the white rectangle holding his fortune and it leaving his hands.

"Our guy said not to have you keep this until the job is done," responded the second bald man, stuffing it wherever he could into his orange jumpsuit.

"Now, Paulie...we will be right behind you for support. But, you have to make this happen. You have enough clout in here to have the blood on your hands and to get away with this," detailed the one.

Paul stood up. He nodded his head, letting the duo know he was ready to get the job done. "No security, we worked it out. The coast is clear for the next ten minutes. We will follow you down. Not too close...but not too far either," said the one.

As he turned around, anyone in the vicinity would be able to see the giant black letters tattooed on the back of his head. "RIRA." This stood for the *Real Irish Republican Army*. The second one had the same letters branded on his wrist. A bit more faded, but the same meaning nonetheless.

These guys were working for somebody on the outside who was dying to see a specific individual on the inside have his throat cut in multiple different directions.

Off he went. Tucking the shank up his sleeve, Paulie sped walked back into the prison building and down towards where he needed to go. The Ides of March was always the best time to strike.

As mentioned by the IRA guys, security was out of his path for a short while. He had to act quickly. There was no time for second-guessing and there were no margins for error.

Step by step, trot by trot, the pretty one whirled past anyone trying to say hi or questioning what he was doing. The clock was ticking...he had to act at a rapid pace. He didn't stop hauling until he saw the signs for "ICU" letting him know he was at his destination.

There weren't many staying in the depths of these hallways. But, that was okay. Paulie only had one target. The man whose first and last name both started with the letter V.

Pretty Paul crept closer and closer to his room, following the sounds of the ECG beeping. It was as if it was an alarm, telling him that it was his time to make a move. He pulled out the piece of wood from his sleeve. Just before he stepped inside, he touched the tip once more to be sure the point was sharp enough to slice through the old man's skin.

The curtain divided the room in half, blocking Vinny's bed from being seen. Even though he was the only one staying in these chambers, the curtains gave a message of "do not disturb" to guests. It was as if he was dead already.

There was only one way to be sure! Inching his way over, Paulie gripped the piece of wood tight. He tussled at the track sets, glancing at his weapon one more time. Carefully opening the curtain, he kept the piece in front of him, ready to strike.

BAM! There was a shank that went to the stomach…but not the way he planned it. He looked down in disarray. All of a sudden, Paulie tried holding his blood that was pouring out profusely onto his orange jumpsuit.

It was when he brought his head up, he saw the most frightening thing ever. Vinny, as healthy as he had appeared in months, standing in front of him. He was holding Paulie's fate with his right hand, deeper than he realized. He even had a smile stretched across his face.

Vinny pulled a honed plastic spoon out with his hand from Paulie's stomach with a vigorous haul on the way out. The pretty one's wooden dagger fell to the floor as he stood in awe, numb of every sense in his body.

Viscously, Vinny came back for more. A stab to the chest! Then the stomach again! Once to the cheek...then to his left eye. Blood was spraying up and everywhere like Old Faithful.

Finally, for the coup de grace, Vinny shoved the spiked spoon deep into Paulie's neck. Jackpot! He slashed open his main artery, cutting through it as if it were a long red chili pepper.

"Not so pretty now, cocksucker!!"

He watched Paul fall to his knees and into the puddle of red beneath him. Choking on the last drops shooting out of his mouth, he fell to his death, face first. SPLASH! Vinny remained standing, grasping the bloody spoon so rigidly, he was shaking.

Coming in from the corridor appeared the two bald men with IRA tattoos who conspired with Paul earlier. Both perplexed and apprehensive, they watched at the menacing marvel Vinny kept on his face. He was silently laughing, staring back at the two while pointing to the pretty one's carcass on the floor, oozing as the seconds unraveled.

It was like gazing at the devil himself. The fire that came out of his eyes was hot enough for them to feel from the door. They didn't know what to do.

He didn't speak a word. However, he didn't need to. The two men both looked at each other, hoping they had the answer on how to counter collectively. Yet, they couldn't come up with anything.

Slowly, they backed up and away from the madness. They kept their eyes glued towards Vinny's direction on their way out. Nonetheless, they didn't want to deal with what they saw before them. To make it even more startling, the security alarms went off louder than an air horn. Anybody who was in the vicinity of what happened was on high alert, demanded to rush to Veccuto's room.

Prison guards came bolting down the hallway past the bald men exiting like they were running the forty yard dash. Vinny remained immobile, laughing...smiling...waiting. He then feasted his eyes on the slaughtered Pretty Paul, grinning wider and wider. He felt more satisfied than he had in nearly three decades. His ultimate revenge plan was complete.

However, it seemed as if he was far from being done with killing. All of a sudden, his smile turned into a scowl. His eyes bulged from their sockets. He held the spoon just a little tighter, shaking as if he were about to erupt.

Coughing and wheezing, Vinny was doing his best to keep his balance as the end came near, right in front of his eyes. He wasn't sure if he was dying or merely dizzy, about to pass out onto the ground. He could see the light, white and bright!

Right before he was wrestled down by the guards coming at him, he whispered his last words to the gory crime scene.

"Nice try, McCool. I'm gonna get ya! Even if it is the last thing I do before I die, you little Irish piece of shit...I'm gonna fuckin' get ya!"

THE END

Made in the USA
Columbia, SC
10 May 2018